Electronic Mail

For a complete listing of the *Artech House Telecommunications Library*,
turn to the back of this book

Electronic Mail

Jacob Palme

Artech House
Boston • London

Library of Congress Cataloging-in-Publication Data

Palme, Jacob, 1941-
Electronic mail / Jacob Palme
Includes bibliographical references and index.
ISBN 0-89006-802-X (hard)
1. Electronic mail systems. I. Title
TK5015.73.P34   1995   94-23898
004.692–dc20   CIP

British Library Cataloguing in Publication Data
Palme, Jacob
Electronic Mail
I. Title
384.34

ISBN 0-89006-802-X

International Standard Book Number: 0-89006-802-X
Library of Congress Catalog Card Number: 94-23898

10 9 8 7 6 5 4 3 2 1

Contents

Preface

This book gives a broad survey of electronic mail. The book explains both the techniques and the uses of this medium. There are chapters about the effects on people and organizations, cost/benefit analysis, functions, standards, markets, ethics, legal aspects, and research. The book can be used as a textbook in education, for people working with or planning to use electronic mail, and for others interested in this area.

Uses, effects, and benefits of electronic mail are discussed in Chapters 1-5. Functions, techniques and standards are described in Chapters 6-8. The market is described in Chapter 9, ethics and law in Chapter 10, and an introduction to research is given in Chapter 11. Chapters are ordered in this way, so that those who want to read through the whole book will have read about techniques as a background for Chapter 9-11. Those who are less technically inclined can, if they find the text too technical in Chapters 6, 7 or 8, skip directly to Chapter 9, read to the end of Section 9.1, and then go directly to Chapter 10.

References to electronic documents are given in the URL format. To download such documents, use a network program that accepts URL as input (for example NCSA Mosaic) and use the command *Open URL*. If this does not work, use an Archie client and use the Find command with the part of the URL after the last "/" only.

The words "he" and "his" when used in this book, refer to both males and females.

Many people have helped me with ideas or with the proofing of the manuscript. I especially want to thank Hans Köhler (Universität Hohenheim, Germany), Carl-Uno Manros (Onsett International, Massachusetts), Markus Kuhn (University of Erlangen), Harald Tveit Alvestrand (SINTEF, Norway), and Sead Muftig (Stockholm University). I take personal responsibility for all errors which may occur in the book.

Chapter 1

Introduction

Systems for electronic mail are already used today by millions of people around the world. In a few years, this may increase to hundreds of millions of people. Electronic mail is not only a replacement for postal mail and telephones, it is a new medium, which will change the way in which people and organizations work.

Many of the electronic mail systems today are already connected together in networks, so that users can send mail to each other, regardless of which mail system each of them is connected to. In the future, almost all systems will be connected in this way. This means that all the electronic mail systems, when connected, behave as one large system. This large system may eventually be comparable in size and complexity to the world-wide international telephone network, but will have more advanced technical functions, and will be more of a data-processing system than the telephone network.

Chapter 2

Electronic Mail and Other Media

People today spend a large part of their time on communication with other people by technical means. Figure 2.1 shows how much time the average Swede spends on the most common technical communication media.

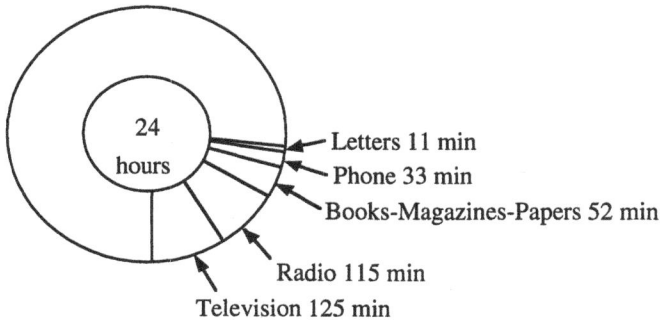

Figure 2.1   Use of technical communication modes.

If you compare the speed with the number of people reached, you get the diagram in Figure 2.2.

What is interesting about the Figure 2.2 is the large empty space in the middle. There are no good conventional media for communicating to groups of 8-1000 people in a day or less. Electronic mail and other computerized media makes such communication possible.

Radio
Television   Newspaper
100000 –   Weekly magazine

10000 –   Book

Number
of   1000 –   Magazine
people
                                        Conference
100 –

                        Meeting
10 –
        Phone   Mail
2 –
    Hour   Day   Week   Month   Year
            Time for the communication

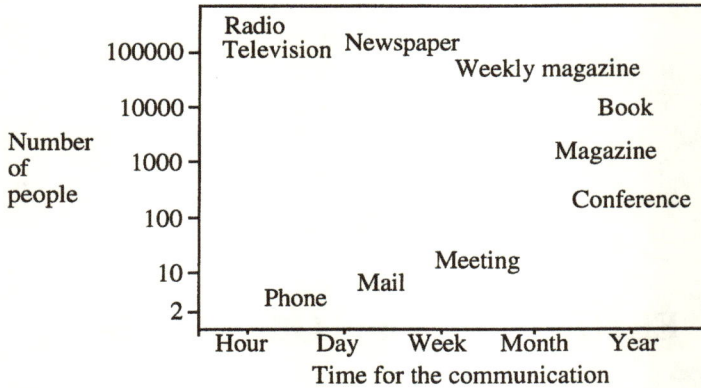

Figure 2.2   Speed and size of the user group in various media.

Figures 2.1 and 2.2 only include well-known, traditional media. New media, whose use is not yet very prominent in statistics for the whole population of a country, include, for example:

- Telex and its more modern variant teletex;
- Fax,
- Group telephone calls (audio conferencing);
- Video conferencing;
- Databases and videotex systems;
- Electronic mail and voice mail systems; and
- Bulletin board systems and computer conferencing systems.

Even if the term "electronic mail" could be interpreted to include most of these media, the term is normally used for those media where the ability of a computer to organize and sort information is used in a more qualified way. That is the way the term is defined in this book. This book is thus not about, for example, telex, teletex, or fax. The book does, however, include group communication via distribution lists, bulletin board systems, and computer conference systems.

Electronic mail, as defined in this book, has the following properties

- The user produces, sends, and usually also receives mail at a computer screen, a terminal, or a personal computer.
- The messages sent have a data structure, which can be handled by a computer. This structure can be more or less advanced: it can, for example, allow the user to ask his computer to find the last received letter from person N about the subject XYZ, or to find the outgoing message, to which a certain incoming message replies.

4

A better term for such systems might be *computer mail*, but since electronic mail enjoys widespread usage, that term will be used in this book.

Another common term for systems in this area is *CMC (computer-mediated communication)*. this term encompasses all computer systems whose primary aim is to relay information between persons. Electronic mail, bulletin board systems, and computer conferencing systems are most common for CMC. Since e-mail is more often embedded in other applications, the borderline between e-mail and other computer applications is not well defined.

Another term in this area is *groupware* or *CSCW (computer supported cooperative work)*. This is software for communication between groups of people. Johansen [1] proposes that different groupware applications can fit into different quadrants of Figure 2.3 [2].

	Same place	Different place
Same time	Ordinary *face-to-face* meetings, but may be supported by computer tools, for voting, producing records, pinpointing issues, etc.	*Video and audio conferences*, supported by computer tools similar to those for same time/same place but operating in a wide-area networked environment.
Different time	*Electronic mail, voice mail* and *computer conferencing* usually belong to this area. Such systems must be able to store messages and a structured organization of such message stores is often useful. The functionality for different time applications is usually similar for same-place and different-place usage.	

Figure 2.3   Time-place functions of different media. After [2].

Electronic mail and related applications are common tools in the *different time* half of Figure 2.3. The term electronic mail is not normally used to refer to *same-time* (see Section 6.3) text communication systems. Thus, electronic mail needs facilities to store messages. Messages are usually stored in personal mailboxes for senders and recipients, but some systems for group communication employ storage areas shared by several users. The storage of messages is further discussed in Sections 6.6 and 6.7.

REFERENCES

[1]   Robert Johansen *Groupware—Computer Support for Business Teams*, The Free Press, New York, 1988.
[2]   Robert Johansen *Leading Business Teams: How Teams can use Technology and Group Process Tools to Enhance Performance.* Addison-Wesley, 1991.

Chapter 3

When Is Electronic Mail Successful?

Few people will obtain a computer just to use electronic mail. *Electronic mail* is usually a fringe benefit of having a computer at your work or home. Many people feel that it is not worth the effort of learning to use a computer just to be able to use electronic mail. If, however, you already have a computer and regularly use it, then it requires little extra effort to use electronic mail. Also, a person who has entered the "wonderful world of computers" often needs to communicate with other people who use computers and electronic mail is a natural medium to use.

Everyone makes a personal choice of whether electronic mail is worth the cost just for him/her (It is seldom successful to try to force electronic mail on people who do not themselves feel the need for it).

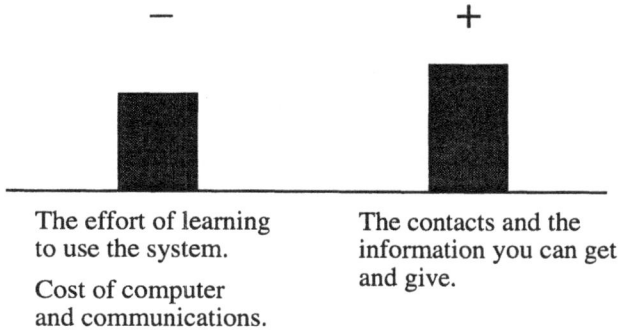

The effort of learning to use the system.	The contacts and the information you can get and give.
Cost of computer and communications.	

Figure 3.1   Factors in a personal decision to use or not to use electronic mail.

Figure 3.1 shows the most important pros and cons in this personal choice. These factors are important, if you want to predict whether the introduction of electronic mail in a group will be successful. If the people involved already use computers and if you can make the electronic mail application easy to use, then this will increase the probability of success. If the electronic mail application allows its users to reach many people and if they find it important to exchange information with these people, then the probability of success will again increase. Note that the pros are related to the volume of e-mail usage, while the cons are volume independent. Thus, higher volume increases the likelihood that the pros will outweigh the cons.

The following criteria are especially important to the success of electronic mail:

- The users should be accustomed to using computers. (Typing capability, however, is of less importance.)
- Each user should have a computer screen at his workplace and not need go to another area to use the electronic mail system.
- People who the users find it important to communicate with should be active users.
- The users should feel a real need to communicate with people who they can reach via electronic mail.
- users should feel a "solidarity" with other active users of electronic mail.
- The total amount of communication offered should be large enough to satisfy the user. This is often related to the number of people the user can reach via electronic mail.

Note that lack of other communication channels is *not* necessary for success with electronic mail. Even though an advantage of electronic mail is that it makes it simpler to communicate across large distances, much electronic mail is in fact between people in the same building or place.

As a consequence of the above factors, one can conclude that the introduction of electronic mail will often *not* be successful in two common cases

- The decision to use electronic mail has been made by people other than the actual users, simply because the decision makers believe that the use electronic mail is a high priority, even though the users themselves find other things more important.
- Electronic mail is introduced on a too small a scale, so that it does not reach the necessary critical mass (see Section 4.6) of users and/or communication volume.

Chapter 4

Value for People and Organizations

4.1 NEW COMMUNICATION OR OLD COMMUNICATION IN A NEW MEDIUM?

Much behavioral-science research has been done on electronic mail (see also chapters 3, 5, and 11). This research has resulted in a considerable amount of data about the effects of electronic mail on people and organizations. One important result is that electronic mail does more than just change the form of communication from other media to computers. The introduction of electronic mail changes communication patterns, so that people communicate with different people more often, and about other subjects than before.

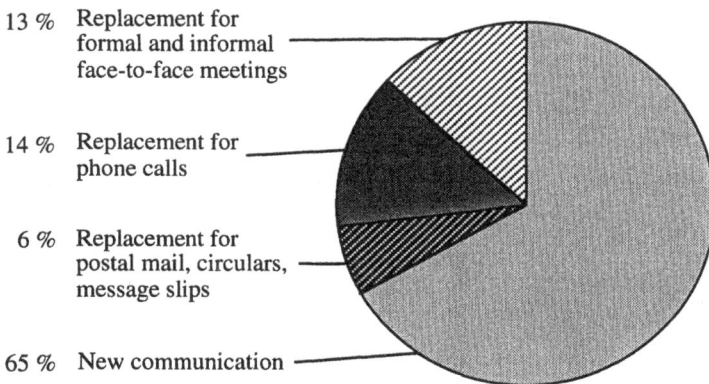

13 % Replacement for
formal and informal
face-to-face meetings

14 % Replacement for
phone calls

6 % Replacement for
postal mail, circulars,
message slips

65 % New communication

Figure 4.1   Is electronic mail a replacement for other media?

Figure 4.1 shows the result of an investigation [1] into the use of an e-mail system, a few years after its introduction. The percentages given show how much of the communication is new communication, that would not have occurred without e-mail and how much is communication that would have occurred with conventional media. The results may seem surprising but will not be so after some consideration. Look at other important media, such as print or telecommunication. If you look at all the communication via books, journals, newspapers, and the telephone, you would certainly conclude that most simply would not occur if these or other similar media had not been available and thus that most of the actual communication, in the printed and phone media, is new communication. If a communication medium opens possibilities for new kinds of contacts that would not have been practical or economically possible without the new medium, then people will take advantage of the new possibilities and change their patterns of behavior.

4.2   CHANGES TO ORGANIZATIONS

Thus most of the communication is new, then electronic mail has changed with whom and about what people communicate. In other words, electronic mail has changed the social behavior in an organization and has probably also changed the social workings of the organization.

How, then, has the behavior of an organization changed? The investigation [1] this looked at how much communication was between people who were close to each other (employed in the same department) and how much was between different departments and with people outside the organization. The investigation compared personally addressed messages and group messages. A group message is a message in which the sender did not explicitly input the names of the recipients when sending the message. Instead, the sender gave only the group name, and the computer then sent the message to all the members of the group. Such a function is available in most electronic mail systems. The result of this investigation is shown in Figure 4.2.

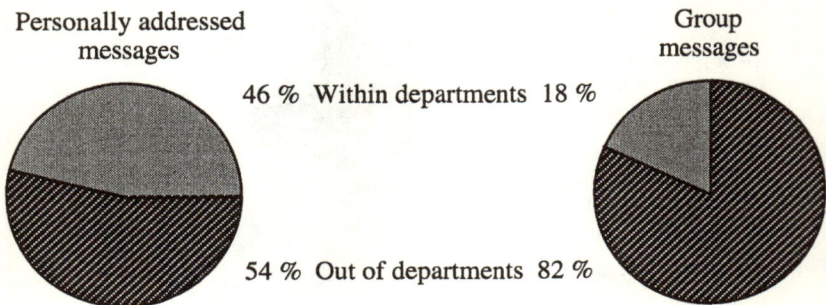

Personally addressed
messages

Group
messages

46 % Within departments 18 %

54 % Out of departments 82 %

Figure 4.2   Use of e-mail to communicate to people who are close or far away.

Figure 4.2 shows an important effect of electronic mail: increased communication between people who are distant geographically or organizationally. Without CMC, [4] finds that a surprisingly large percentage of the contacts of company employees are with other people less than a 100 feet away. Other investigations [2] have shown similar results and also found that electronic mail increases the contacts which do not follow the hierarchical organizational charts, that is, contacts between people other than coworkers and between bosses and their subordinates. The change may not always be as radical as shown in Figure 4.3, which shows the tendencies of change in an organization when electronic mail is introduced.

Hierarchical organization　　　　Network organization

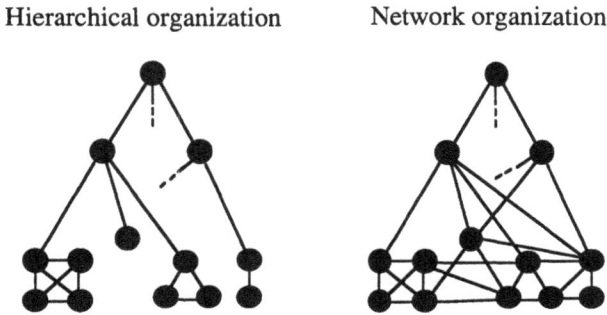

Figure 4.3　　Organizational effects of electronic mail.

As an example [3] tells the story of a large American company, where an employee had an idea for a new product and told other people in an electronic communication group about it. Other employees in different locations jumped at the idea, and a smaller group of people with a special interest in the idea was formed to discuss the design of the new product. If you analyze this example, you will see that it only took a few days from the idea to the formation of a group of experts, with members from different parts of the company, to the development of the product. If the company had used traditional communication patterns, several months would have passed before the new idea had filtered up and down through the organization and caused such a geographically distributed group of experts to be formed.

4.3　WILL ELECTRONIC MAIL IMPROVE COMPANIES?

Are these changes to organizations good or bad? A complete answer to this question cannot be given, but some investigations, for example [4], show that those development groups that had many geographically diverse contacts, were more successful than groups whose contacts were mostly within one area. The explanation for this is believed to be that small, closed groups tend to be conservative, and continue to do things in the same old ways. They have difficulty coping with change and accepting new ideas. Such adaptation is necessary if an organization is to succeed in a changing world.

4.4 EXCHANGE OF EXPERIENCE USING ELECTRONIC MAIL

One large area of electronic mail is the exchange of experience between experts in different places, within one organization or between different organizations. Examples include:

- Users of the same computer product;
- Researchers in the same area;
- Lawyers specializing in a particular legal field; and
- Doctors specializing in a certain area of medicine.

This has become a common application for electronic mail because it simply was not possible with any other medium to have contact every day for a reasonable cost between a geographically distributed group of experts. (See Section 5.5.) The cost with other media would have been prohibitive; electronic mail has a particularly low cost when compared to alternative media.

4.5 THE CHANGING ROLES OF SUPERVISORS AND MANAGERS

Experience at one e-mail user [1] was that communication within the system was as common for supervisors as for nonsupervisory personnel, and was a little more common for people who were less than 40 years old. At ordinary, face-to-face meetings with participants from different departments, supervisors and people older than 40 were strongly overrepresented. Thus electronic mail also gave young employees and non-supervisors an opportunity which before had been available only to older employees and supervisors. See, for example, Figure 4.4.

These results are due to the fact that electronic mail systems usually are designed to give equal control over the communication to all users. In this way, electronic mail is similar to phone and postal mail, which also are egalitarian. If, instead, an electronic mail system is designed primarily to support the communication needs of the supervisors, then the result will be different. At the GMD organization in Germany, an electronic mail system, COMEX, was specially designed to fit into the hierarchical organization of the company. As a result, the system benefited supervisors the most.

12

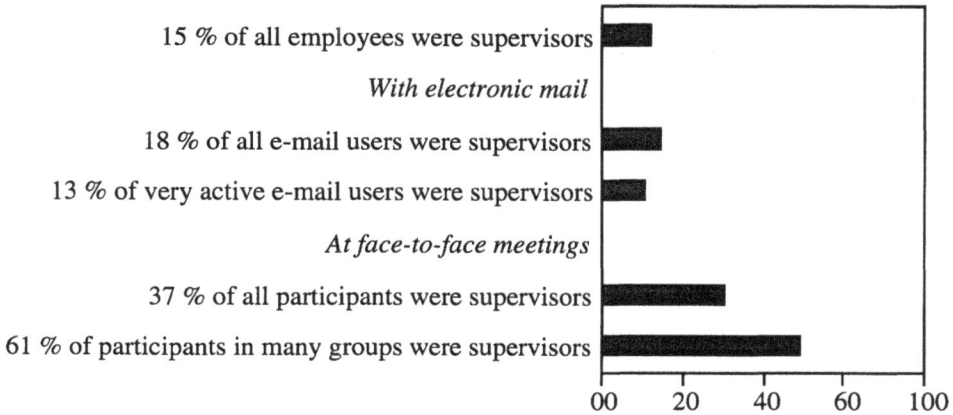

15 % of all employees were supervisors

With electronic mail

18 % of all e-mail users were supervisors

13 % of very active e-mail users were supervisors

At face-to-face meetings

37 % of all participants were supervisors

61 % of participants in many groups were supervisors

Figure 4.4   The percentage of supervisors in e-mail as compared to face-to-face meetings in a large research agency [1].

The changes in the workings of an organization described above will also influence the role of supervisors. One role of a supervisor is to move information along the traditional channels of communication in an organization, for example, between subordinates and supervisors. Another role is to find the right person to perform a certain task. These roles are, to some extent, taken over by the computer when electronic mail is used.

Different supervisors have different reactions to the introduction of electronic mail. Many experience positive effects

- Supervisors are freed from mundane work, since the computer system will perform some tasks that they previously had to be perform themselves. (Supervisors are often overwhelmed by such tasks.)
- Supervisors can use the computer to encourage discussion of an issue and collect the ideas of many employees, reducing the risk that some important aspect of the issue is forgotten.
- The computer helps supervisors monitor what is happening in his organization.

Other supervisors react negatively to the introduction of electronic mail. They feel their position of control threatened. They are afraid that employees will use the system to push the organization in unsuitable directions. They may also be afraid that the computer system will make it easier for employees to confront them and raise questions they would rather not respond to.

4.6   GROUP SIZE AND THE CRITICAL-MASS HYPOTHESIS

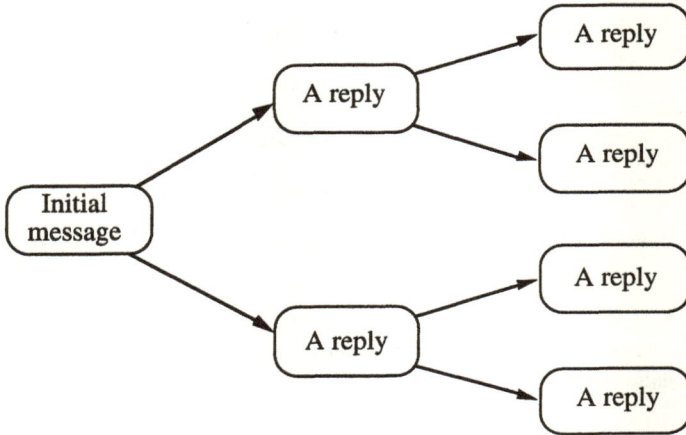

Figure 4.5   Chain reaction of group discussions in electronic mail.

Electronic mail commonly uses either distribution lists (see Section 7.4) or computer conferencing systems/bulletin board systems (see Section 6.7) for group communication. The lower size limit for a successful group for the exchange of experience is usually between 20 and 50 active participants. (Groups for other tasks than experience exchange can be successful with much smaller group sizes.) This is probably because the activity in these groups is a kind of chain reaction. Much of what is written is a response to a previous message. Assume, hypothetically, that the probability for each group participant to reply to a message is 0.05. With N participants in the group, each message will on average generate $0.05 \times (N-1)$ new messages. If the group size is 21 participants, then this figure will make 1. Thus, with fewer than 21 participants in the group, on average, each message will generate less than 1 new message, so that the chain reaction is subcritical. If the group size is larger than 21 participants, each message will, on average, generate more than one message, and we get a sustained chain reaction. Of course, the real figures are not always exactly 0.05 and 21, but the principle still applies: group size must be above a certain threshold if activity within the group is to be sustained.

Figure 4.5 shows how a chain reaction of messages can arise if each message on average causes more than one replying message.

The effects of group communication on group size is discussed further in Section 5.5.

4.7   EXAMPLES OF OBSERVED EFFECTS OF E-MAIL/CMC

This section provides some examples of observed effects of CMC (e-mail with group communication support) on organizations. Most of the examples here and in Section 4.8 are taken from [5].

A salesman wants to sell the product ABC to a customer in the XYZ branch. He uses the CMC networks in his company to inquire about other customers in the XYZ branch who have bought the ABC product. This example shows how CMC networks are used to find information available in other parts of the company. Note that the information to be found was not found in a computer data base. The search was not done on information in the computer, but in the knowledge of other employees connected to the network.

As an alternative, the company could have a data base with this kind of information. However, this can be very costly compared to the usage of the data base. CMC networks can thus be more efficient than preestablished data bases when a company's information needs cannot be well defined in advance, such as to improve the capacity of the organization to cope with new, unanticipated problems.

In another example [6 as quoted in 5] Tandem computers installed a network of 8,000 personal computers for a large company. A serious problem occurred during the installation, a problem which could have stopped the whole installation process. Through use of CMC networks, it was easy to find a Tandem employee who could solve the problem, and it was resolved within 24 hours.

Unexpected problems often occur in routine work, and CMC is a valuable tool to quickly assemble the information needed to solve such problems. Note that this is very different from the communication provided by company newsletters. Such newsletters give the same information to everyone and only contain a small collection of all possible information. CMC networks, on the other hand, let people ask for information specific to their needs, which means that they get the information relevant to their problems when the information is needed.

4.8   COORDINATION AND DECISION-MAKING

In preparing for decisions, it is important to assemble all facts, ideas, alternatives, and consequences before making the decision. CMC has been found to be more efficient than face-to-face meetings in assembling information, because more people can be reached more quickly and at reasonable costs [7]. CMC has also been found to be more efficient for at coordinating the work done at different places in an organization [8]. Traditional media, like travel, face-to-face meetings, courses, inventories, and company regulations, are not always very efficient in coping with such coordination problems. Travel may be too expensive. The main advantage of CMC is that it goes on all the time in parallel with other activities. Whenever you have a problem, you can immediately reach a group of people who can help you.

The lack of body language, voice inflection, etc. increases the risk of misunderstandings. Locked situations will more easily occur in CMC, where people stick with their initial opinions and are unable to agree. CMC may need to be combined with face-to-face or phone communication in such cases.

CMC can increase feelings of "togetherness" and understanding with other people in an organization. Without CMC, people tend to extend such feelings to only a few people with whom they interact daily. While employees are generally more loyal to their own branch office than to the whole company, CMC can integrate geographically distributed people more integrated into the activities of their company [9]. CMC usage increases the loyalty and positive feelings to the whole company [10].

For a merger between companies to be a success, it is important to integrate the employees into the whole new company, while preserving their individual knowledge and experience. Reference [5] reports that connecting all the employees to a common e-mail network was an important tool in this process.

Investigations show that CMC allows a person to participate simultaneously in more parallel group processes and have a more flexible range of contacts. Increasing the number of parallel group processes in this way has even been shown to increase the mental health [11].

CMC also increases the contacts with people outside a company [1, 2, 12]. This is important because people are surprisingly willing to help each other even if they work in different organizations. Such cooperation patterns make companies more able to follow trends and avoid getting stuck in old and inadequate ways of solving problems [4, 5].

CMC has also been found to be a useful tool for distance education [13-16].

REFERENCES

[1] Palme, Jacob, *Experience with the use of the COM computer conference system*. QZ UniversitetsData AB report C10166E. Revised 1984. Reprinted 1992.

[2] Köhler, Hans, *Inflytande och datorbaserade kommunikationssystem* (Eng.: Influence and computer-based communication systems), Teldok report 27, April 1987, Stockholm, Sweden: Televerket, 1987.

[3] Kiesler, Sara et al., "Social Psychological aspects of computer-mediated communication," *American Psychologist*, 39, 1123-1134.

[4] Allen, Thomas J., *Managing the Flow of Technology: Technology, Transfer and the Dissemination of Technological Information within the R&D Organization*, Boston, MIT Press 1977.

[5] Sproull, Lee and Kiesler, Sara, *Connections: New Ways of Working in the Networked Organization.* MIT Press, Boston 1991.

[6] *E-mail Delivers Tandem's Competitive Edge*. Unpublished manuscript as quoted in [5].

[7] Diehl and Stroebe, "Productivity Loss in Brainstorming Groups: Toward the Solution of a Riddle." *Journal of Personality and Social Psychology*, 53, 1987, 497-509.

[8] Fanning and Raphael, *Computer teleconferencing: Experience at Hewlett-Packard.* Proceedings of Conference on Computer-Supported Cooperative Work, New York, The association for Computing Machinery, 1986, pp. 291-306.

[9] Eveland and Bikson,"Work Group Structures and Computer Support: A Field Experiment." *Transactions on Office Information Systems*, 6(4), 354-379, 1988.

[10] Huff, Sproull, Lee and Kiesler, Sara, *An Experiment in Electronic Collaboration.* In J.D. Goodchilds, *Interacting by computer: Effects on Small Group Style and Structure.* Symposium conducted at the meeting of the American Psychological Association, Atlanta, 1989.

[11] Thoits, "Multiple identities and psychological well-being." *American Sociological Review*, 48, 174-263, 1983.

[12] Adrianson, Lillemor, *Psychological Studies of Attitudes to and Use of Computer-Mediated Communication.* Göteborg Psychological Reports, University of Göteborg, Sweden, 1987.

[13] Mason, Robin and Kaye, Anthony, *Mindweave—Communication, Computers and Distance Education*, New York: Pergamon Press 1990.

[14] Kaye, Anthony, *Collaborative Learning through Computer Conferencing: The Najaden Papers.* Heidelberg: Springer-Verlag, 1992.

[15] Hiltz, Starr Roxanne, "Constructing and Evaluating a Virtual Classroom" In Lea, Martin, *Contexts of Computer-Mediated Communication.* Harvester Wheatsheaf, 1992.

[16] Hiltz, Starr Roxanne, *The Virtual Classroom: Learning Without Limits Via Computer Networks*, Norwood, Ablex Publishing, 1995.

Chapter 5

Cost/Efficiency Analysis

5.1   HOW COST/EFFICIENCY ANALYSIS CAN BE USED

There are several reasons for making a cost/efficiency analysis of electronic mail. The analysis can be a basis for decisions on

- Whether and how to introduce electronic mail into a company;
- What kind of system to obtain;
- How to use an electronic mail system; and
- Changes in the organization of work as a result of the introduction of electronic mail.

5.2   CAN THE PRODUCTIVITY OF OFFICE WORK INCREASE?

When techniques for word processing, electronic mail, etc., first began to be used, James Bair [1] analyzed the potential for improvement in the efficiency of office work. He noted that, during a ten-year period, productivity had risen much faster in industrial production than in office work, as shown in Figure 5.1. He then looked at the possible gains in starting to use word processing systems, which today is still the most common computer application. He looked at how much of the time is actually spent writing text. His results are shown in Figure 5.2.

Increase in productivity during ten years

Blue collar worker

White collar worker

| 0 | 20 | 40 | 60 | 80 | 100 |

Thousands of dollars invested per worker

Blue collar worker

White collar worker

| 0 | 5 | 10 | 15 | 20 | 25 |

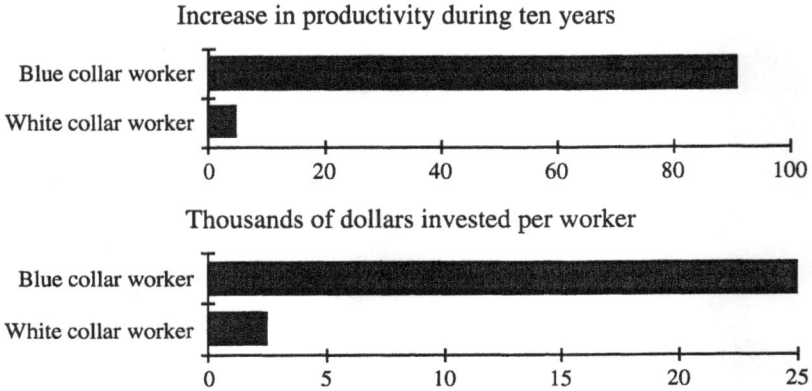

Figure 5.1   Comparison of productivity increase for clerical and industrial work. From [1].

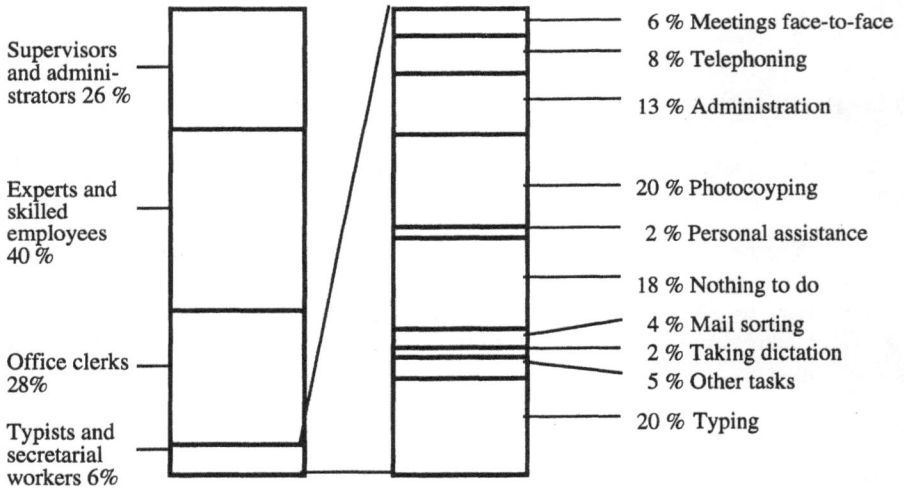

Supervisors and admini-strators 26 %

Experts and skilled employees 40 %

Office clerks 28%

Typists and secretarial workers 6%

6 % Meetings face-to-face

8 % Telephoning

13 % Administration

20 % Photocoyping

2 % Personal assistance

18 % Nothing to do

4 % Mail sorting

2 % Taking dictation

5 % Other tasks

20 % Typing

Figure 5.2   Percentage of personnel costs for different activities in office work. From [1].

Figure 5.2 shows that typing was only 20 percent of the working time for person-nel and 6 % of the total wage costs. In total, Bair said that typing represented 2 percent of the wage sum in an office. Bair concludes that the benefit from word processing systems is very low. Today, knowing how word processing has changed office organi-zation, with people typing their own texts instead of using a typist, we might say that Bair's reasoning is faulty. He only looked at the possible improvement within an exist-

20

ing organization of work and did not take into account the improvements possible by changing the organization of work—having people typing who did not type before.

Still, Bair's reasoning is interesting, since he also looks at where real efficiency gains are possible. What kind of office work is so common, that improvements would really result in large savings? The work time of supervisors and administrators is distributed as shown in Figure 5.3.

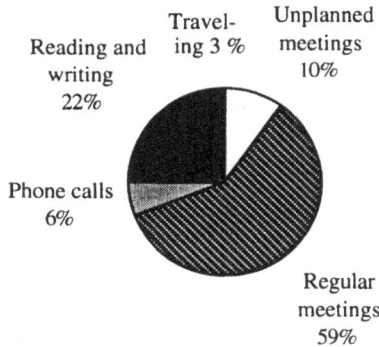

Figure 5.3   Fraction of the working time managers spend on different activities. From [1].

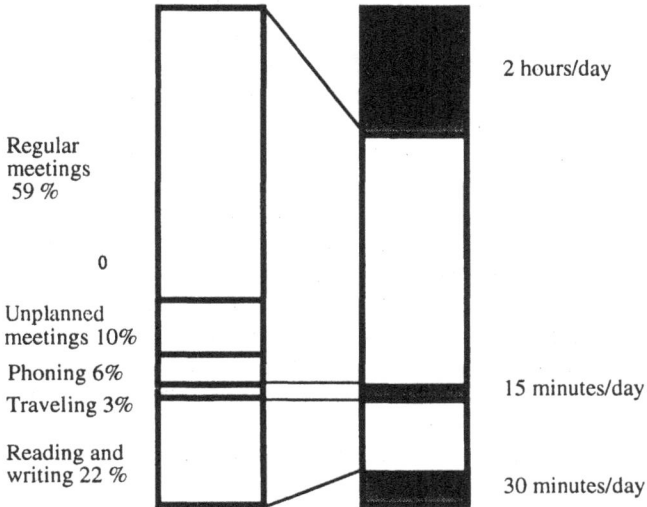

Figure 5.4   Comparison of productivity increase for clerical and industrial work. From [1].

Bair also says that a supervisor might improve his efficiency as shown in Figure 5.4. One can see that the largest improvements in efficiency in the figure is for meetings of various kinds. This is the basis for the current interest in groupware (see Section 7.5 and Chapter 11). For electronic mail, the largest gain will occur when it is used for group communication. Thus, according to Bair, offices should obtain qualified electronic mail systems with good support for group communication, rather than word-processing systems.

Bair's analysis shows the potential for improving office work, it does not measure how this potential can be realized. A restriction of Bair's method is that it only looks at cost savings for existing work patterns and does not show the gains from new organizations of work made possible by the new media. The introduction of word-processing systems connected to common data bases has, for example, made possible a new way of working with texts that Bair's method cannot measure. But Bair's results are still interesting, however, and give us something to think about, even 15 years later.

5.3 COMPARISON WITH TELEPHONE CALLS

According to Bair, only every fourth phone call reaches the intended person: there are three unsuccessful attempts for each successful call. The total working time for the caller, the callee, and all other involved people (exchange operators, people taking messages, people answering coworkers phones) is shown in Figure 5.5. The time cost for each successful phone call is 20 minutes, compared to 4.7 minutes for an electronic mail message [1 and 2]. If four electronic mail messages can produce the same result as one phone call, then the electronic mail system is only slightly more efficient. If the task can be completed with less than four messages, then electronic mail is certainly more efficient. If more than five messages are necessary, then the phone will usually be more efficient. All this assumes that you only want to reach one single person. Since the high costs are for people, not for equipment, the comparison is not particularly sensitive to the technical costs of computers and phone calls.

Figure 5.6 shows when phone calls or electronic mail are most efficient, assuming that each electronic mail message, taking 4.2 minutes to write and 0.5 minutes to read, replaces 1.2 minutes of the time for phone calls. The figure shows that phone calls are hardly ever the most efficient way to reach more than one person. Theoretically, two phone call might be more efficient than electronic mail if each phone call lasted more than one hour, but you very seldom want to discuss the same topic by phone for more than an hour each with two different people.

One can thus conclude that electronic mail is almost always more efficient in terms of time spent if you reach more than one person, or, when you only need to reach one person, if the task can be completed with less than four or five messages.

Three unsuccessful attempts: 9 minutes

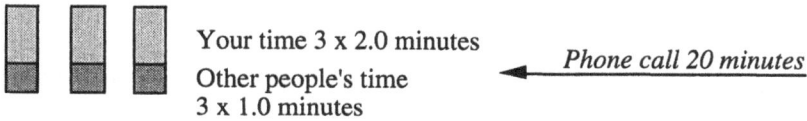

Your time 3 x 2.0 minutes
Other people's time
3 x 1.0 minutes

Phone call 20 minutes

One successful call: 11 minutes

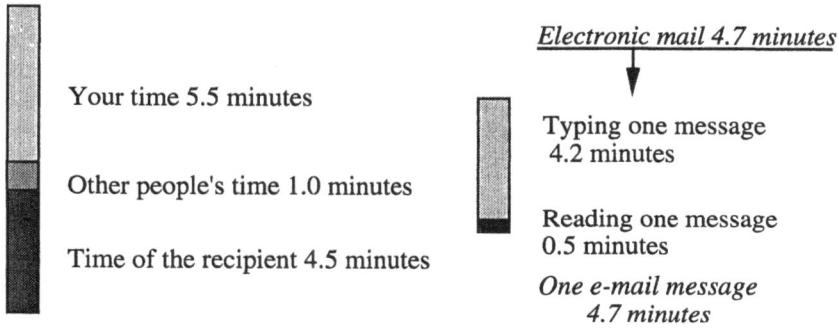

Your time 5.5 minutes

Other people's time 1.0 minutes

Time of the recipient 4.5 minutes

Electronic mail 4.7 minutes

Typing one message
4.2 minutes

Reading one message
0.5 minutes

*One e-mail message
4.7 minutes*

Figure 5.5   Total working time spent on one phone call versus one e-mail message.

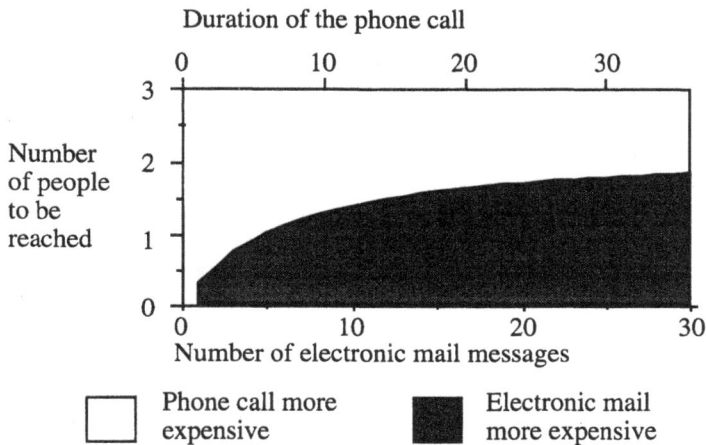

Duration of the phone call

Number of people to be reached

Number of electronic mail messages

☐ Phone call more expensive

■ Electronic mail more expensive

Figure 5.6   Comparison of the cost of phone calls versus electronic mail.

5.4 COMPARISON WITH POSTAL MAIL, POST-IT NOTES, TELEX AND FAX

On average, it takes four minutes to write a message in an electronic mail system and half a minute to read it [1]. These short times are possible because the computer supports the writing and reading. For exmaple, you do not have to supply your name or the date of the letter. With some systems, filing and archiving of outgoing and incoming messages is also automatic. You need not print the letter on paper and put it in an envelope. Often, you need not even supply the name of the recipient, since most electronic mail messages are replies to earlier messages, and the recipient names are then copied automatically. During typing, the computer supports simple ways for you to correct typing errors. Some systems even supply automatic spelling and grammar correction. The result will look neat with little effort.

Compared to an average of four minutes to write an electronic mail message, the average time to produce a postal letter is half an hour. Scraps of paper with messages on them are faster to produce, but still more time-consuming than electronic mail messages. This does not mean that electronic mail is always more efficient. Postal letters are used for formal communication with high demands on correctness and neatness, and this will, of course, be more costly to produce. Electronic mail is used for more informal communication, and it is in fact more of a replacement for phoning than for postal mail. An electronic message is also usually sent faster than a postal letter. Most electronic mail messages are available to the recipient only a few seconds or minutes after they were entered.

The cost of sending electronic mail is for short messages roughly similar to the cost of sending postal messages. Most electronic mail messages are short: the average length of a message in a system was about six lines (not including the message heading) [1].

Telex and fax functions similarly to, but faster than, postal mail. They are as costly to produce as postal mail, except for some systems which support the sending of fax messages in a manner similar to electronic mail systems.

Telex and fax are also much less efficient than electronic mail when communicating with groups of people. Another advantage of electronic mail is that you can easily insert data produced by a computer, and the recipient can easily use this data on his computer. An advantage of fax is that you can send pictures and existing paper documents. Most electronic mail systems today do not yet support this. Most existing systems for electronic mail do not support the signing of letters as well as postal mail and fax do.

The large difference in quality between electronic mail, postal mail, and fax means that in reality they are not competitive systems. The choice of medium is usually obvious, and the different media support different communication needs.

5.5 COMPARISON WITH FACE-TO-FACE MEETINGS

Much of the communication in electronic mail systems is group communication. Most electronic mail systems have some built-in support for group communication (see Section 6.7), ranging from simple distribution lists to advanced computer conferencing systems. Even in those systems that do not support group communication, there is almost always a command to write a reply to a multirecipient message, such that the reply is sent to all recipients of the previous message. Thus you do not need to input the names of all the recipients again. This means that the previous message is in fact used as a kind of implicit distribution list. Even this simple aid supports and is often used for group communication.

Electronic mail is used so often for group communication because it is particularly efficient for many types of group communication; this will be explained further below.

Group communication using electronic mail is very different from ordinary meetings. Even audio and video conferencing and group phone calls are more similar to face-to-face meetings than to electronic mail. The important difference is that, in ordinary meetings, all communication is concentrated to a short time period (usually one or two hours). All communication must be done in this short period, or it will have to wait for the next scheduled meeting, which might be a week or a month later. If you forget one aspect of an issue, have to look up a fact, or get an idea the next day, then it has to wait until the next meeting. With electronic mail, the process is not concentrated in a fixed meeting period. Participants enter the system when they have time, read what others have written, give their own views, and connect again at a later time.

Electronic mail is more efficient for some kinds of group communication for the following reasons

- You save the cost and effort of travelling and gathering everyone in the same place at the same time.
- Each participant has greater control over his own communication: what to read, when to read it, what to read carefully, what to skip, and when to write his own comments. If you prefer, you can think about an issue and reply the next day.
- Since you write slower but read faster than listening and talking in voice communication, written communication is more efficient if the size of the group is larger than about five people.

This last point is very important, and is illustrated by the example in figure 5.7, which compares a meeting of twelve people with the same amount of communication via electronic mail. The figure shows the total spent effort for all the participants of the group to transfer the information given in an average message. As is shown in the figure, much less time is needed for the same communication with electronic mail, if the group size is larger than five participants.

The shorter reading time with electronic mail is caused not only by the fact that you actually read faster than you listen, but also because you can control your own reading more than your listening: it is easier to spend less time on less-important texts and to read carefully what is most important to you.

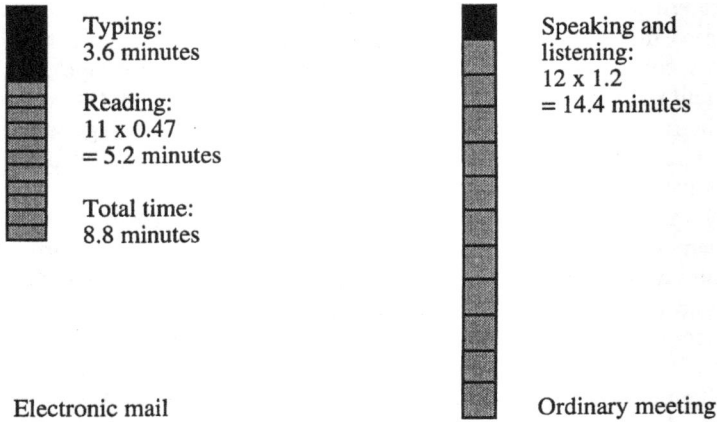

Electronic mail

Typing:
3.6 minutes

Reading:
11 x 0.47
= 5.2 minutes

Total time:
8.8 minutes

Ordinary meeting

Speaking and listening:
12 x 1.2
= 14.4 minutes

Figure 5.7   Comparison of the time spent giving and receiving information in written versus spoken communication in a group with 12 participants.

The results described above are not only a matter of efficient use of time, they are also important psychologically. Everyone knows that it is difficult for face-to-face meetings to work well if the number of participants is larger than about 5 to 8 people. Typical problems of meetings with many participants are:

- The meeting takes more time than planned;
- Everyone does not have time to say what they want;
- There is not enough time to cover all items on the agenda as fully as needed; and
- Many people feel that too much of their time is spent in meetings, and within these meetings on discussion of issues they already know or are not interested in.

There are psychological advantages to face-to-face meetings too, especially for certain kinds of issues. This is discussed in the end of Section 5.7.

This result can also be understood by looking at Figure 5.7, and comparing the additional cost of including one more person in the communication process with electronic mail. This additional cost is less than half of the corresponding cost at a face-to-face meeting. Thus, with electronic mail, you can choose to include more people, at more reasonable additional cost than with face-to-face meetings.

Figure 5.7 only covers the time the participants actually participate in the meeting. Other costs (gathering everyone at the same time and place, travel, computer, etc.) are usually higher for face-to-face meetings than for electronic mail. The technical costs for simultaneous audio conferences are comparable to those of electronic mail, while video conferences are much more expensive.

Note, however, that the travel cost per meeting minute is smaller the longer a face-to-face meeting lasts. As an example, I have estimated the cost of a meeting assuming that two-thirds of the participants do not have to travel and that one-third must travel 150 kilometers. The estimate includes working time, computer time and travel costs. If more or fewer people have to travel, if the travel distances are larger or smaller, or if you use other prices, the result will differ. The result, with given assumptions, are shown in Figure 5.8.

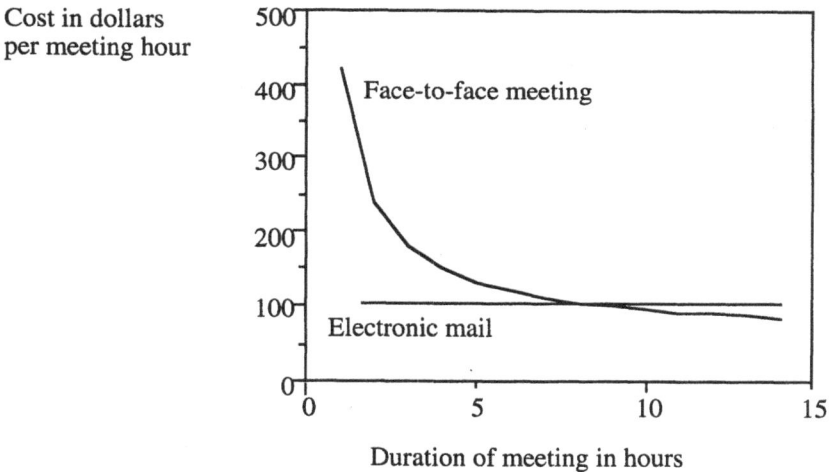

Figure 5.8   Comparison of cost for e-mail versus face-to-face meeting with five participants.

Figure 5.8 shows that a face-to-face meeting will cost more than electronic mail if the duration of the meeting is less than a whole day. If the meeting is more than one full day. This is, of course, the reason why face-to-face meetings where participants have to travel usually are held at large time intervals, and last for a longer time. It is obviously a disadvantage if you can only meet a few times a year. With electronic mail, an issue that needs 15 or 30 minutes of discussion can be taken up immediately, and there is no need to wait for the next scheduled meeting.

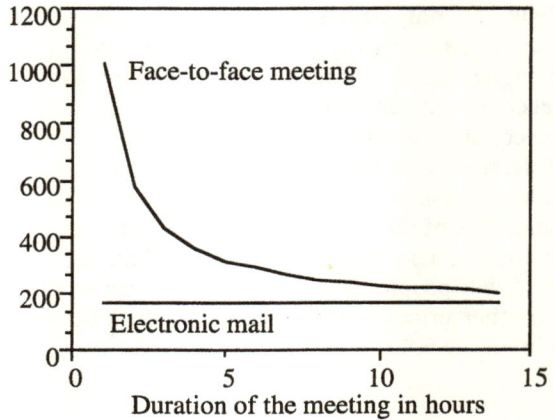

Figure 5.9   Comparison of cost for e-mail versus face-to-face meeting with twelve participants.

Figure 5.9 shows that, with twelve participants, electronic mail will be less expensive even if the duration of the meeting is two full days.

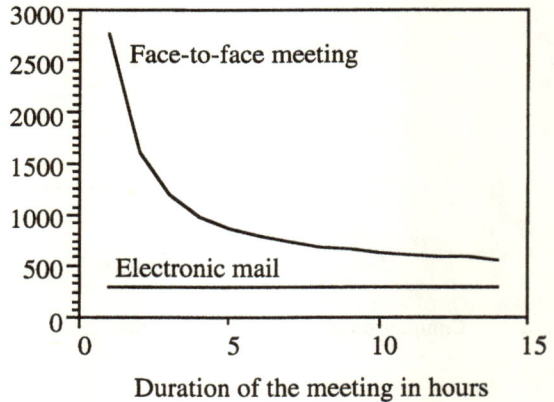

Figure 5.10   Comparison of cost for e-mail versus face-to-face meeting with 33 participants.

Figure 5.10 shows that, with 33 participants, face-to-face meetings will be so expensive that such meetings in fact are very seldom organized. Symposia, lectures, conferences, etc., are of course exceptions. My assumptions are not valid for such meetings, however, since I have assumed that all participants have roughly equal rights to speak. At symposia and lectures, this rule does not hold: the speakers have more opportunities to talk than the other participants. In this way, higher efficiency is

28

achieved for larger group sizes. This is an important difference between electronic mail and face-to-face meetings: discussion with equal rights to "talk" is possible through CMC even with 33 or more participants.

Some may object that this is irrelevant, since large face-to-face meetings with equal speaking rights are seldom held, but the reason such meetings are so seldom held is that before electronic mail, there was no efficient medium for them. If electronic mail provides an efficient medium for large meetings, the result will be opportunities that simply could not be realized otherwise. The more people can participate in a discussion, the more people can be kept informed, the more people get a chance to have their say, the less is the risk of forgetting some important factor. A survey of users of an e-mail and computer conference system showed that a large majority of its users agreed with these statements [3].

An interesting factor to note is that, in a face-to-face meeting with 5 participants, each participant is allowed to talk for an average of 20 percent of the time. In an electronic mail meeting with 33 participants, each participant also spends 20 percent of the time giving information, writing messages, etc. See Figure 5.11.

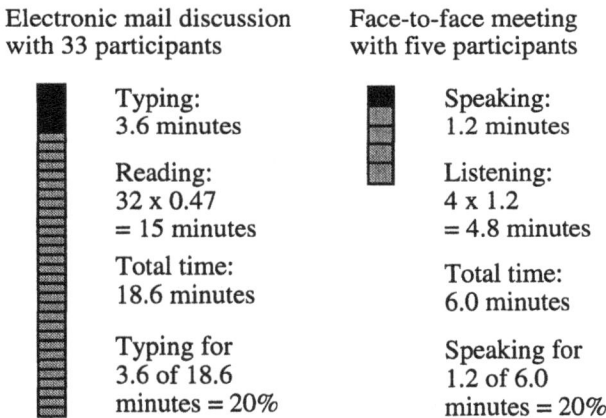

Electronic mail discussion
with 33 participants

Typing:
3.6 minutes

Reading:
32 x 0.47
= 15 minutes

Total time:
18.6 minutes

Typing for
3.6 of 18.6
minutes = 20%

Face-to-face meeting
with five participants

Speaking:
1.2 minutes

Listening:
4 x 1.2
= 4.8 minutes

Total time:
6.0 minutes

Speaking for
1.2 of 6.0
minutes = 20%

Figure 5.11   Number of participants to get roughly 20 percent giving and 80 percent receiving per participant.

Maybe human communication (with equal speaker rights) works best psychologically if the participants can be active and give information at least 20 percent of the time. This could be the reason why face-to-face meetings seem to be most efficient with group sizes of about 3-7 people, while group communication using electronic mail or computer conferencing systems seems to be efficient in groups of 20-100 people or more.

5.6 COMPARISON WITH AUDIO AND VIDEO CONFERENCING AND VOICE MAIL SYSTEMS

The communication in audio conferencing (group phone calls) and video conferencing is spoken, just like at face-to-face meetings. Also like face-to-face meetings, everyone has to participate at the same time. However, participants need not be at the same place, as with ordinary face-to-face meetings. This means that much of what is written in Section 5.5 comparing electronic mail to face-to-face meetings is also valid for audio and video conferencing.

Research on these media [4] shows that the difference in efficiency between audio and video conferencing is rather small. The much higher cost for video conferencing seldom gives a corresponding improvement in the quality of the communication. According to [4], audio conferencing is a suitable medium for routine meetings held to solve simple tasks.

Voice mail systems are functionally similar to electronic mail and are sometimes combined with electronic mail. Existing voice mail systems, however, do not usually provide facilities for organising and structuring information as that are as good as in more advanced electronic mail systems. The cost of storing information is also much higher for voice mail systems. Voice mail also seems psychologically inappropriate except for short messages to a small number of recipients. The advantage of voice mail systems is that they can be used from an ordinary voice phone, so no access to a computer is necessary. This can be of special value for people who travel a lot.

5.7 WHEN IS ELECTRONIC MAIL THE BEST MEDIUM?

Considering the discussion in Section 5.5 and 5.6, electronic mail is more efficient than other communication media in the following cases

- Electronic mail costs less than a phone call when you have to reach more than one person, or, when you only have to reach one person, if the issue can be concluded with a maximum of four messages averaging 6 lines/message.
- Electronic mail costs less than postal mail and messages on scraps of paper with notes on them, except for very long messages.
- Electronic mail costs less than face-to-face meetings for large group, or if some participants have to travel to the meeting and the duration of the meeting is less than a full day.

The smaller the issue is, and the more people who have to be reached, the more efficient electronic mail will be. If you are a member of a geographically distributed group, who need to spend a few minutes every day exchanging information and resolving small, simple issues, then electronic mail may be the only viable medium.

Practical experience with the use of electronic mail shows that it is mostly used for resolving small, simple issues and for group communication. This shows that users have an intuitive understanding of when electronic mail is the most suitable medium, even though they have not made a formal comparisonas this chapter has.

In addition to these conclusions, electronic mail is usually more efficient if the recipient processes the information in a computer, especially if the message is partly formatted with fixed fields (like a bill or a travel expense statement), which will be handled by a computer at the receiving end.

Much of this chapter has examined monetary and temporal costs of using electronic mail and other media. Of course, there is more to communication than money and time. However, as mentioned above, the amount of time a user spends using various media has important psychological impact on their social interactions. In addition, it is obvious that different media have different qualitative aspects. The difference between electronic mail and face-to-face meetings have been investigated in several studies [3, 5, 6]. These and other studies show that electronic mail has advantages and disadvantages compared to other media. The following are the advantages of electronic mail:

+ You can give and take information when you have time. You do not have to interrupt other people as you do when calling. You can participate more easily in communication when you otherwise cannot be easily reached, as when you are travelling, on holiday, etc.
+ It is easier to give precise factual information.
+ The recipient gets the information in a written format which can be reused or archived.
+ Equality between people increases, more people are allowed to have their say, there is less risk of one single person dominating.

The following are the disadvantages of electronic mail:

− It is more difficult to persuade others, and thus to reach consensus. With e-mail, difficult and controversial issues will more often lead to a war of positions which can only be resolved in a face-to-face meeting. The lack of body language, voice inflections and facial expressions help explain this effect. Thus, negotiations can be difficult to conduct via electronic mail.
− It is more difficult to conduct a formal decision process through electronic mail.

A project often consists of three phases:

(1) Preparation: Collecting ideas, solutions and alternatives; examining the consequences;
(2) The decision making process; and
(3) Execution and realization.

Electronic mail is more suitable in phases (1) and (3) than in phase (2), since an important aspect of decision making is to reach consensus about a decision which all parties are expected to support in the execution phase.

31

5.8 THE VALUE OF CHANGED COMMUNICATION PATTERNS

Chapter 4 showed that electronic mail is often used for new communication, not as replacement for old communication. This makes it more difficult to estimate the benefits of electronic mail. The situation is illustrated by Figure 5.12 [7]: It is based on real data from the use of electronic mail in a computer-intensive company. Even though this company used electronic mail to a large extent, all the potential benefits of electronic mail were not realized at the time of the study, since many of the organizations with which the company worked did not use electronic mail. The gains from electronic mail thus can be asumed to be larger when the use of electronic mail is more widely used.

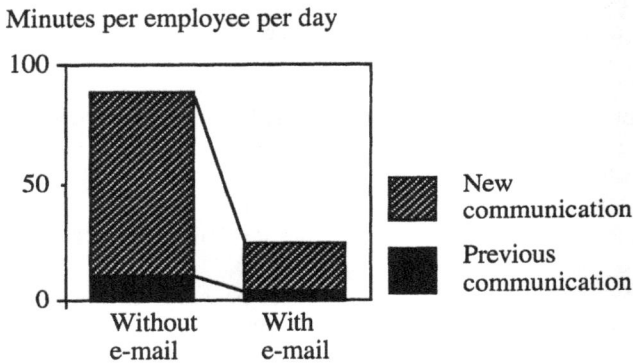

Minutes per employee per day

New communication

Previous communication

Without e-mail

With e-mail

Figure 5.12   Comparison of time used for communication using e-mail and previous media.

The black bar in Figure 5.12 shows how much a previous communication could be done faster via electronic mail. Previously, this communication took 10 minutes a day, and it can now be done in 4 minutes, a saving of 6 minutes per employee per day. The lined part of the bar shows the new communication which took place only after electronic mail was introduced. An average employee spent 20 minutes per day on such communication, but if this communication had existed before then it would have taken 78 minutes. Thus, the left lined bar is hypothetical; it is the time that employees would have needed without electronic mail.

Assuming the organization and its employees choose to use media in an optimal way, the benefits for the organization by using electronic mail will at least be the time savings over older forms of communication, that is, 6 minutes per employee and day. The benefit of the new communication is less than the reduction of 78 minutes of work to 20 minutes, since if this communication had been worth 78 minutes, then it also would have occurred without electronic mail. This is the upper and a lower limit to the gain due to electronic mail—a gain of 64 minutes per employee per day and a gain of 6 minutes per employee per day, respectively. The difference is large, because most of

32

the potential gain from electronic mail from new communication and from changed communication patterns, not simply using a new medium for old communication. The value of this new communication is more difficult to quantify.

The new communication may have the following kinds of benefits for the organization:

- More people can get information and give their ideas, issues will be more fully examined, and the risk of forgetting some important aspect will be reduced.
- Employees in different parts of the organization can work with each other more easily and feel more in solidarity with the common goal.
- A more decentralized organization of the company is possible. Everyone need not work in at the same place in order to work together.
- Increased contact with the outside world makes it easier to accept new ideas and disseminate one's own views. The organization is less likely to act on old, outmoded views and methods.

It is difficult to put a monetary value on these kinds of changes, but at the same time, they are the largest and most important advantages of electronic mail.

The above discussion is based on the assumption that the employees of a company will intuitively choose to use the best medium in an optimal fashion. My experience is that electronic-mail users quickly learn when the new medium is suitable and use it appropriately. However, this may be based on what is best for the individual employee, rather than what is good for the company as a whole. For example, individual employees may put higher value on increasing their own competence than their employers do. The possibillity of efficiency loss because of private usage of office e-mail is discussed in Section 10.1.4.

REFERENCES

[1] Bair, James, *The Impact of Office Automation*, in , in Uhlig, Farber, Bair, The Office of the Future. North-Holland 1979.
[2] Palme, Jacob, *Experience with the use of the COM computerized conferencing system*, Research report at the Swedish Defence Research Institute, 1984.
[3] Adrianson, Lillemor, *Psychological studies of attitudes to and use of computer-mediated communication*. Göteborg Psychological Reports, University of Göteborg, Sweden, 1987.
[4] Williams, E. *Experimental comparisons of face-to-face and mediated communication: a review*, Psychological Bulletin, Vol. 84, No. 5, 1977, 963-976.
[5] Hiltz, Starr Roxanne and Turoff, Murray: *The Network Nation: Human Communication via Computer*, Addison-Wesley, Cambridge, 1978; MIT Press 1993.
[6] Hiltz, Starr Roxanne and Kerr, Elaine, *Studies on computer-mediated communication systems: A synthesis of the findings*, New Jersey Institute of Technology, Newark, Research Report No. 16, 1981.
[7] Palme, Jacob, "Cost-benefit analysis of computer-mediated message systems." In *Information Processing 86*, Proceedings of the IFIP 10th World Computer Congress, pp 1021-1023, North-Holland, Amsterdam 1986.

Chapter 6

User Functionality with Electronic Mail

6.1 PERSONALLY ADDRESSED MAIL

Personally addressed mail is the basic functionality of electronic mail. The users enter the electronic mail system, input the text of messages, input the names of one or more recipients to which the messages are to be sent, and then give the commands to deliver the messages. The recipients also regularly connect to the electronic mail system, asking if there are any new messages for them. They can usually get a list of all unread messages, with one line per message, which in a compact format provides the sender's name, the date, and a few words from the subject/title of the message. The user can then, select from this list which messages to read. An example of such a list is shown in Section 12.3.

When recipients have read a message, they are given the opportunity to perform various actions in relation to the message:

- Write a reply to the sender of the message;
- Write a reply to the sender and all other recipients of the message; (if the message has only one recipient, then these two functions are identical)
- Forward the message to one or more new recipients, with or without an added comment.
- Archive the message—systems often allow messages to be stored in folders (see Section 6.6).
- Remove the letter from their own mailbox.

Most message systems provide a personal "mailbox," a personal area in the computer for each user which holds incoming messages and often outgoing messages. Unlike postal mail some electronic mail systems allow the sender to retract already-sent messages, but usually only before they have been delivered or before they have been seen by the recipient.

Most systems will make a copy of a message to the mailboxes of the sender and the recipients and sometimes to a central data base. Some systems store all messages in a central data base, which is not under the direct control of the sender or recipients. A system can, of course, be designed to appear as if each recipient has his own copy of a message, even though in reality the messages are not copied. Systems with a central data base can also be designed in such a way that the central storage influences user functionality, for example, providing a function for a sender to physically remove a message from all its recipients.

Messages in a personal mailbox are usually saved there, until the recipient approves their removal. There are then two principles which the systems can use to purge this data base

(1) All messages are manually deleted by the user. Usually, when users receive a message, they can give a command to save it or delete it immediately.
(2) Messages are purged automatically after a specified time. Users can mark certain messages to protect them from being deleted.

Automatic purging of old messages saves user time. Without such purging, there is a risk that users will purge too much and will then have difficulty finding an old message they want to reexamine. New users may feel more secure without automatic purging, but experienced users will know how to use the facility to protect messages they want to save.

Recipients are not usually told that they have new messages, until they enter the mail program. There are sometimes functions to remind users of new incoming messages, for example, every time they switch on their screens or log in to a server computer host. Some systems have a lamp on the phone, which starts to blink as soon as new mail have arrived. Some users do not like this function, and in some cases the system providers have had to include a switch to disconnect this lamp or put small hoods over them.

6.2   AUTOMATIC MAIL

Some systems have functions for automatically generating an answer to all or some incoming mail. A common variant allows, for example, people who are on holiday, to have the mail system generate an automatic reply to all messages, telling the sender that they are on holiday. A badly designed facility of this type can cause trouble. In the worst possible case, replies are sent to all the members of a distribution list for each new ordinary message sent to the list. If the message comes back from the list and causes a new automatic-reply to be sent, an explosion of messages can occur. When two people, who both have this kind of automatic answering facility, an endless chain of automatic answers can ensue.

The best solution to this would be a standard requiring a special mark on such automatically generated messages. Systems could then be designed so that an automatically generated message would never cause a new automatic message to be created. Such a facility was introduced in the 1992 version of the X.400 messaging standard[1]. For a special class of messages, the "notifications," the first (1984) version of X.400 had this facility, but it supports only a limited set of such notifications, and there is, for example, no notification type in X.400(1984) is suitable for telling people that you cannot read their mail immediately (if you are on holiday for example).

6.3   SIMULTANEOUS TEXT COMMUNICATION

Most electronic mail is used in an asynchronous fashion, where senders and recipients write and read independently of each other at different points in time. Some systems also support simultaneous or synchronous communication, that is, a real-time dialogue between two or more persons. In some advanced systems, the screen is split into several windows, where you can simultaneously write in your window and see what the other person is writing in his window. Systems which support simultaneous text discussions between two or more people are called *chat* or *talk* systems. The most well-known such service is the *IRC (Internet Relay Chat)*, a distributed chat/talk system encompassing thousands of simultaneous users all over the Internet.

Experience with electronic mail shows that, even though such a facility for simultaneous real-time communication is valuable, electronic mail will still mostly be used for asynchronous messaging. The reason is that the asynchronous functionality is actually one of the main advantages of electronic mail. If you are to communicate simultaneously, most people prefer a phone call.

6.4   MULTIMEDIA DOCUMENTS AND VOICE MAIL

The basic function of most electronic mail systems is the sending of pure text. Some systems can send documents that can contain more than text: for example, sound, graphics, animated graphics, movies, spreadsheets, and computer programs. A problem with such systems is that they are not yet supported in a standardized way by messaging software packages. There is therefore a risk that all recipients of a message cannot use all parts of the message, unless they all use the same messaging software. Multimedia will probably be more common with more advanced user equipment in the future.

In a more advanced multimedia system, there is a requirement that picture, sound, and voice be coordinated, so that you can hear a spoken comment to a picture at the

---

1   X.400 is a standard for electronic mail developed jointly by ITU/CCITT, the organization for telecommunication companies, and ISO/IEC, the international standards organization. X.400 is more fully described in chapter 8.4.

same time as you see the picture. Such coordination is not supported by the X.400 messaging standard, but is to some extent supported by the MIME[2] messaging standards.

If a message includes a computer program, the system can be designed so that this program is more-or-less automatically executed when the user attempts to read it. These are called *active messages*. For example, such messages can put a series of questions to the user and show different information depending on previous replies of the user to such questions. The system may also store the answers to a series of questions in an automatic reply to the sender of the active message.

There are obvious security risks with active messages. Systems with this facility have to plan carefully their security features, so as not to allow active messages which will erase files or bring a computer virus into the computer. An example of the problems which can occur happened during Christmas 1986. The active messagewas a program which showed a Christmas tree on the screen. The program at the same time duplicated itself to all e-mail addresses it could find. The BITNET (Because-It's-Time Network) was overloaded with thousands of such messages.

Voice mail systems are electronic mail systems for spoken messages. They are mostly use as a kind of advanced answering machine or by travellers who want to leave short messages without carrying any computer equipment. One important advantage of written electronic mail over voice mail is the efficiency gained with textual communication to several recipients (see Section 5.5). Thus, voice mail is often not very suitable for multirecipient messages. Existing voice mail systems are usually not coordinated with textual electronic mail systems. This may change, however, since the 1992 version of X.400 contains built-in support for voice mail.

6.5   OFFICE DOCUMENTS (EDI), FORMS, WORK FLOW APPLICATIONS

6.5.1   Formatted Fields in Message Bodies

The common format of electronic mail is a heading and a piece of text, where the heading contains structured information about sender, recipient, etc. The text, which comes after the heading is usually called the *body* of the message. In some cases, the body is also structured fields. Such messages resemble forms with different fields to fill in.

The advantages to this are:

- You can ensure that certain information is present in certain kinds of letters;
- The receiving computer can automatically interpret the contents of such fields;
- The information can be put into a data base or used for sorting and searching;

---

2   MIME is the part of Internet mail standards which supports graphics, voice, etc. in messages (see Section 8.6.6.)

- The information can be used for more specialized uses, for example, an order for a ticket may cause the booking of a seat, the printing of a ticket, etc.

6.5.2 E-Mail to and from Humans or Computers

Electronic mail may be sent primarily by a human or a computer, and the recipient may primarily be a human or a computer. Of course, there is always a human behind everything a computer sends or receives, so this is only a matter of to what extent a computer automatically handles the production and receipt of a message. Figure 6.1 shows different degrees of human involvement in the production and receipt of messages.

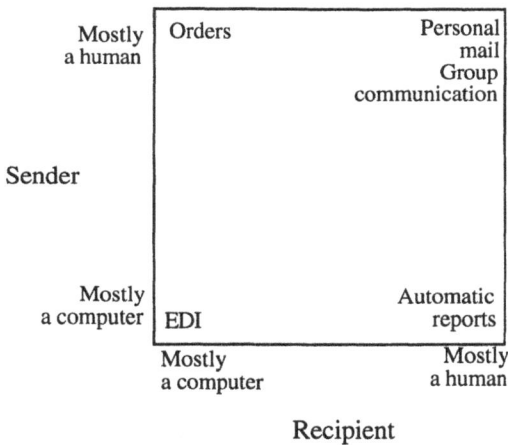

Figure 6.1   Communication from and to humans or computer programs.

When electronic mail is used for communication between computers rather than between humans, it is called office documents or electronic data interchange (EDI).

Systems may also be a combination of human input/output and computer control. Examples include:

- Form-fill-in on the screen, where the user manually fills in the fields of a form, but the computer checks the data, for example, checking the format and check-sum in social security numbers;
- Access control that allows only certain people to fill in certain fields, for example, the authorization of a payment;
- A document can pass through several versions, where different people enter information into different fields and then forward the document via e-mail according to prescribed rules.

In some cases, EDI messages are forwarded in specialized networks, like the booking networks of the airlines and the SWIFT network banks use to send money (electronic funds transfer, EFT). The format of these documents is often particular to each area. For example, European car manufacturers have a special format called "Odette" for communication between car manufacturers and their suppliers.

Office documents can be coordinated with other electronic mail. As an example, take the case of a person ordering a computer program from a supplier. The program may then be sent in a three-part message, one part with the program, one part with the user manual, and a third part containing the bill in an EDI format, so that the recipient can instruct his computer to pay the bill electronically.

For more information about EDI, see [10]. The March 1993 issue of *Byte* magazine contained several articles on the use of e-mail for communication with computers [8, 9].

6.5.3 Combining Formatted and Free Text Messages

One might also find it natural to combine ordinary electronic mail with structured fields. An incoming letter to a company, might, for example, have an appendix with extra fields to control the handling of mail within the company, who is to handle it, what is to be done with it, how the handling is to be terminated, etc.

The border between electronic mail between humans and data transfer from computer to computer is thus not very well-defined, since there is usually a human somewhere behind computer-produced messages.

In 1990, X.400 was extended with X.435, a special part on the forwarding of EDI through ordinary X.400 mail networks. This may mean that more EDI will be handled through the ordinary electronic mail networks in the future. However, X.435 prescribes that office documents should have a special format (in X.400 called *content type*). This means that a mixture of EDI and interpersonal mail in the same message is not permitted. The standard does, however, allow for an EDI message to refer to a separate interpersonal message or the reverse. X.435 is thus mostly suited to applications in the lower left corner of Figure 6.1 rather than applications combining humans and computers as source or recipient.

6.5.4 Work Flow Applications

"Work flow applications" is another term often used for applications where messages are sent wholly or partly to and from computer programs. For example purchase orders, travel expense reports, sales-proposals, etc. Work flow can also be used to designate e-mail with extended functions to clarify who is going to do what, and when. A person sends a message asking someone to do some work. The person asked replies with acceptance, rejection, or a modified proposal. Formatted fields in the messages specify what is to be done, what has been agreed on, when tasks are to be completed, etc. [7].

This information might also be stored in a data base, which produces automatic reminders when tasks are to be completed.

It is well-known that ordinary free-text e-mail has problems in handling negotiations and agreements, since interactive cues like voice inflection and body language seem to pay an important role in face-to-face communication. See Section 4.8. One could say that these kinds of work flow applications attempt to solve this problem with e-mail, by introducing explicit fields in messages to more clearly indicate what users have agreed on through the messages they exchange.

Experience with such applications is that it is difficult to get people to accept using an ordinary e-mail system for ordinary e-mail and a separate system for work-flow applications. Users want all the functionality in one system with a coherent user interface. Many users also dislike work-flow systems, because they feel constricted by the formalism. Thus, even though work-flow applications provide standard fields for certain information in messages, users prefer systems where they can skip using these standard fields in cases where the fields are not suitable [6].

There has also been some controversy over these systems. Some claim that the systems are based on "fascist" views of human communications, and others extol the systems as a major advance in getting better controlled work flow in organizations. Obviously, the design of such systems is a sensitive matter, and systems built on too narrow views of human communications may indeed be perceived as "fascist" by their users. But it ought to be possible to design systems where these additional features are perceived as an optional and useful aid to users rather than as constricting regulations.

6.6   FOLDERS AND ARCHIVES

Most message systems store incoming messages in some kind of temporary data base or message store, often called a *mailbox*. Many message systems have functions for storing messages in data bases. This can vary from sorting messages into folders to advanced information retrieval systems, where the documents are given keywords and other methods of classification. The message stores can be common to several people, for example, the central archiving of official mail to and from a company or government agency. Note, however, that the term *message store* in X.400 has a specific meaning a personal store for just one user.

Sometimes the term *store* is used for short-term storage of messages, while the term *archive* is used for long-term storage, perhaps indefinitely. Archives are sometimes moved to mountable media such as magnetic tapes or optical disks.

Message stores are often arranged in a hierarchical manner, with folders within folders, such as the filing systems on most computers or the document store defined in the document filing and retrieval (DFR) standard. Sometimes, the same document is allowed to belong to more than one folder, as shown by the dotted lines in Figure 6.2. Access control is often connected to this tree structure, so that only certain people are allowed to go into a certain subbranch of the tree.

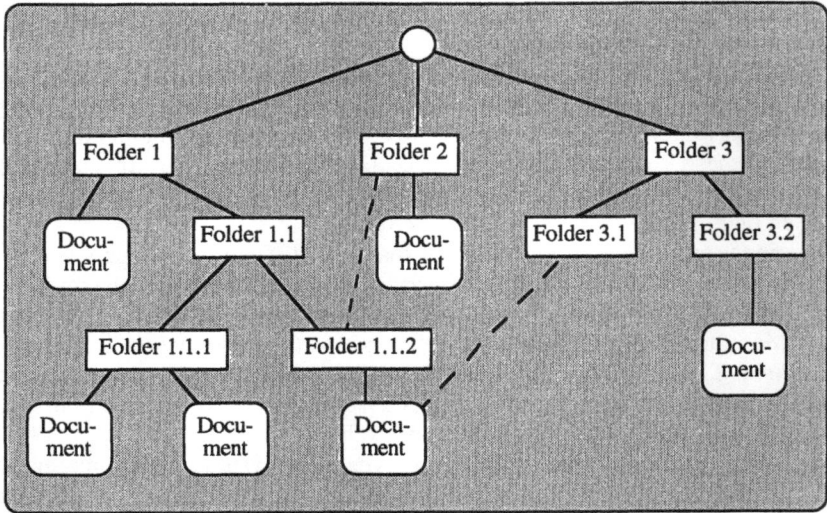

Figure 6.2   Folder organization of document data bases.

Note that the "conferences" or "bulletin boards" and "conversations" in computer conferencing or bulletin board systems have a similar utility as folders in message stores. See Section 6.7 and 7.5.

6.7   GROUP COMMUNICATION

The analysis in Chapter 5 showed that electronic mail was most efficient media for communication in three cases: (1) small simple messages, (2) EDI and other computer-interpretable messages and (3) communication between more than two people. Indeed electronic mail is used a great deal in these three areas, and good electronic mail systems should support all three areas, or at least support more than just interpersonal mail.

Communication between more than two people is called *group communication.* Some electronic mail systems have tools for group communication. Examples include the following:

- *Multirecipient messages:* the sender can send a message to more than one recipient at the same time.
- *Multirecipient replies:* when replying to a multirecipient message, the sender can request that the reply is sent only to the sender or to all recipients of the message you are answering.
- *Reply links:* a series of messages, which are replies to each other, are linked in the computer, so that the user can easily scan or get an overview of the discussion between a group of people. Such a series of linked messages on the same

42

issue is called a *conversation*. Some systems have special built-in support for conversations. This support might allow you to skip certain branches of a conversation, to scan through all messages in a conversation, or to forward all messages in a conversation to additional recipients.

- *Personal distribution lists:* in his personal area in a computer a user can store lists of people to whom the user often writes messages, and he will then only have to give the name of the list in order to send a message to all the people on the list.
- *Public distribution lists:* this works in the same way as personal distribution lists, but these lists are stored in a public area, so that several senders can send messages to the same list of recipients.
- *Circulation lists:* messages are circulated and read in a certain order by recipients. This allows those who appear early in the list to add comments which are then read by those who appear later in the list.
- *One-of-a-group-reads:* messages may be addressed to a unit containing more than one person, but the unit may be organized so that normally only one person in the group reads and answers each incoming message. This is used, for example, for help desks, where customers are served by a group of assistants.
- *Computer conferences (meetings) or bulletin boards:* there are two main differences between computer conferences and distribution lists:

  (1) The recipient views read and unread messages sorted by conference, sometimes also sorted into *topics* or *conversations* within conferences, and this helps the recipient in deciding what and when to read.
  (2) There is a common store of messages for a group. This not only means that participants can search for old messages, it also means that new members in a computer conference can be allowed to read what was written before they became members of the conference.

An important function of computer conference systems is *news control*. This is the facility in the computer to know which messages a person has or has not seen, which aids a user in finding only the new messages. This may be obvious if you view computer conferencing as a kind of electronic mail system. But some systems have very rudimentary or no news control at all. Such systems are sometimes called *bulletin board* systems, but many systems called bulletin board systems can also provide good news control.

A facility in computer conferencing systems also allows it to provide an access control system suitable for group communication and involving different kinds conferences:

- *Open or public conferences*, in which any user can make himself a member;
- *Closed or private conferences*, with various kinds of control over who may participate;
- *Write-protected conferences*, with an editor or an editorial board deciding what is published; and

- *Selection conferences*, containing a selection of the most interesting entries from other conferences.

Electronic mail systems that do not have advanced support for group communication are still often used for group communication. Such systems usually make it as easy for the sender to send a message to a hundred recipients as to one single recipient. But they do not give the recipient facilities to cope with the large flow of information which this may cause.

Figure 6.3 shows the situation for the recipient in systems with distribution lists but no advanced support for handling the incoming information flow. Figure 6.4 shows how a recipient experiences a good computer conferencing system. The incoming messages are sorted into conferences and within the conferences into conversations.

Figure 6.3   Information overload when incoming messages are not well organized at delivery.

By providing a well-structured data base for messages, computer conferences are somewhat similar to text data-base systems such as Videotex (Minitel) and information-retrieval systems[3]. A difference is, however, that the latter systems organize their users into two categories of people—information suppliers, who can add information to the data bases, and information recipients, who retrieve the information. Videotex systems even have different kind of terminals for these two categories.

---

3   Videotex are systems for access to computer services, using a special simple and inexpensive terminal. They usually have a data base of numbered pages. Users can access pages by giving their numbers. Many pages contain references to other pages, which can then be reached by short-cuts of only one digit. Pages can contain information to the user, or can contain executable programs providing various services.

Letters   Meeting A   Meeting B   Meeting C

Seen

Un-
seen

Structuring of the
message flow
increases recipi-
ent control

Figure 6.4   Structuring of messages in computer conferencing systems.

The relation between electronic mail, conference systems, and information retrieval can be understood by looking at which possibilities the sender (including editors and intermediaries) and recipients have to control the communication process. See Table 6.1.

Table 6.1
Division of Control Between Senders and Recipients

Medium	Sender facilities	Recipient facilities
Information retrieval systems, videotex systems	The sender controls the classification of messages and sometimes also sets access codes controlling who may read the messages	The recipient decides what to read by the formulation of search queries.
Computer conferencing systems	The sender controls to which conferences a message is sent, and chooses to enter them into closed or public conferences	The recipient decides in which order to read different conferences, and to some extent which conferences to participate in
Interpersonal mail	The sender has full control of exactly who is allowed to read the messages	There are usually very limited facilities for the recipient to control the incoming information flow

This can be simplified as in Figure 6.5, which shows the balance between senders and recipients in different media.

45

Personally
addressed
messages

Computer conferencing

Videotex and
information-
retrieval systems

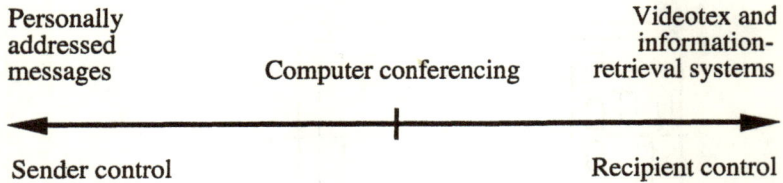

Sender control

Recipient control

Figure 6.5   Balance of control between sender and recipient with different media.

For more information about various functions in group communication systems, see [11, 12].

6.7.1   Examples of Existing Electronic Discussion Groups

There are tens of thousands of electronic discussion groups. Below is a list of just a few, selected to show that it is not only researchers in technical sciences who use these tools:

6.7.2   Examples of LISTSERV Distribution Lists

U47C2@ WVNVM.WVNET.EDU	The culture and history of England before 1100 C.E.
ANTHRO-L@UBVM.BIT.NET	Anthropology
BALT-L@ UBVM.CC.BUFFALO.EDU	Information exchange in Baltic countries' languages
BUBBA-L@ KNUTH.MTSU.EDU	Language and culture of the southern United States
CHAUCER@ UNLINFO.UNL.EDU	Geoffrey Chaucer and medieval English literature and culture
CONTEX-L@ UOTTAWA.BIT.NET	Cross-disciplinary analysis of ancient texts
CPS-L@HEARN.BIT.NET	Interdisciplinary studies of the Pacific regions
CUBA-L@ UNMVMA.BIT.NET	Cuba today (Spanish/English)
EARLYM-L@ AEARN.BIT.NET	Medieval, renaissance and baroque music
ELENCHUS@ UOTTAWA.BIT.NET	Christian thought and literature in Late Antiquity
ESPORA-L@ UKANVM.BIT.NET	History of the Iberian Peninsula
GERLINGL@ UIUCVMD.BIT.NET	Older Germanic languages (to 1500)
HESSE-L@UCSBVM.BIT.NET	Life and literary works of Hermann Hesse

6.7.3 Examples of Usenet News Newsgroups

alt.books.reviews	alt.folklore.herbs
alt.chinese.text.big5	alt.folklore.info
alt.chinese.text	alt.folklore.science
alt.comp.mac	alt.folklore.urban
alt.culture.alaska	alt.horror.cthulhu
alt.culture.argentina	alt.horror.werewolves
alt.culture.austrian	alt.horror
alt.culture.electric-midget	alt.humor.best-of-usenet.d
alt.culture.hawaii	alt.humor.best-of-usenet
alt.culture.indonesia	alt.humor.oracle
alt.current-events.bosnia	alt.news-media
alt.current-events.haiti	alt.psychology.personality
alt.current-events.russia	alt.rave
alt.current-events.somalia	alt.sexual.abuse.recovery
alt.current-events.usa	alt.skinheads
alt.discrimination	alt.soc.ethics

6.7.4 How You Become a Member of a Distribution List

There are no standards for how to become a member of a distribution list. Two practices are, however, very common.

6.7.5 The LISTSERV Way

Suppose you want to become a member of a distribution list, whose e-mail address is listname@host.bit.net. You then write an e-mail message addressed to listserv@host.bit.net and write in this message a single text line with the text:

```
SUB listname Your Own Name
```

For information about other commands you can give, such as how to unsubscribe from a list, download archived messages from the list, etc., write a message to the same recipient, listserv@host.bit.net, with the single word HELP in the text of your message. For more information about Listserv, see Section 6.10.

6.7.6 The Listname-Request Way

Suppose you want to become a member of a distribution list, whose e-mail address is listname@host.bit.net. You then write a message to listname-request@host.bit.net and write in the text of the message something like "Please add me as a member of this mailing list." The e-mail address with the name of a distribution list with "-request" added to it can also be used for other communication with the list manager.

6.8 FILTERS

A filter is a function which sorts incoming messages automatically (before the recipient reads them) into different folders. Usually, filters are placed in the stream of incoming messages for a certain person. To some extent, filters and computer-conference systems provide similar facilities. In conference systems, messages are presorted by conference when shown to the user. With filter-supported systems, incoming messages may be sorted by which distribution list they arrive from, providing a similar facility: the recipient gets messages sorted by topic and can read them one topic at a time.

In addition to sorting by the distribution list, filters can also sort by author, sender and words in the subject or the text of a message. In one well-known system, Usenet News, it is customary to keep the subject line of messages unchanged throughout conversations (except adding the character sequence "Re: "), and a user who does not want to read any more messages in a certain conversation can tell the system to filter out all messages with that content in the subject line.

A problem with filters is that most filtering systems are not very easy to set up. The filtering conditions are specified as boolean conditions. Many filtering systems also apply the filtering conditions in sequential order, so that the effect of one filtering condition will depend on its order in the list. This makes it even more difficult to set up filtering conditions.

An important topic for research in the messaging area is how to make filters more user-friendly. Several techniques are being tested: new user-interface design, use of artificial-intelligence methods to find filtering conditions, and use of transfer of information between users. This would mean that if two users have similar interests, messages liked by one of them may be recommended by the filter to the other. Such transfer is, of course, difficult to realize in practice. A variant of this is the principle of moderators or editors, who perform a human evaluation and selection of the most valuable messages. This principle is, of course, well-known in the publishing world, where magazine and newspaper editors perform the function. Intelligent e-mail systems might possibly be better than magazines or newspapers, because they can make different selections for different users.

There are similarities between information filtering and information retrieval, but there are also differences [1].

Filtering is done by applying filtering conditions to attributes of the messages being filtered. These attributes can be the author, distribution list, other people's opinion of the message, etc. To get better filtering, it is necessary to scan the text of the message. Such scanning can be done either by looking for the occurrence of certain words or by trying to "understand" the text. However the general problem of making a computer understand written text has not yet been solved, even by artificial intelligence researchers. Looking for the occurrences of certain words is problematic because there are often different words and phrases used to designate the same concepts. A filter may, for example, search for messages containing the word "persuade" and then not find messages which contain the word "convince" instead. A thesaurus can be used to find synonyms, but this is not sufficient to solve the problem.

Note that people may be more interested in finding new messages and presenting new ideas and concepts than in finding messages about things they already know. Thus, a filter based on their present knowledge may not be ideal for doing this.

A perfect filter will never be designed. Anyone searching for valuable information will always have to accept some less valuable information. Two terms used to describe this problem are *precision* and *recall* [2]. "Precision" means the percentage of retrieved messages which are of value, and "recall" means the percentage of all interesting messages which are retrieved. It is obvious that a more liberal filtering condition will often give higher recall but less precision, and a more stringent condition will often give higher precision but less recall.

One interesting system, the information lens system [13], uses a quite different approach. When you write a message in the information lens system, you do not normally address it to a certain group of recipients. You just address your message to "anyone who may be interested in it." On the recipient side, you do not subscribe to certain distribution lists or become a member of certain computer conferences. Instead you just use your personal filter, which will then scan everything you are allowed to read and supply you with everything that fits the filtering conditions.

Many of the ideas in this section appeared originally in [3]. This paper also contains more complete references on filters and filtering.

6.9   ANONYMITY AND PSEUDONYMITY

In general, messages in e-mail are not anonymous. There are, however, some systems which provide some kind of anonymity or pseudonymity service. This service is usually provided in such a way that information on who wrote the message is still stored somewhere. This means that if, for instance, police asked for this information, the information could be provided. Storing the information somewhere will allow e-mail to be sent to the author of an anonymous message even though the sender of such messages may not know the real name of this sender.

On the Internet there are about ten anonymous servers, also called anonymous remailers [16, 18]; the most popular is in Finland at anon.penet.fi [17]. This server works by receiving e-mail and forwarding it to the final destination with a pseudonymous author name. It is possible, however, to send messages to this pseudonymous name, and the anonymous server will then forward the message to the original sender. Thus, people can exchange messages without knowing the other person's real name. You can, of course reveal your real name when writing to an anoymous name. Message size is for anon.penet.fi limited to 48Kb.

Differences for other anonymous remailers are: The format of commands is not the same for all anonymous remailers. Some allow messages longer than 48Kb. Some do not support pseudonyms. Some provide higher security by allowing encrypted messages between the user and the server. For more information, see [15].

Anyone with some knowledge about the simple mail transfer protocol (SMTP) (see Section 8.6.2) can easily connect to an SMTP server and send a faked message. In

49

the same way, network news transfer protocol (NNTP) (see Section 8.8) can be used to send a faked entry to Usenet News. This is not 100 percent secure and system administrators do not always like such activities and might try to find out who you are.

Opinions on anonymity are varied. Some claim that anonymity fosters irresponsible behaviour, others claim that, at least in certain cases, anonymity allows freer exchange of information. This is said to be true especially for people employed in large companies, who may be restricted in what they are allowed to say if their messages are not anonymous.

Ethical aspects of anonymity is discussed in Section 10.1.5, and legal issues of responsibility for anonymous messages are discussed in Section 10.11.

6.10   MAIL SERVERS

A mail server is a computer program which can receive and send e-mail. A mail server will perform some service to the people who send messages to it. The most common services provided by mail servers are

(a)   Managing a distribution list, which in addition to distributing messages to list members includes adding and removing members from the list; and

(b)   Managing a data base, allowing users to retrieve and sometimes submit documents to the data base.

These kinds of services can, of course, also be provided via direct client-server connections. Such direct connections are usually nicer to use, since users get more direct feedback. If you have to wait for an e-mail reply, this may take a few minutes.

The reason why mail servers are used in spite of this disadvantage is that direct client-server connections are normally only possible if the user has a client in the same network as the server. However, many people can send e-mail through gateways to a net, without having full access to that net. Such people may have to use mail servers.

There is no standard for the commands to give to a mail server, but usually if you send a message to the mail server with the single word "help" as the only text of your message, then the mail server will reply with a summary of commands you can give to it.

A very common mail server is called Listserv [5], written by Eric Thomas. Below are some examples of the most common commands which you can send in e-mail messages to a Listserv server

Listserv Commands for Handling Distribution Lists

(Boldface in the list indicates an allowed abbreviation of the command.)

subscribe   Join a distribution list

unsubscribe	Leave a distribution list
list	Get a list of distribution lists available from this list server
list **global**	Get a list of distribution lists available everywhere
review	Get more information about one particular list
query	Find out your own subscription settings to a list
set	Change your subscriptions settings to a list
confirm	Confirm that you want to stay on a list
stats	Get statistics on a list
register	Register your name and e-mail address with a list server

Listserv Commands for Handling Document Retrieval

index	Get a list of available documents
get	Get a document
afd	Subscribe to a copy of a document, every time it is changed
query file	Get more information about a particular document
give	Send a document to someone else than yourself
pw	Change your password

6.11 DIRECTORIES

Just as a telephone directory holds the telephone numbers of people you can call, an electronic mail directory contains addresses for electronic mail. Since electronic-mail systems are computer-based, their directories are often available via the computer instead of printed on paper. This means that the result of the directory search can be used directly for addressing your message.

Because of this, many electronic mail systems provide directories. Just as there are personal address and phone number books, internal company directories, and public directories, electronic mail systems can provide personal, local, or general directories. A personal or local directory can also contain external addresses that you frequently use. Some systems automatically add into the personal or local directory names of people sending mail to you or names you use in sending mail.

Electronic mail addresses are often long and clumsy, especially with the X.400 standard, the addresses with the SMTP standard are, for example, usually longer than phone numbers. This makes it difficult for you to type in the whole address correctly, thus the need for a directory system which finds the proper electronic address and automatically inserts it as recipient.

Global directories can be based on a distributed data base, where your search query, if necessary, is automatically routed to the directory of the area or company that contains the required address. The X.500 Directory System standard developed by ITU and ISO is meant to be used for such a globally interconnected system of directories. It is described further in Section 8.5. Another standard for directory systems is the Whois standard [4], now being upgraded to Whois-plus.

Compared to other data base systems, directory systems do not have very strong requirements for consistency or timeliness: reliable access is more important.

A sensitive issue with directories is the willingness of companies to hand over their internal "phone books" for use in public directory systems. Companies may not want to give out so much information about their internal organization. One solution might be to strip all organizational information before giving out the remaining information. A similar problem occurs for companies providing public electronic mail services. The directories for such companies are their customer lists, and many companies regard their customer lists as closely guarded company secrets. Such problems are one reason why the efforts to develop global directory services have had difficulties.

6.12   COWORKING WITH OTHER MEDIA

Some electronic mail systems provide coworking with other communication media, such as postal mail, telex, teletex, fax, telegrams, videotex, voice mail systems and beepers. It is often easier to provide transmission from electronic mail to other media than vice versa. Because of this, most coworking services with postal mail, fax, voice mail, and alert systems are one way: from electronic mail to these systems, not the reverse. With telex, telegram and teletex, which work with text in a digital format, coworking is easier to provide in both directions.

Messages from these media, however, lack the comprehensive structured envelope and header information that exists in electronic mail. This means that electronic-mail addressing information has to be added manually, which makes such services expensive and less reliable.

Beeper systems can usually only receive and display a few characters on a very small display, so they will often only be sent very short messages, or just an indication that there is electronic mail to collect. This, however, is expected to change in the future with more powerful hand-held combined computers, beepers and cellular phone systems.

6.13 RELIABILITY AND SECURITY

6.13.1 Risks and Reliability Requirements

Below are some risks which may require special protective measures in electronic mail systems:

- *Denial of service* occurs when a message does not reach its recipients. If a message cannot be delivered, the sender should always be informed. Messages should never disappear into "black holes."
- *Masquerade* occurs when some entity successfully pretends to be another entity, for example: sending a message with false sender information. This could be used for false orders or to trick the recipient into divulging secret information.
- *Nonauthorized access* occurs when messages are read by unauthorized recipients.
- *Data modification or destruction* is the illegal or unintentional modification or deletion of messages.
- *Repudiation* occurs when some entity falsely denies submitting or receiving a message or sending a message with certain claimed contents.
- *Traffic analysis* occurs when unauthorized persons deduce secret information by using statistics of the message flow between legal users.
- *Deduction of information* is the deduction of secret information from publicly available information, such as statistics. *Traffic analysis* is a special case of this threat.
- *Illegal activities* occur when electronic mail is used for various kinds of illegal or harmful activities, such as the planning of crimes (See Section 10.7), fraud, transmission of computer viruses, etc. (Section 6.4 describes one such case.)

A more complete list of security risks can be found in [14]. An introduction to security issues on the Internet can be found in [16].

Most electronic mail services today provide very low security. In Internet mail, most servers allow any user to masquerade as an SMTP sender and send faked messages. Many mail clients allow senders to put any name in the originator (From:) field of outgoing messages. Now and then, cases occur, usually at universities, where young students send faked e-mail messages (for example, messages from less-liked teachers purporting to ask for resignation).

The only protection used much is the trace, which is sent together with messages to show which way the message is forwarded. This trace is easily faked. There are defined methods for getting high security in e-mail, using cryptographic techniques. In Internet mail, these methods are called *privacy enhanced mail* (PEM) or *pretty good privacy* (PRP), see Section 8.6.7. They are, however, not yet much used, as of this writing.

One should note, however, that it is even easier to fake ordinary postal mail. Despite this, faked postal mail messages are surprisingly seldom serious problems. People tend to require more security measures in computerized systems than in manual systems. There is also a tendency for abusers to wrongly believe that anything which is not stopped by security measures in the computer is therefore legal!

6.13.2 Cryptographic Security Services

Cryphthographic methods are most known for their basic usage to encrypt a message so that non-authorized people cannot read it. Modern cryphthographic techniques, described in Section 7.6, can, however, be used for many other important security services. Some wellknown such services are:

- *Digital signatures*, methods to ensure that a message was really signed by the purported originator of the message.
- *Digital seals*, methods to ensure that the contents of a message has not been tampered with.
- *Digital authentication*, methods to ensure that someone else is not masquerading for a certain person or agent.
- *Digital authorization*, methods to ensure that only authorized people or agents can use protected services.

There are also other, less secure methods of achieving some of these services, for example, the well-known method of authentication through the use of ordinary passwords.

6.13.3 Notifications

Notifications are services for a sender that check whether a message has reached its intended recipient or not. A *delivery notification* informs the sender that the message has been delivered, and a *nondelivery notification* informs the sender that it has not been delivered. Electronic mail networks cannot always produce such notifications when a message is sent. Because of this, the notifications are sent back to the sender as a special kind of return message.

A good electronic mail system should always (unless the sender explicitly relinquishes this requirement) inform the sender if a message cannot be delivered. But sometimes a fault, such as a disk crash, cam cause messages to disappear without any notification to the sender (such situations are often called *black holes*). However, if the sender has requested a delivery notification, the fact that it has not arrived within a reasonable time can indicate to the sender that the message has been lost, even when no nondelivery notification appears.

It is, of course, advantageous to the sender if his mail software automatically recognizes incoming delivery and nondelivery notifications and handles them in suitable ways. The sender may prefer not to be informed every time such a notification arrives, but to store them so that later the sender can ask the system to provide a report about which recipients have received their messages. Notifications usually indicate that a message has reached the mailbox of the recipient, but some systems also provide notifications when a message has been read by the recipient, or, rather, when it has been shown on the screen of the recipient.

Getting Wanted and Unwanted Nondelivery Notifications

```
Date: Sat, 22 Jan 94 14:29:32 +0100
From: Mail Delivery Subsystem <MAILER-DAEMON@vall.dsv.su.se>
To: jpalme@ester.dsv.su.se
Cc: Postmaster@vall.dsv.su.se
Subject: Returned mail: User unknown


     ----- Transcript of session follows -----
While talking to byrd.mu.wvnet.edu:
>>> RCPT To:<listerv@byrd.mu.wvnet.edu>
<<< 550 <listerv@byrd.mu.wvnet.edu>... Addressee unknown
550 <listerv@byrd.mu.wvnet.edu>... User unknown


     ----- Message header follows -----
Received: from ester.dsv.su.se by vall.dsv.su.se (5.61-bind 1.4+ida/4.0)
        id AA19781; Sat, 22 Jan 94 14:29:32 +0100
Received: by ester.dsv.su.se (4.1/SMI-4.1)
        id AA21595; Sat, 22 Jan 94 14:29:31 +0100
Date: Sat, 22 Jan 1994 14:29:30 +0100 (MET)
From: Jacob Palme DSV <jpalme@dsv.su.se>
Subject:
To: listerv@byrd.mu.wvnet.edu
Message-Id: <Pine.3.89.9401221422.B21558-0100000@ester>
Mime-Version: 1.0
Content-Type: TEXT/PLAIN; charset=US-ASCII
```

Figure 6.6   Example of a nondelivery notification as delivered in Internet mail.

The figure shows that nondelivery notifications are often diffiult to understand if you are not an expert on electronic mail protocols. Getting a a nondelivery notification from some recipient to whom you never sent any message can be especially confusing. See Figure 6.7. What happens is that you send a message to a distribution list, and there is a delivery problem in delivering the message to one of the members of this list. For large distribution lists, such delivery reports should, of course be sent to the manager of the list, not to the originator of the message. However, it is not uncommon for mailers to mistakenly send the nondelivery notifications to the originator. This is also discussed in Section 8.4.18.

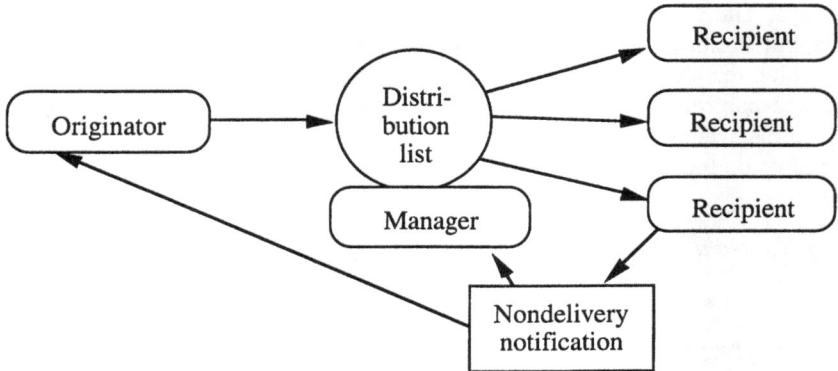

Figure 6.7   Sending error reports till distribution list manager or to the originator.

6.13.4 Closed User Groups

Some message systems try to achieve higher security by storing in the computer rules governing who is allowed to communicate with whom, for example, by establishing *closed user groups*, whose members can only communicate with each other. As electronic mail becomes more widespread, and as messages with topics unanticipated by the original system planners are sent to many different people, such usage restrictions will become difficult to implement, since the computer-stored rules about whom may communicate with whom about what will have to be updated very often.

Another meaning of *closed user group* refers to groups, where all information about a certain kind of communication within the group is invisible outside the group, but where communication about other topics outside this group is allowed. This meaning of the term may be more useful. However, a computer can find it difficult to check the topic of a message in order to control whom you may send it to.

6.14 ROLES

Electronic mail is usually sent and received by humans. But a communication entity (sender or recipient) may also be a computer program. A human can also receive or send a message as a private message or as a message to or from a certain *role*, such as to the manager of a certain organizational unit. There may be a need to have different electronic mailboxes for different roles for the same person. The mailbox for the role of supervisor may, for example, be handled by a deputy when the supervisor is away. The access rights for a person may also vary with the role.

56

Electronic mail systems today usually do not give much support for roles, but this may change in the future, since much research into of computer support for office procedures is based on the concept of roles.

The term *agent* is often used in electronic mail. An agent is a person or a computer program which uses or provides network services, like electronic mail. Examples of agents are the user agents (UAs) who represent users. An agent may perform different functions in the electronic mail system. It may, for example, create or send a message. Note that author and sender need not be the same person. Many electronic mail systems separate information about the sender (also called originator) and author of messages. The agent can also be a recipient of electronic mail and perform other controlled roles such as controlling access, approving a message for distribution, registering users, etc.

REFERENCES

[1] Belkin, N.J. and Croft, W.B., "Information filtering and information retrieval: two sides of the same coin?" *Communications of the ACM*, Vol. 35, No. 12, pp. 29-38, 1992.

[2] Salton, G. and McGill, M.J. *Introduction to information retrieval*, New York, McGraw-Hill 1983.

[3] Pargman, Daniel, *Creating a humane information flow*, Masters Thesis, Uppsala University, Uppsala, Sweden 1994.

[4] Feinler, E. et al. *NICNAME/WHOIS*, Internet RFC 954.

[5] EARN Association *LISTSERV User Guide*, 1993. Published by EARN Association. Available from URL ftp://aun.uninett.no/uninettinfo/brukerhjelp/listserv.guide, 1993.

[6] Carasik, R.P., "A case study of CSCW in a dispersed organization" CHI'88 Proceedings, May 15-17, Washington D.C., pp 61-66, 1988.

[7] Flores, F. et al.: "Computer systems and the design of organizational interaction," *ACM Transactions on Office Information Systems*, April, 153-172, 1988.

[8] Reinhardt, Andy, "Smarter E-mail is coming." *Byte*, March 1993, pp 90-96.

[9] Udell, Jon. "The Vines advantage," *Byte*, March 1993, pp 98-108.

[10] Hendry, Mike, *Implementing EDI*. Norwood, MA: Artech Books 1993.

[11] Turoff, Murray, "Computer-mediated communication requirements for group support," *Journal of Organizational Computing*, 1, 86-113, 1991.

[12] Palme, Jacob, "Computer conferencing functions and terminology," in *Collaborative Learning through computer conferencing* (ed: Tony Kaye), Heidelberg: Springer-Verlag, 1992.

[13] Malone, Thomas W., *The information lens, an intelligent system for information sharing in organizations*. CHI'86 Proceedings, Association for Computer Machinery, 1986.

[14] Muftic, Sead et al., *Security architecture for open distributed systems*, New York, John Wiley & Sons, 1993.

[15] Ghio, Matthew, *FAQ on anonymous remailers*; to retreive send an e-mail message to mg5n+remailers@andrew.cmu.edu. Also available by Gopher.

[16] Detweiler, L., *Identity, privacy and anomymity on the Internet*. Privacy & Anonymity on the Internet FAQ. Available on the Internet from URL ftp://relay.cs.toronto.edu.pub/usenet/comp.answers/net-privacy or ftp://rtfm.mit.edu:/pub/usenet/news.answers/net-privacy.

[17] Helsingus, Johan "Julf", *Anonymous help;* to retrieve send an e-mail message to help@anon.penet.fi with the word "help" in the text of the message.

Chapter 7

Techniques for Electronic Mail

7.1   TRANSMISSION OF MESSAGES (ROUTING)

When the mailboxes of the sender and of the recipient are in different computers, the message must be transmitted between the two computers. There are two main methods for this as shown in Figure 7.1: *direct connection* and *store-and-forward*.

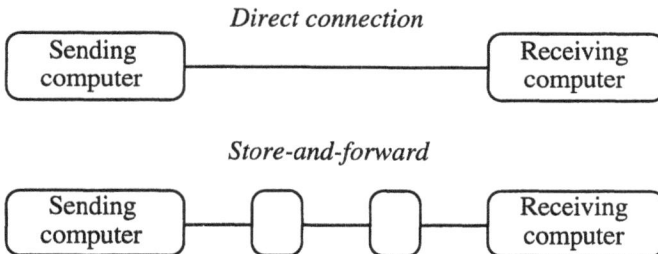

Figure 7.1   Comparison of direct connection and store-and-forward routing.

When a direct connection is used, the computer of the sender and the recipient are interacting directly with each other. The sending computer transmits the message and then gets a confirmation that the message has been received. If something goes wrong before this confirmation has been received, the sending computer will try to retransmit the message until it gets a confirmation. (Large messages can be split into separately confirmed parts, so that the whole message need not be retransmitted if something goes wrong, but this does not change the basic principle.)

59

Figure 7.2 shows how transmission is done during a direct connection, or, if store-and-forward transmission is used, how transmission is done between two intermediate stations on the way from the sender to the recipient:

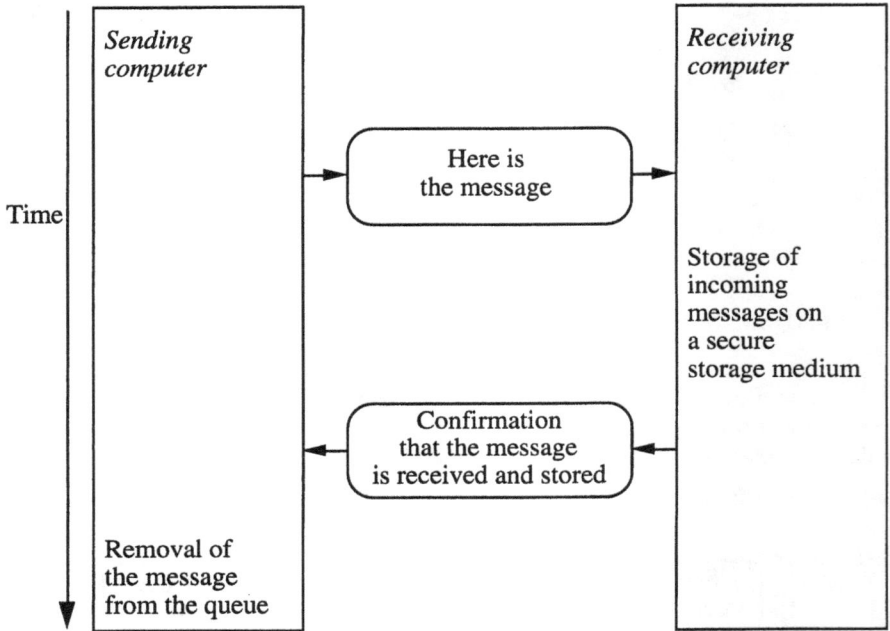

Figure 7.2   Transfer of responsibility during one transmission step.

When the store-and-forward method is used, the sending computer transmits the message to the nearest intermediate station, MTA. When the entire message has been copied to secure memory in the intermediate station, the sending computer gets confirmation of this. This confirmation means that the main responsibility for getting the message delivered is transferred from the sending computer to the intermediate station. This station copies the message in the same way to the next station until the message arrives at the receiving computer.

Note that a direct connection may use a *packet switching net*. This means that the message is transferred in small packets, which are temporarily stored in intermediate stations. But logically, the connection is direct, since the sending computer has responsibility for the message until the receiving computer takes over.

The advantages of direct connections is that it gives better security and reliability, and that the sender can get a more immediate confirmation that the message is received. With the store-and-forward method, the risk may increase that a message can disappear, due to a failure like a disk crash or overflowing queues in each of the intermediate stations. In spite of this, many nets for electronic mail use the store-and-forward method, since it has the following advantages

+ You can split the computers into mailbox handlers, which interact with the users, but need not know very much about mail sorting and mail-sorting computers, that specialize in the routing of mail. Also the mail-sorting computers can further be specialized, for example, one computer for sorting mail within a company, one for national mail, and one for international mail. Different companies can run these computers, each specialized in its task, as is shown in Figure 7.3.

The proponents of direct transmission say, however, that, special units knowledgeable about routing and addressing can help the sending computer to find the best route to use in a direct connection.

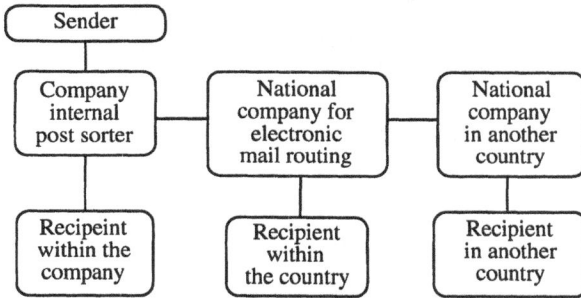

Figure 7.3   Division of responsibility between e-mail providers.

+ If a message is to be transmitted to several recipients far from the sender but close to each other, only one copy of the message need be transmitted to a relay station that is close to the recipients. The message does not need to be split into copies for each recipient, as is shown in Figure 7.4.

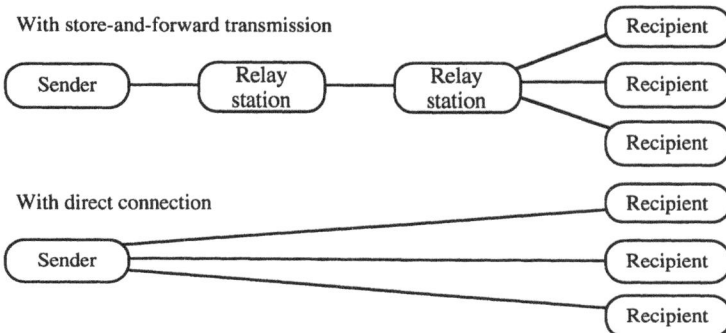

Figure 7.4   Optimization gain with store-and-forward to multiple distant recipients.

+ There are different standards for electronic mail interchange. With store-and-forward, some relay stations can act as bridges between nets using two different standards, translating mail between the formats used in the two standards, as shown in Figure 7.5.

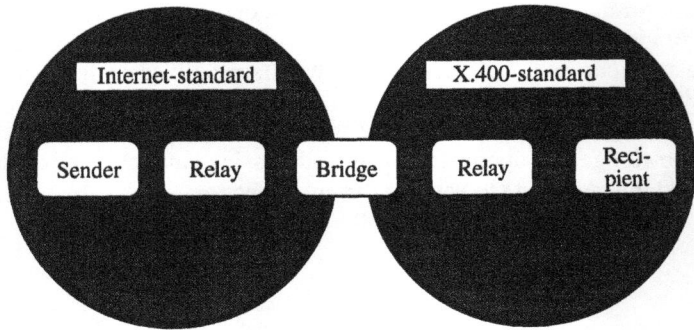

Figure 7.5   Use of relaying in bridges between different network standards.

Even when the store-and-forward method is used, reliability and speed will increase if the number of relay stations between sender and recipient is kept small. Some nets, such as Fidonet and BITNET, have been configured so that they sometimes need many intermediate relay stations. This can give less reliability. If some of the links between the relay stations, as in the earlier days of the Unix-to-Unix-copy (UUCP) network, are not on-line all the time, but instead use batch transmissions between stations a few times a day, the total delay can be long. Today, UUCP is closely linked to Internet and uses fast and direct Internet links for its main highways, so that delays because of batch transmission will only occur in remote by-roads.

Store-and-forward techniques are sometimes more expensive, since each intermediate node wants a cut of the income. The fact that Internet mail costs less, since it uses more direct transmission and less store-and-forward, may be one factor explaining why Internet mail has been more successful then X.400 mail.

When direct connection is used, the system of the sender may let the sender wait until the message has arrived and then immediately confirm the delivery to the sender. Direct connection may also use *spooling*, which means that the transmission is handled by a background process, so that the sender can do something else during transmission. Pros (+) and cons (-) of spooling are:

- The sender gets no direct and immediate confirmation that the message has been delivered.
+ The sender need not wait during the transmission. If the message has several recipients in different computers, this can take time.

+ If no connection can be established because of a temporary network failure, the sender must, if spooling is not used, remember to resend the message at a later time. If a spooling process handles the transfer, this process can automatically retry until the message can be transferred without bothering the user. This advantage with spooling is especially marked for a message to multiple recipients.

Most message system designers choose some kind of spooled transmission, obviously finding that the advantages outweigh the disadvantages.

When a message reaches an MTA, which cannot deliver the message directly to the mailbox of the recipient, it must find another MTA closer to the recipient, that is, find a route towards the recipient. This process is called routing. The process may be controlled not only by efficiency criteria, but also by a wish to keep as much of the income from the transmission with the service provider that chooses the route. Security criteria may also cause certain routes to be chosen for security-sensitive information.

Routing can be static or dynamic. *Static routing* means that routing is controlled by static routing tables. *Dynamic routing* means that information about system congestion and server availability can be used to change the routing based on the current traffic situation.

Bad routing may cause a message to be sent endlessly back and forward between two or more MTAs. To avoid this, messages often include a trace list of the MTAs which it has passed, so that such loops can be stopped. Internet also uses a technique for resolving names in name servers that cannot create loops (see Section 8.6.3).

Normally, each MTA which receives a message determines the next step in its routing to the next MTA, which will then determine the following step from that MTA, and so on. An alternative method sometimes used is called *Source routing*, which means that the originators (or their MTAs) direct several routing steps in advance. Source routing is indicated by the use of relative addresses (see Section 7.6.3).

On the use of relative addresses for routing, see Section 7.2.3. On the use of name servers for routing, see Section 7.2.4. On the routing methods used in Internet, see Section 8.6.3.

7.2 NAMING AND ADDRESSING

7.2.1 Domain Naming

Identifiers, preferably globally unique identifiers, are useful in many ways in electronic mail. Three common uses of such identifiers are for:

(1) A *name*, a globally unique designation which can be used to look up information about an object in a data base such as a directory system;

(2)   An *identifier,* a globally unique designation used to identify duplicates of the same object and to handle references from one object to another (such as from a reply to the message it is a reply to); and

(3)   An *address,* a globally unique designation used for routing a message through an electronic mail network.

Addressing is simple when a message is sent betweer two recipients connected to the same MTA. It becomes more complex in large heterogeneous nets.

The most common kind of electronic mail addresses are *domain addresses.* Domain addresses are being used more and more in message systems, both those based on the Internet and those based on the X.400 electronic mail standard (see Section 8.4.21). A domain address is similar to a postal address, in that the address is split into several subfields, such as department, company, street address, city, county, country, etc., each narrowing the field of potential recipients further.

A domain address for Per Persson in the sales office of the company ABC in Australia may, for example, be:

```
Per_Persson@SALES.ABC.AU
```

This address indicates that within the domain AU (internationally standardized code for the country Australia) there is a subdomain ABC.AU, and within the subdomain ABC.AU there is a further subdomain SALES.ABC.AU. See Figure 7.6.

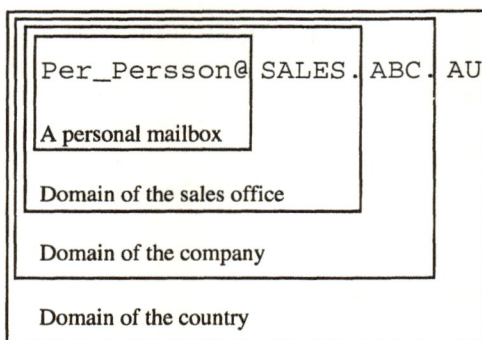

Figure 7.6   Principles of domain naming.

Domain addresses are usually printed on paper or shown on a computer screen in the order used in Figure 7.6, going from the innermost domain towards more general domains. This order is used by ARPAnet, Internet, UUCP, and the national nets of most countries and is the recommended usage according to a new annex in the 1992 version of the X.400 standard. (X.400 tries to avoid standardizing the user interface, but the printing of addresses is an exception. See Section 8.4.21.) The reverse order, with the

64

outermost domain first, as with phone numbers, is used by some systems such as Memo (see Chapter 9.2.1) and the British academic network Janet.

Sometimes, the routing is directly controlled by the domain address. This would mean, in the example above, that a message for Per Persson is sent first to a general Australian mail office (AU), then to the mail office of the company (ABC), then to the mail office of the sales department (SALES), and then to the mailbox of Per Persson. But routing need not be directly controlled by the domain address. The general British mail office may, for example, know that different departments of the ABC company are in different cities, and route using this information so that messages to SALES.ABC are routed a different way than messages to ACCOUNTING.ABC.

In order to choose routes in ways other than exactly following the domains in the address, the mail stations (MTAs) must have tables, that indicate the best route to different recipients. Similar tables are often used by many MTAs, and are therefore sometimes stored in special service agents called *directory systems* or *name servers*. OSI (open systems interconnection) directory systems are described in Section 8.5, and Internet domain name servers are described in Section 8.6.3. More information about domain naming in Internet is given in [1].

7.2.2 The Outermost Domain

Usually, the outermost domain in a domain address is the country, just as with ordinary postal addresses or phone numbers. The country code, however, is abbreviated to two characters, according to an ISO standard for two-character country codes. The code is FR for France, DE for Germany and GB for Great Britain, for example. One deviation from this principle is that the outermost domain for Great Britain is in Internet mail usually UK (short for United Kingdom) instead of GB.

In Internet domain addressing, an alternative to the country is used mainly for e-mail addresses in North America and also sometimes for international organizations. For these addresses, the outermost domain is instead one of the following three-character codes:

COM   for commercial companies
EDU   for schools and universities
GOV   for other government agencies
INT   for international and multinational organizations
MIL   for military organizations
NET   network providers and gateways
ORG   for organizations

For example, an American domain name may be "alnitak.usc.edu" for a department within the University of Southern California (usc), while an European domain name may be "brunel.ac.uk" for Brunel University within the academic community (ac) in the United Kingdom (uk). Thus, if you encounter a domain address ending with a three-character code, it is probably a North American host or a multinational entity.

65

X.400 does not allow such multinational domain names. All ADMD and PRMD names in X.400 must be relative to a particular country. However, one X.400 user, SITA (the international organization for commercial airlines) has tried to use a country code of "WW" (for World-Wide) as the outermost domain in X.400 for itself as an international organization. Whether this will lead to a permanent change in real or de-facto usage of X.400 is not clear at this time.

Note: The use of "NET" to address recipients in other networks through gateways is discouraged. With properly set up name servers, routing by logical names of recipients can often replace such addresses.

7.2.3 Relative Addresses

Domain addresses are *absolute* addresses. An absolute address the same address for a certain recipient, irrespective of where the message is sent from. Another type of address is called a *relative* address. A relative address indicates one or more relay stations on the route to the recipients. This would be roughly equivalent to indicating the postal mail address of a person as: "First to London, then from London by train to Nottingham, then by truck to the University, then by mailman from the University to the Computer Science department."

There are three commonly used formats for relative electronic mail addresses. All the three addresses in Figure 7.7 indicate the same relative route but in a different printed format

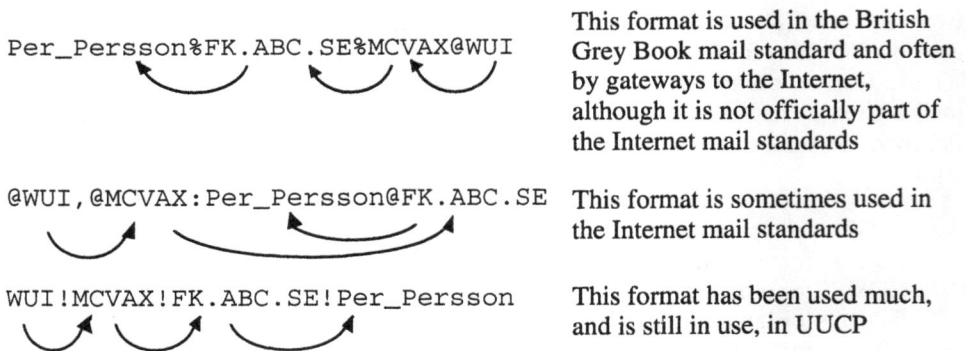

```
Per_Persson%FK.ABC.SE%MCVAX@WUI
```
This format is used in the British Grey Book mail standard and often by gateways to the Internet, although it is not officially part of the Internet mail standards

```
@WUI,@MCVAX:Per_Persson@FK.ABC.SE
```
This format is sometimes used in the Internet mail standards

```
WUI!MCVAX!FK.ABC.SE!Per_Persson
```
This format has been used much, and is still in use, in UUCP

Figure 7.7 Various formats for writing relative addresses. The arrows show the order in which the message is to be transferred.

Combinations of several of these formats in one address may occur sometimes. For example, an address of the format:

```
MCVAX!FK.ABC.SE!Per_Persson@WUI
```

may according to RFC 822 be interpreted as:	`MCVAX!WUI!Per_Persson@FK.ABC.SE`

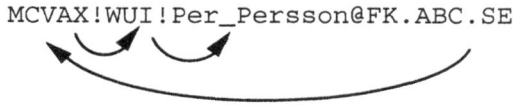

but may according to older UUCP practice be interpreted as:	`MCVAX!WUI!Per_Persson@FK.ABC.SE`

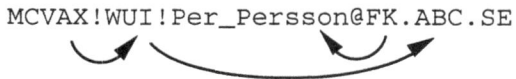

Internet [ ] recommends that such ambiguous relative addresses should not be used, but that if they occur, the RFC 822 interpretation is preferred.

The uppermost format in Figure 7.7, which employs percent (%) signs, is used to a large extent in areas where such usage is not officially standardized, for example, in Internet and BITNET. This format will occur particularly often when a message passes a gateway between two nets. An example is given in Figure 7.8.

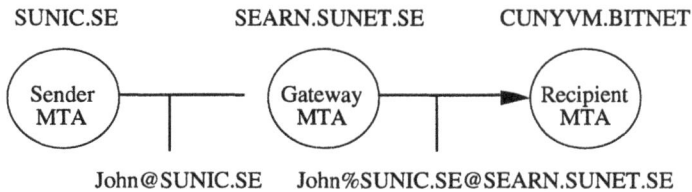

SUNIC.SE   SEARN.SUNET.SE   CUNYVM.BITNET

Sender MTA ——— Gateway MTA ——▶ Recipient MTA

John@SUNIC.SE   John%SUNIC.SE@SEARN.SUNET.SE

Figure 7.8   How gateways produce %-type relative addresses.

A message from a sender John@SUNIC.SE passes a gateway from Internet to BITNET. The address of the sender is given as John@SUNIC.SE before the gateway, but the gateway translates this into John%SUNIC.SE@SEARN.SUNET.SE when transmitting the message to BITNET. Thus, the gateway takes the original sender address, replaces the @ with a %, and appends @ followed by the name of the gateway.

In BITNET, when a reply is sent from the recipient to the sender, the reply is first sent to John%SUNIC.SE@SEARN.SUNET.SE. BITNET views this address as a user named "John%SUNIC.SE" at a host named "SEARN.SUNET.SE." Thus, from a BITNET viewpoint, the whole Internet is in this case seen as local names in SEARN.SUNET.SE. When the reply reaches SEARN.SUNET.SE, this MTA will strip out @SEARN.SUNET.SE and look at the rest, John%SUNIC.SE. It will translate this back to John@SUNIC.SE and forward the reply to the original sender.

This example shows that neither the Internet nor the BITNET will actually view this address as relative. In BITNET, the address is an absolute address of a user named John%SUNIC.SE in the host SEARN.SUNET.SE. Only the gateway itself recognizes the translation between % and @. Thus, fundamentalists can proudly claim that "our messaging standard does not use any relative addressing" even though relative addresses are sometimes transported in their net.

There are many disadvantages of relative addresses. You cannot print your address on your business card in the same way for all recipients. You have to indicate a different address depending on to whom you are giving your address. There may also be problems with sending a return message. This is illustrated in Figure 7.9.

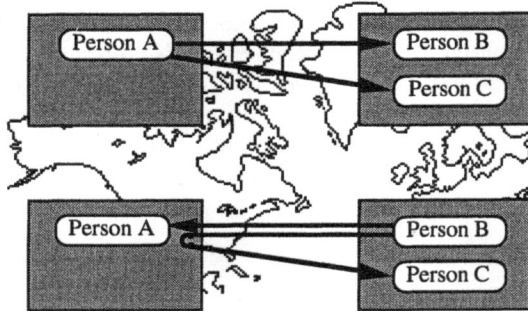

Figure 7.9   Inefficiency for replies to interpersonal messages with relative addresses.

Suppose that a person A in America sends a message to two recipients B and C in Europe and that this message uses relative addressing via some American gateway. This means that when B gets the message, the relative address to C is given via this American gateway, so that if B sends a reply to C, this reply must be routed unnecessarily twice across the Atlantic. There are two disadvantages of this. Firstly, it means unnecessary costs and delays, as was shown in the example above. Secondly, the American net may refuse to transmit messages from a European sender to another European recipient, since the American net may have to pay for part of this unnecessary transmission.

To avoid such problems, intelligent mail sorters sometimes try to be intelligent and remove unnecessary routing in a relative address. Such optimizations may be necessary, but they are error prone. If the node names are not globally unique, and you remove the relative address, you may route the message to the wrong MTA.

A problem similar to that in Figure 7.9 can occur when distribution lists are used, as in Figure 7.10.

In this example, a person A in Europe sends a message to a distribution list in America. The letter reaches a recipient B in Europe via the list. If relative addressing is used, a reply from B to A may have to be transferred via a gateway in America as in Figure 7.9.

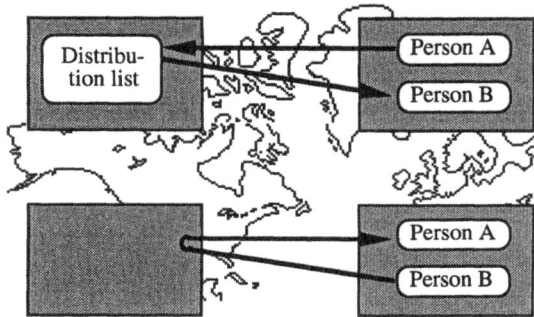

Figure 7.10   Inefficiency for replies to distribution-list messages with relative addresses.

Everyone agrees that relative addressing is bad. Why then does it crop up again and again? The reason is that electronic mail is handled by different electronic mail networks, connected via gateways. Since each net has limited knowledge of the internal structure of another net, it can often only address a recipient in another net via a gateway between the nets, and the inclusion of such gateways into addresses makes them relative.

7.2.4   Use of Domain Addresses for Routing

Domain addressing can be used for routing messages. Two examples of how this can be done are Figure 7.11, using a store-and-forward technique (common for X.400) and Figure 7.12, using name servers (common in Internet mail).

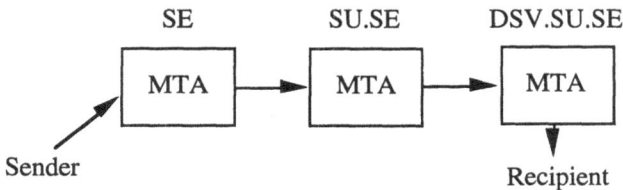

Figure 7.11   Direct routing based on domain addresses.

Figure 7.11 shows how a message may be forwarded via MTAs serving different domains closer and closer to the recipient. Of course, it is also possible for the SE MTA to forward directly to the DSV.SU.SE MTA.

69

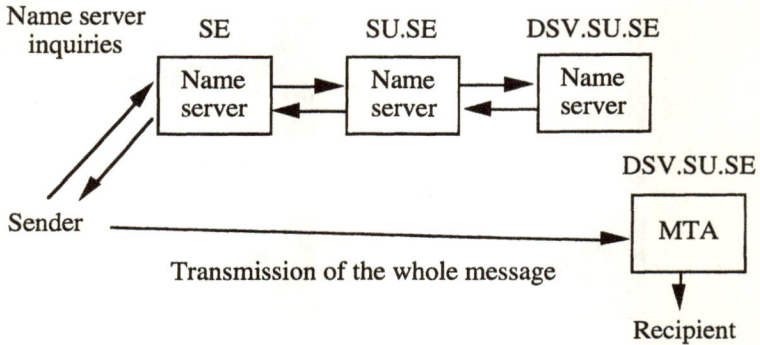

Figure 7.12   Name server look-up followed by direct transmission.

Figure 7.12 shows how a series of name servers that know host addresses in domains successively closer to the recipient can be used to find the network address of the recipient MTA host. The sender can then transmit directly to the recipient MTA. Of course, the name servers for SU.SE and DSV.SU.SE might be combined into one name server. And the name server for SE can store names and addresses, so that after a second inquiry for the address of DSV.SU.SE, the SE name server can answer directly without forwarding the query to SU.SE. The technique of keeping names passing through a name server is called *caching*. Cached addresses should only be kept for a limited time, since they may otherwise become out-of-date.

The technique described in Figure 7.12, where each successive name server connects to another name server, is called *chaining*. Another also commonly used technique is called *referral*. With referral, the searcher will successively connect to a series of name servers until the right one is found. For more information about chaining and referral, see Section 8.5.2.

7.2.5 How to Find E-Mail Addresses

The easiest way to find someone's e-mail address is usually to ask the person. Other methods are:

- Send an e-mail to mail-server@pit-manager.mit.edu and include in the message the text "send usenet-addresses/name" where "name" includes words you can expect in the name of the person you are looking for. This will search a data base of all names which have appeared as senders of Usenet News messages.
- Use the Internet Gopher to connect to e-mail address directories, such as Whois and X.500 servers.
- If you know the name of an e-mail host where the person you are looking for is located, try to send an e-mail to "postmaster@host" where "host" is replaced by the person's e-mail host.

A much more complete guide on how to find e-mail addresses can be found in [2].

7.3   ARCHITECTURE OF ELECTRONIC MAIL SYSTEMS

Various topologies exist in electronic mail networks, whether they use store-and-for-ward techniques or direct connections. This was discussed in Section 7.2.

The local message system can also have different architectures. What differs is mainly how much is stored and done in the personal computer or workstation of the recipient and how much is done on servers shared between several users. The numbers in Figure 7.13 show four different places where the interface between the workstation of the user and shared servers can be placed.

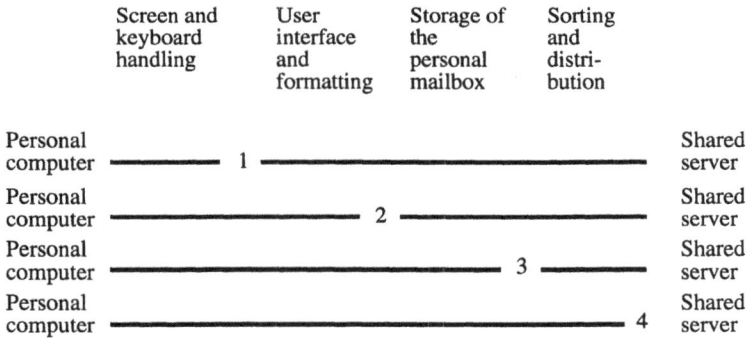

Screen and keyboard handling	User interface and formatting	Storage of the personal mailbox	Sorting and distri- bution	
Personal computer ——— 1 ———————————————————————				Shared server
Personal computer ————————————— 2 —————————				Shared server
Personal computer ————————————————————— 3 ——				Shared server
Personal computer ——————————————————————————— 4				Shared server

Figure 7.13   Various divisions of responsibility between client and server.

Two often used system architectures are shown in Figure 7.14.

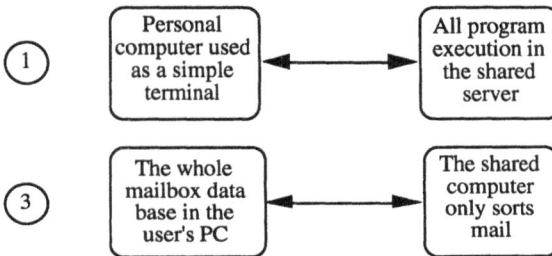

Figure 7.14   Two common architectures. Numbers in this figure refers to Figure 7.13.

71

The latter of these architectures allows for a nicer, graphical user interface and shorter response times. The most common protocol using this division is called P3 in X.400 and POP in Internet mail. A disadvantage of that solution is that storage of mail in the user's personal computer may be more expensive and less reliable. Another disadvantage is that the user will only have access to his mailbox when sitting at a certain personal computer or workstation. Problems will occur if users want to access their mailboxes when traveling or if they want access at home and at work. Because of this, the architecture shown in Figure 7.15 is sometimes used as an alternative and has support in the 1988 version of the X.400 standard (see Section 8.4.4) under the name P7. In Internet mail, the most common protocol of this kind is called IMAP. A disadvantage with this design is that unless the transmission line between the work station and the server is fast, then response times may be slow.

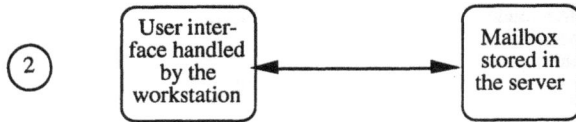

Figure 7.15   Remote mailbox protocol. The number in the figure refers to Figure 7.13.

7.4   DISTRIBUTION LISTS

Expansion of Nested Distribution Lists

Nested distribution lists (see Figures 7.16 and 8.21) occur when one list is a member of another list. If, for example, list B is a member of list A, then a message sent to list A will be distributed to all members of both list A and B. A message sent directly to list B, however, will not reach the members of list A, unless A also is a member of B.

There are two techniques for handling distribution lists:

- *Sender UA expansion.* The mailbox software (user agent software) of the sender finds the list of the members of the list and sends it directly to them. If the lists are nested, the sender UA will successively and recursively find the lists of members of the sublists, all the way to the final recipient. With this method, the message will thus be converted to an ordinary multirecipient list. The message will also have ordinary users, and not lists, as recipients, before the message leaves the sender UA .

- *Expansion at the list location.* The sender's UA sends the list to the list-expansion agent or to the domain which is responsible for the list. The list is then expanded at this location. Expansion means the replacement of the name of the list with the names of the members of the list. With nested lists, the message is then forwarded to the domains of the sublists, which perform the secondary expansion, and so on if there are sublists to the sublists.

Consider a person who is a member of both lists. With the second method, this person will probably receive two copies of the same message. With the first method, such duplicates can be eliminated during the expansion. In spite of this, expansion at the list location (the second method) is most common, and is the only method for handling distribution lists which is supported by the X.400 standard (from the 1988 version). One reason why the X.400 standard supports expansion at the list location is that this expansion will be more efficient when handling large, geographically distributed lists. Assume, for example, that a group has 100 European and 100 American members. With two nested lists, one for the European and one for the American members, the message need only be sent to one single recipient when crossing the Atlantic. If the whole list is expanded by the sending UA, at least 100 recipient have to be listed when crossing the Atlantic, which will make the transfer more expensive. See Figure 7.16.

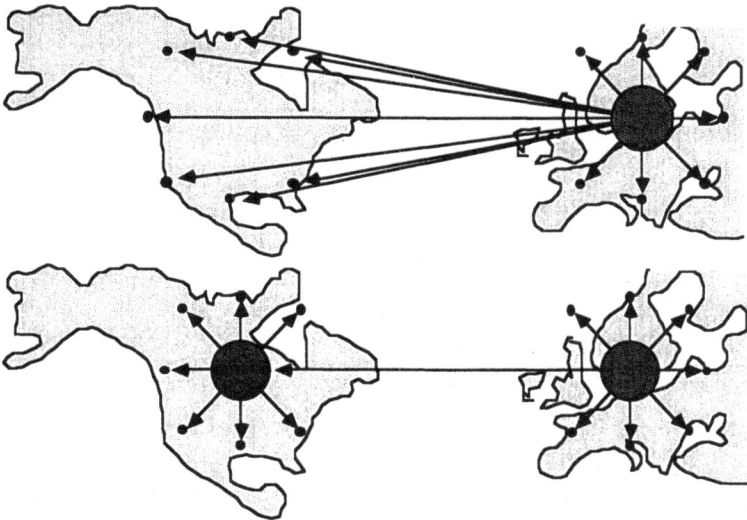

Figure 7.16   Advantage of using nested distribution lists (bottom) vs. nonnested (top).

Other advantages with expansion at the list is that it is easier, to support distributed control of the membership of a group—each sublist can have its own management. This can, of course, can be a disadvantage when central control of the membership is required.

Loop Control for Nested Distribution Lists

If two lists are directly or indirectly members of each other, there is a risk that the same message will be looped back and forward indefinitely between the lists. There are several different techniques for avoiding this:

(1) Full expansion by the originating UA.

(2a) A trace list of all the distribution lists passed is put on the envelope of the message. A distribution list can then refuse to accept, incoming messages, that have the name of the distribution list itself as part of the trace list on the envelope of the message.

(2b) Using a variant of method (2a), each distribution list will instead refuse to send a message to another distribution list which is included in the trace list of the message.

(3) The registration system for distribution lists is designed in such a way that no list will ever be a member, directly or indirectly, of itself.

(4a) Each distribution list stores the message-IDs of all messages passing through the list. When the same message returns once more to the list, the list checks the message-ID of the message and stops the loop if a message with the same ID has already passed through the list. (Message-ID is also known under the term IPM Identifier.)

(4b) This is a variant of method (4a), where a checksum of the content of the message is used instead of the message-ID.

The X.400 standard for electronic mail uses method (2a) and recommends use of method (2b) as an addition to (but not as a replacement for) method (2a). The advantage of method (2b) is that it saves some unnecessary transmission. However, method (2b) is not as reliable as method (2a), because the same electronic mail address can have different forms, and therefore the comparison used in method (2b) may not work. It is easier for a list expander to recognize a name which it itself puts on an envelope than a name which some other list expander puts on an envelope.

Comparing methods (4a) and (4b), method (4b), use of a checksum, has the advantage that it caters for systems where the message-ID is corrupted (something which is not unusual), but has as the disadvantage that two different messages may accidentally get the same checksum. A further problem with the message-ID is that two messages with the same message-ID may not always be identical (see Section 8.4.13). Finally, some mail systems to not generate globally unique message-IDs on the messages they produce.

Method (4a) is often used by computer conferencing systems, sometimes combined with the other methods. For example, Usenet News mainly uses method (4a).

Programs that send messages through gateways from Internet e-mail to Usenet News will assign Message-IDs to messages lacking such IDs. This can cause the same message to get different Message-IDs by different gateways.

The Listserv software has very powerful methods for avoiding loops, primarily based on method (4b).

In practice, many existing distribution lists have no loop control mechanism except that the people who manage the list manually try to avoid producing loops.

Other Distribution List Issues

For information on how to become a member of distribution lists, see Section 6.7.2.

Techniques for handling distribution lists in the X.400 messaging standard are discussed in Section 8.4.18 and techniques in the Internet messaging standards are discussed in Section 8.6.5. Mail servers for managing distribution lists are discussed in Section 6.10.

Management of large distribution lists is not easy. The manager will receive each day nondelivery notifications for messages from the list which cannot be delivered, and requests for addition and removal of members from the list. It is sometimes difficult to identify the item in the list of members which such a notification or request refers to. Sometimes, they are actually members of a sub-distribution list. The problems of managing large distribution lists is more fully discussed in [3].

7.5 COMPUTER CONFERENCING AND BULLETIN BOARD SYSTEMS

Computer conferencing and bulletin board systems often have a common storage area for messages of many recipients. An important feature in such systems is what is known as *news control*. News control is the mechanism for helping a recipient to find only messages he has not yet read. A method used by many such systems is to store a pointer indicating how far a person has read in a conference for each member and each conference, as shown in Figure 7.17.

Using this method, you do not need to store for each person and each entry whether this person has seen or not seen this particular entry. A disadvantage is that if people read entries in nonchronological order, then the computer will not know what they have or have not seen. The pointer, indicating how much you have seen, only stores a number or a time. If there are several copies of the same conference at different hosts, for each host this pointer or time must, refer to the ordinal number or the time of storage at that particular host.

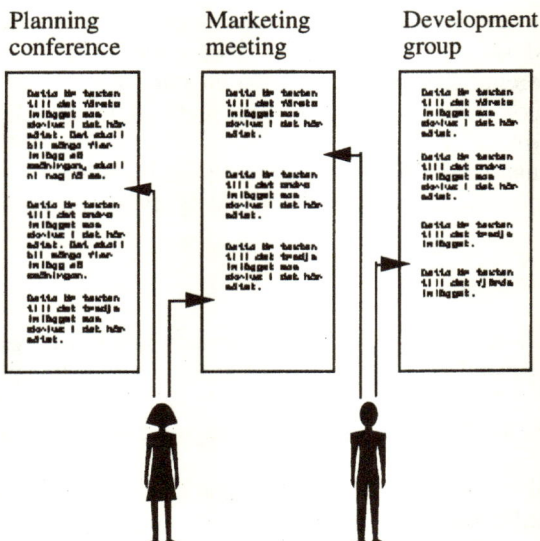

Planning conference   Marketing meeting   Development group

Figure 7.17   Common principle for news control in many computer conferencing systems.

Newer conference systems try to avoid the problem of having to read messages in chronological order in order for news control work. This can be done in several ways:

- Storing an exception list of messages you have read in nonchronological order.
- Storing an exception list of messages you have bypassed in nonchronological order.
- Storing a complete data base for each message that you have seen.

7.6 CRYPTOGRAPHIC SECURITY TECHNIQUES

7.6.1 Cryptography

Cryptography is a technique for protecting data (messages) during certain phases of its processing. It is important to note that processing of the encrypted information is not usually possible except after decryption. This means that cryptography is mostly useful only if there are unreliable phases of message handling and if there is no processing of encrypted information during these unreliable phases. Communication lines between sender and recipient, or between two message transfer agents (MTAs) are examples of such areas where encryption can be valuable. Cryptography can also be used to provide some other special security services like digital signatures, digital seals, etc. This will be described in Section 7.6.3.

There are two types of cryptographic systems: symmetric and asymmetric. Symmetric systems are based on the use of a secret key. Only the sender and the recipient have access to this key. Since a secret shared by many people is difficult to protect, this means that symmetric encryption is most useful if it is applied to only one specific connection line between two specific units and only those two units have access to the secret key.

A problem with symmetric cryptographic systems is the transfer of secret keys between these two units. This transfer cannot use the same unsecured channel which is to be protected by encryption. In addition, new keys must be exchanged regularly, since symmetric cryptographic systems are usually only safe if each key is used for a limited period of time. These problems can be reduced or solved by using so-called *asymmetric* or *public key* cryptographic techniques.

To understand this idea, one should note that protection by cryptographic systems includes two transformations of the text: encryption at the sending side and decryption at the receiving side. For both of these transformations, a transformation algorithm and a key are needed. The key is usually simply a series of digits or bits. Some cryptographic algorithms use different keys for encryption and decryption. The two keys are related in such a way that the decryption key will decrypt messages which have been encrypted with the encryption key. One of the keys is called the secret key. The other key is called the public key and need not be kept secret. The public key of the recipient is used by the sender to encrypt the message. The algorithm used is very time-consuming (years of CPU time on a supercomputer) to derive the secret key from the public key. Anyone with access to the public key can then use it to encrypt information, which can then be decrypted only by the agent holding the secret key. Public key encryption can, of course, be used only for transmissions in one direction, since the public key is publicly available. For transmission in both directions, two sets of keys are necessary, one for each direction.

Public key systems solve the security problems which occur when the same encryption key must be available in many places. Only the public key needs to be distributed in this way. This also solves the problem with transporting secret keys, since only the public key need be transported. However, one must ensure that the sender is not given a false public key, since the agent who provides a false public key would be able to decrypt the messages. To safeguard the delivery of correct public keys, certification authorities (see Section 7.6.4) are used.

A problem with public key encryption is that, for very short messages, someone might guess what the original message was, encrypt it, and compare this with the transmitted encrypted message. To safeguard against this, random bits are usually added to the message. Another problem is that no authentication is provided, so anyone can send a message and encrypt it with the public key. Thus, public key encryption is often combined with digital authentication.

A disadvantage of public key encryption is that the encryption algorithms often consume more CPU-power than secret key encryption. Because of, they are not usually used to encrypt large amounts of data. Instead, public key encryption is used to encrypt smaller pieces of data, such as passwords and checksums. Public key encryption is also used to transmit the encryption keys to be used in ordinary symmetric (secret-key) encryption algorithms, which are then used to encrypt the bulk of the information to be transmitted. This solves the problem of transporting secret keys for symmetric encryption. Another disadvantage of public key systems is that a lot of harm can occur if the secret key is stolen or intentionally revealed. With symmetric cryptographic schemes, this risk is reduced by switching to a new cryptographic key at regular intervals. But this is more difficult with public keys, since they are often widely distributed.

Secret keys and passwords may be stored on plastic cards. They can then be transferred to the computer only when they are to be used. This reduces the risk of unauthorized access by, for example, a so-called *Trojan horse*, a program gains access by claiming to perform certain tasks, but which also secretly performs other, sometimes damaging, tasks. Even higher security can be achieved with *smart cards*, which are cards with a built-in microprocessor. With such cards, the secret key need never be moved from the card, since the cryptographic algorithm can be performed by the processor in the card. The card can be designed so that it is never possible to take out the secret key from the card, thus reducing the risk that the secret key gets divulged. A problem is that the most popular public key algorithm, the RSA algorithm, is too complex to perform by many smart cards. Such cards therefore often use a simpler algorithm, such as the *videopass* algorithm, which, however, is not a public-key algorithm.

Cryptography can provide many useful security services, but one should be aware of the restrictions and realize that not all security problems can be solved by this method. Useful uses of cryptography includes

- The transmission of information via an insecure cable, satellite or radio link between two MTAs. The information is transformed inside the message transfer agent, so this will not protect the information from a person who has gained unauthorized access to an MTA.
- The transmission between a sender and a recipient who have agreed to encrypt their messages. Encryption and decryption algorithms are needed only by the sender and the recipient, so this method will also protect against unauthorized MTA access. However, the envelope information cannot be encrypted, since this information is needed by the MTAs to forward the message to the right recipient.

A disadvantage of the method in the second example is that the data needed for transferring messages cannot be encrypted within the MTAs. Some companies believe that this information should also be protected, since outsiders might deduce which projects two companies are working on together by looking at which people in each company are exchanging messages. One way of protecting this data by cryptography is shown in Figure 6.18.

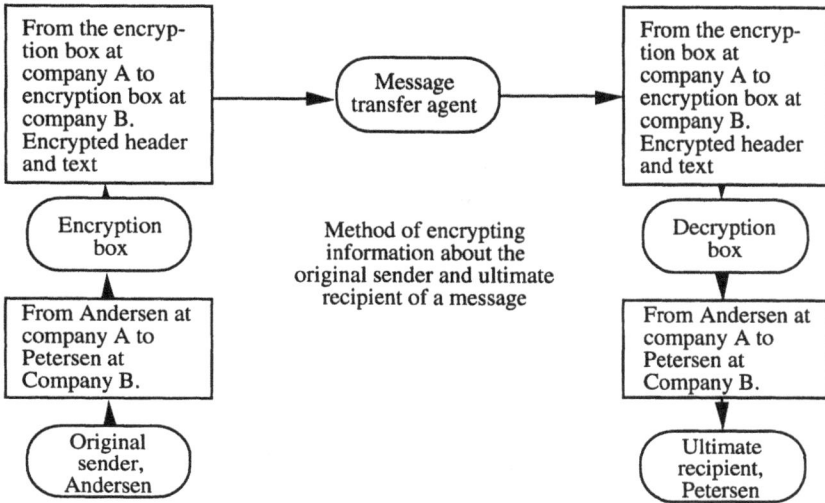

Figure 6.18   Protection against flow analysis.

More detailed descriptions of cryptographic techniques are given in [5].

7.6.2 Digital Authentication and Authorization

Authentication is a technique of verifying that a person or a unit is who or what it claims to be. *Authorization* is the use of authentication to allow authorized access. Examples of uses of authentication include:

- To verify that the sender of a message is correct (see also section 7.6.3).
- In economic transactions, to make electronic agreements valid and to order payments from accounts (see also Section 7.6.3).
- To ensure, when two MTAs connect to each other, that each of them is the MTA it claims to be. Otherwise, a false MTA may illegally download messages intended for the proper MTA, or send false messages. This will provide higher security if the line between the MTAs is less secure than the internal workings of the MTAs themselves.
- When a user agent (UA), client process supporting a single user, connects to an MTA to download and upload messages.

The three most common methods for electronic authentication are:

(a)   Passwords. The verifier requires a password from the identifier and checks this against a password stored in some control data base. The data base of passwords is usually stored in an encrypted form. This encryption can be

79

done using a noninvertible algorithm (an algorithm whose result cannot easily be reversed) since decryption is not necessary. The identifier's password can be encrypted before it is compared with the stored encrypted password.

(b)   Specially designed networks. Such networks can provide certain identification procedures or parameters. For example, the network may provide the identity of the caller to the called party.

(c)   Public key cryptography, as in Figure 6.19.

The verifier	*The identifier*
Generate a random number.	
Encrypt it using the public key of the identifier.	
Send the encrypted random number to the identifier.	Decrypt the encrypted number.
	Return the decrypted number.
Check that the initial random number is returned.	

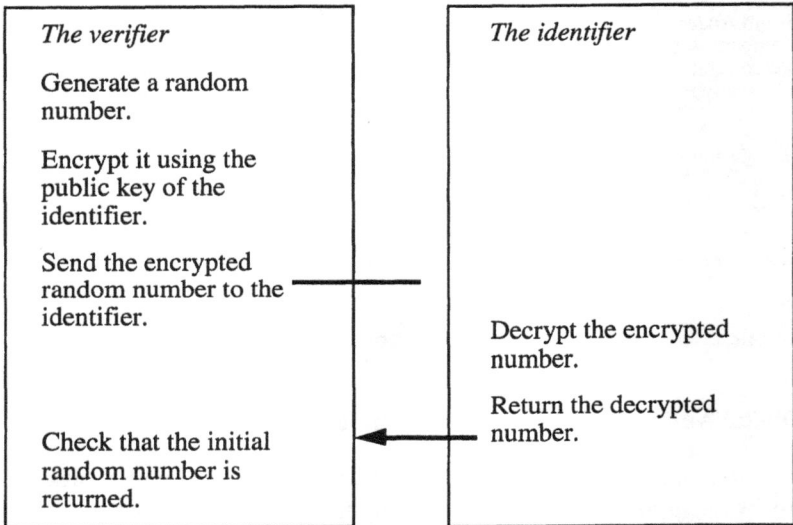

Figure 6.19   Authentication using public key cryptography.

The protection of messages on a transmission line, for example, between two MTAs or between a UA and an MTA, can be classified into three levels of increasing security:

(1)   The agents identify each other using noninvertible forms of ordinary passwords. This is called *weak authentication*.

(2)   The agents identify each other using public key encryption algorithms. This is called *strong authentication*.

(3)   Strong authentication is combined with encryption of all messages during the whole transmission.

7.6.3 Digital Signatures and Digital Seals

Digital signature is a method of safe-guarding that a document really comes from the claimed originator. It will thus protect against (a) insertion of false documents, and (b) sender repudiation of messages. *Digital seal* is a method of ensuring that the content of a document is not modified in transmission. It protects against the corruption of a document during its transmission.

Different algorithms exist for electronic signatures and seals, which may vary in:

- Whether they require interactions backward and forward between a sender and a recipient (this is not easy to provide if the messages are stored at intermediate locations during their transmission from sender to recipient);
- Whether a neutral third party (storing either cryptographic keys or the whole document) is used in proving the authenticy of the document;
- Whether the method can be used bilaterally between a certain given pair of senders and recipients, or be used to prove the authenticity of documents available to several recipients.

In order to avoid long execution times and to reduce redundancy during the transmission, these algorithms usually do not really protect the whole document, but rather a checksum of the document. Therefore, it is important to find a method of computing a checksum, which makes it difficult to falsify a document, that is, to produce another document with the same checksum as the document to be protected. There are several of these algorithms available today: some of them standardized by ISO, called message authentication code (MAC) like MAC-16, MAC-32, and MAC-64, and some of them standardized in the U.S., called message digest (MD) like MD2, MD4 and MD5.

7.6.4 Certificate Authorities

In order to verify digital signatures and to use other cryptographic features, a user must be able to verify the authenticity and originality of public keys. Even if the key is not secret, as with open key cryptography, there is still a risk that the key may be falsified. Because of this, there is a need for certificate authorities, reliable agents which distribute secure keys and other information. Such certificate authorities create certificates in a form specified by the X.509 standard and store them either in local data base or in X.500 directories (see Section 8.5). Since certificate authorities themselves need be certified, they may be arranged in hierarchies (similar to the hierarchies used in domain naming, see Section 9.3.9) where a lower authority is certified by a higher authority.

REFERENCES

[1] Su, Zaq-Sing and Postel, Jon, *The domain naming convention for internet user applications*. Internet RFC 819.

[2]   Kamens, Jonathan I., *How to find people's E-mail addresses*, available from URL ftp://rtfm.mit
      .edu.pub/usenet-by-group/comp.mail.misc/FAQ:_How_to_find_people_s_E-mail_addresses.
[3]   Westine, A. and Postel, J: *Problems with the Maintenance of Large Mailing Lists*. Internet RFC
      1211, March 1991.
[4]   Horton, Mark R.: *UUCP Mail Interchange Format Standard*. Internet RFC 976.
[5]   Davis, D.W. and Price, W.L., *Security for computer networks*, New York, John Wiley & Sons,
      1989.

Chapter 8

Standards

8.1 STANDARDS IN GENERAL

You can reach almost all other phones, all over the world, from a single phone, and you can send postal mail to almost anyone all over the world. Thus it is a desirable feature of electronic mail that you to be able to reach all other electronic mail users independently of where they are and what electronic mail system they use. To make this possible, a standardized format for the exchange of messages between different electronic mail systems is needed. Electronic mail requires a complex system of different standards: a standard for coding different kinds of information (for example, text (see Section 8.2)); general network standards (see Section 8.3.2 and 8.3.3); and general electronic mail standards (see Section 8.3.3 and 8.6).

A *protocol* is a specification of how two different systems are to communicate with each other via some kind of network. A protocol often has conversational rules, which prescribe what is sent first by one of the systems in one format and what the response can be from the other system, etc. Protocols are often part of standards.

There are many different organizations which develop standards used for electronic mail. Some important organizations are:

- *International Telecommunications Union (ITU-T formerly CCITT)*, the international standards organization of Telecom companies.
- *International Standards Organization (ISO)*, with representatives from national standards organizations in different countries. Some important members of ISO are AFNOR in France, DIN in Germany, BSI in the United Kingdom, ANSI in the United States of America and IPSJ in Japan. ISO makes its standards in the information technology area together with the International Electrotechnical Commission (IEC).
- *Internet Engineering Task Force (IETF)* the organization responsible for standards development for the Internet. Internet, however, often uses ISO standards that are sometimes modified for IETF needs.

83

- *Regional standards organizations*, like ETSI, the European standards organization.
- *Computer companies,* like Microsoft, IBM, Lotus, and Apple.

ISO and ITU-T cooperate closely in development of computer network standards, and most of their standards are identical or almost identical. For more information about standards making organizations, see [45].

There has been much discussion about the different methods employed by ISO versus IETF in making standards. The main difference is that IETF requires at least two independent implementations before a standard is accepted as a full standard. Another difference is that IETF uses electronic mail as a communication tool during standards making much more than ISO and ITU. With ISO and ITU, more work is done during meetings; with IETF, meetings are held mainly to discuss controversial issues and confirm work which has been done outside the meetings.

It has been stated that the IETF method of requiring two implementations before accepting a standard will result in bugfree, simpler, and easier to implement standards. For more discussion on this see [13, 42].

8.2 TEXT FORMATS

Most of the information transmitted via electronic mail contains text. Also, in standards, the word "text" has an extended meaning compared to ordinary language, and is used also to refer to graphics, digitized sound and other formats which are not in ordinary language called "text." Thus, "text" in standards usually means any data representation of the content of the message being transmitted (as different from the data representation of the heading and the envelope of the message) and a message need not consist of letters and digits only.

8.2.1 IA5 (ISO 646, ASCII)

The acronym "ASCII" (American Standard Code for Information Interchange) is often used, not quite correctly, to represent a family of different character-set standards, based on an international reference version whose official name in ISO is ISO 646. ITU uses the name IA5 for this character set, and since ITU has a strong position in the area of electronic mail standards, this book will use IA5.

IA5 uses 7 bits for each character and contains 95 printable characters (including space, which is logically a "printable character"). This is not enough characters for all languages. It does not, for example, contain the character "Ö" in German, "Ø" in Danish, "é" in French, or "¿" in Spanish. In order to cover national needs, each country has its own variant of IA5 which replaces certain characters with national characters. ISO 2022 is a standard which allows the sending of a message with a mixture of characters for different languages. This is done by including certain *escape sequences*. These escape sequences indicate a switch from one character set to another, such as between the different national variants of IA5. Escape sequences also allow switching between Nonlatin character sets such as Greek, Cyrillic, Arabian, Chinese or Japanese. Thus, for example, the character sequence "<escape sequence for the Swedish variant>\<escape sequence for the Danish variant>\" will actually be printed as "ÖØ," since "\" is a character which is replaced by "Ö" in the Swedish variant of IA5 and by "Ø" in the Danish variant of IA5.

The earliest standards for electronic mail (RFC 822 and the 1984 version of X.400) did not, however, specify the use of such escape sequences. This means that the same string will look different when viewed by mail systems in different countries. For example, to an American recipient the Swedish name "Björn Ågren" will look like "Bj|rn]gren." Thus, IA5 is not a very good standard for characters in electronic mail, even though it is still the mostly used standard as of this writing (1994).

8.2.2 Newer Character Sets

Because of the limitations of IA5, there are several newer character sets. The most important are:

- *ISO 8859* (Also known under the name *ISO Latin 1*). This standard uses eight bits for each character, allowing twice as many different characters as in IA5. In ISO 8859-1, IA5 has been extended with many national characters and other often-used characters. ISO 8859-1, however, cannot handle all characters, not even the various national variants of the Latin alphabet. Because of this, there are national variants of ISO 8859, just as for IA5. ISO 2022 escape sequences are then necessary to switch between them. Character sets close to ISO 8859-1 are used as one possible method of character representation in VT220 terminals and in the X-OPEN UNIX standards.
- IBM PC/MS-DOS, and Macintosh have each defined their own eight-bit character sets, none compatible with ISO 8859. MS-DOS has several different eight-bit character sets, the most common of these (in Europe) is called *CP850* (*Code Page 850*). Macintosh uses the same eight-bit set in most countries, but has a mechanism that allows a different character set in each font, and thus uses special fonts when characters not in the basic character set are needed. Microsoft Windows, however, uses ISO 8859 as its main character set standard.
- T.61 is a character set from ITU and is based on sequences of eight-bit characters (sequences of octets). It is different from ISO 8859 in that it sometimes uses two octets for a single printable character. In this way, T.61 allows more than 300 different printable characters. Thus T.61 will handle all national variants of the Latin alphabet without using escape sequences. T.61 does need escape sequences for non-Latin alphabets like Greek, Arabic, Cyrillic (Russian), and Kanji (Japanese).

- *ISO 6937* is an ISO-variant of T.61, which is not used much in electronic mail.
- *ISO 10646* is the latest ISO standard, which uses between one and four octets (logically always four octets) to represent each character. Four octets can represent a very large number of different characters, and ISO 10646 is intended to serve for all existing and future character-set needs. As of this writing, ISO 10646 is not yet in widespread use in electronic mail.

The 1984 version of X.400 used either IA5 or T.61 as its main character sets for ordinary text . Of these, T.61 is a much better standard for sending messages between countries. With T.61, the German name "Müller" will, for example, look the same in other languages.

Many computer manufacturers, for example, Digital Equipment and the X-OPEN group, have recommended ISO 8859. The reason they prefer ISO 8859 to T.61 is that it is much easier to represent text in programs and data structures if there is a single octet for each printable character. (But if ISO 2022 escape-sequences are necessary, then there is no longer a single octet for each character.)

It is probable that some of the more powerful character sets, like T.61, ISO 8859, or ISO 10646, will eventually replace IA5 as the common character set in electronic mail. It is not clear which of them is going to be the winner. A few years ago, T.61 looked like the winner, but some recent standards work recommends ISO 8859 combined with ISO 1022 escape sequences and ISO 10646, possibly the most powerful of the standards, may be what will be used at some later stage.

As of this writing, many e-mail systems send ISO 8859 text but label it as IA5, which is against the e-mail standards and adds to the present confusion. This confusion has got worse in the last years (1991-1994), since earlier one knew that text sent as IA5 really was IA5.

8.2.3 Printable String

If your goal is to be able to send electronic mail so that it looks the same everywhere in the world, then you have to use a character set which all computers can display and generate. Because of this, within the ASN.1 standard, a character set called *printable string* has been defined. It contains only the following characters:

A...Z, a...z, 0...9, space (" "), apostrophe ("'"), parentheses ("( )"), plus ("+"), comma (","), dash ("-"), period ("."), colon (":"), equals sign ("=") and question mark ("?").

The 1984 version of X.400 uses the printable string character set in electronic mail addresses. This means that "Björn Müller" will have to represent his name as "Bjorn Muller" or "Bjoern Mueller." The 1988 version of X.400 allows T.61 to be used as an alternative in some electronic mail addresses, but its use is not yet widespread.

8.2.4 ODA, SGML, and Postscript

Office document architecture (ODA) is an ISO standard for the exchange of documents between word processing systems. It allows different codes for different fonts and font sizes, and it allows a mixture of text and graphics with full layout information, etc. The text of this book would, for example, be possible to represent with ODA. ODA is today (1994) not often used in electronic mail.

Another ISO standard for text formatting is standardized general markup language (SGML). While ODA uses a binary format, SGML uses a pure text file with formatting commands in textual format. SGML is directed more towards publishing, while ODA is directed more towards word processing, but the border between these areas are not very sharp. SGML has become very popular in the last few years, since the popular Internet service World Wide Web uses an application of SGML called hypertext markup language (HTML) as its main document format.

An important difference between ODA and SGML is that SGML specifies only the logical structure of a document (what are text bodies, what are headings, what are subheadings, etc.), while ODA allows the specification of both logical and physical representation (what should be at the top of page 10, etc.) Another well-known format which specifies only the physical format is Postscript. Postscript is often used to communicate with printers. The same document in Postscript format, however, will be many times larger than in other formats, and because of this Postscript is not commonly used as an e-mail format.

8.2.5 EDIFACT

Electronic data interchange for administration, commerce and transport (EDIFACT), ISO 9753, is a standard for machine-processable business documents like orders, bills, customs documents, etc. See also Sections 6.5 and 8.4.23.

8.2.6 Other Text Formats

In its first (1984) version, the X.400 standard allowed messages to contain sound or fax (a kind of bit-mapped graphics). Vector graphics were, however, not included, and a standard for formatting sound in text was not ready until in the 1992 version of. Vector graphics can, however, be transmitted as a part of ODA formatted documents. The 1988 version of X.400 (see Section 8.4.22), as well as the 1992 MIME extension (see Section 8.6.6) to the Internet mail standards, allow a multitude of different kinds of data to be sent in mail messages, such as sound, pictures, video, multimedia and so forth.

8.3 The OSI Model

The Open Systems Interconnection (OSI) model is a general model for defining computer communications applications and standards. Many different standards for different applications are based on the OSI model. The main competitor of OSI is the transmission control protocol/Internet protocol (TCP/IP) used by the Internet, but TCP/IP is also based on layering and it is possible to combine layers from OSI and TCP/IP.

8.3.1 OSI Layers

The main principle of the OSI model is that computer communication is split into seven layers. The layers in the OSI model are:

Layer 7: application layer
Layer 6: presentation layer
Layer 5: session layer
Layer 4: transport layer
Layer 3: net layer
Layer 2: link layer
Layer 1: physical layer

To understand the concept of layering, one can compare it to the design of computer applications which do not use computer communication. A popular way of providing a neat structure for such a program is to have a bottom layer which provides basic utility routines. Modules which combine the facilities of the bottom layer into more powerful but also more application-specific modules are then built on top of this layer. The top layer in such a program controls mainly the use of the modules in the layers below. The OSI model is a way of introducing the same idea to distributed applications, that is, applications using computer communication.

One important difference between distributed and nondistributed applications is that, for the distributed applications, there are several separate program processes on different computers which work together and thus must interact with each other. See Figure 8.1.

The arrows in the figure represent interaction between software components on two different computers. However, the real, physical communication is done only at the lowest layer, between the two bottom layers in the figure. The communication between the two middle layers is done only by using modules in the bottom layer. Thus, the middle layer may use modules in the bottom layer but add more structure to them. That is the reason the upper arrows in the figure above are dashed, they represent indirect communication, accomplished by use of the bottom-layer modules.

Note that this does not mean that a computer program using a layered model must be internally structured into layers: the program can also have other structures. But the protocol for communication is logically modeled as if the program had this layered structuring.

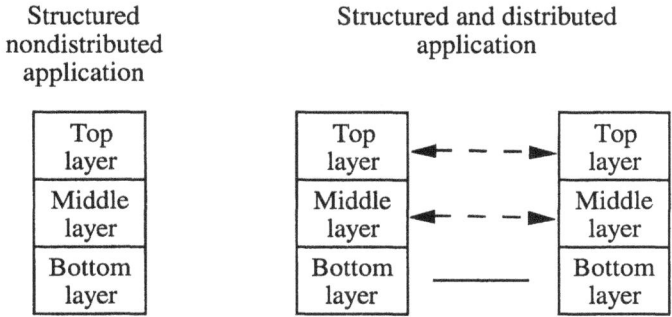

Figure 8.1 Principle of layering of structured protocol definitions.

Another way of understanding this is to look at the information units communicated at a certain level N in a multilayered protocol. The information conveyed consists of two parts: control information, which is needed specifically for this layer, and data, which is just seen as a bit string at this layer. The internal structure, which in reality exists in this bit string, belongs to higher levels and is not understood at layer N. See Figure 8.2.

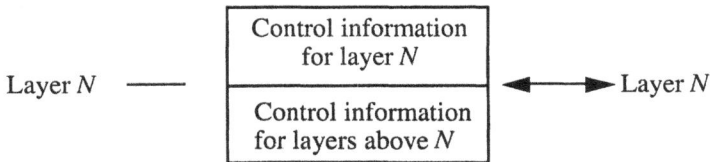

Figure 8.2 Data as seen from layer N.

In order to communicate, the layer N modules make use of the modules on the layer below, layer N - 1. When layer N - 1 transports data, it can be seen as in Figure 8.3.

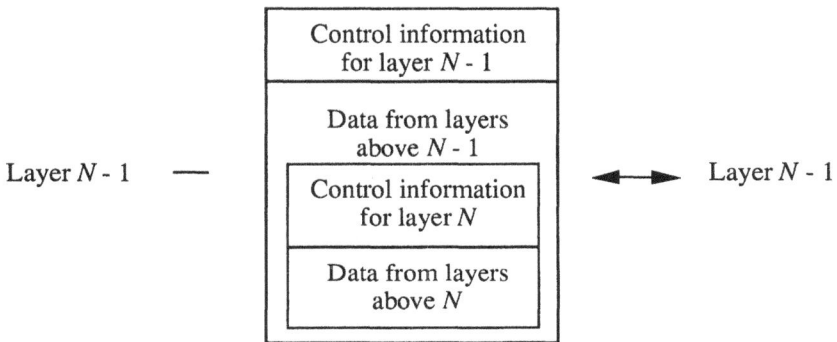

Figure 8.3 Data as seen from layer N - 1.

Note that the control information, which was understood in layer N, is only seen as "data," an unstructured bit stream, in layer N - 1.

Figure 8.4 shows how more and more information is added to a message when it passes from layer to layer in the sending node. In the receiving node, layer by layer of information is stripped from the message in the reverse order.

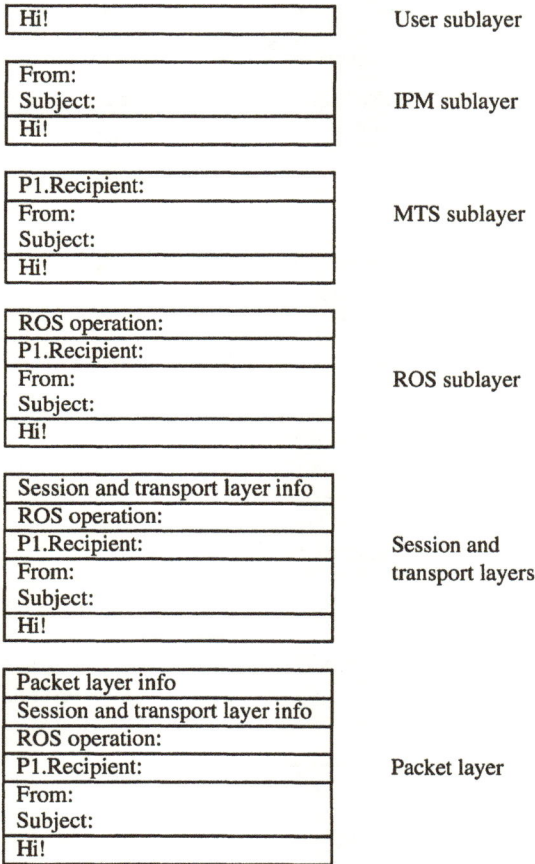

| Hi! | User sublayer |

| From: |
| Subject: |
| Hi! | IPM sublayer |

| P1.Recipient: |
| From: |
| Subject: | MTS sublayer |
| Hi! |

| ROS operation: |
| P1.Recipient: |
| From: |
| Subject: | ROS sublayer |
| Hi! |

| Session and transport layer info |
| ROS operation: |
| P1.Recipient: |
| From: | Session and |
| Subject: | transport layers |
| Hi! |

| Packet layer info |
| Session and transport layer info |
| ROS operation: |
| P1.Recipient: |
| From: | Packet layer |
| Subject: |
| Hi! |

Figure 8.4   Information added to data transmitted in successive layers.

If the structuring into layers is strict enough and the layers are well-defined, then it should be possible to combine modules of any protocol at one layer with any protocol at a lower layer. See Figure 8.5 (which is simplified, in that in reality there are more than two layers).

The X.400 messaging standard usually uses the X.25 standard at lower layers:	The SMTP messaging standard usually uses TCP/IP at lower layers:	But it is also possible to use X.400 with TCP/IP at the lower layers, as specified in [1]:	Or it is possible to use SMTP with X.25 at lower layers, as specified in [2]:
X.400 X.25	SMTP TCP/IP	X.400 TCP/IP	SMTP X.25

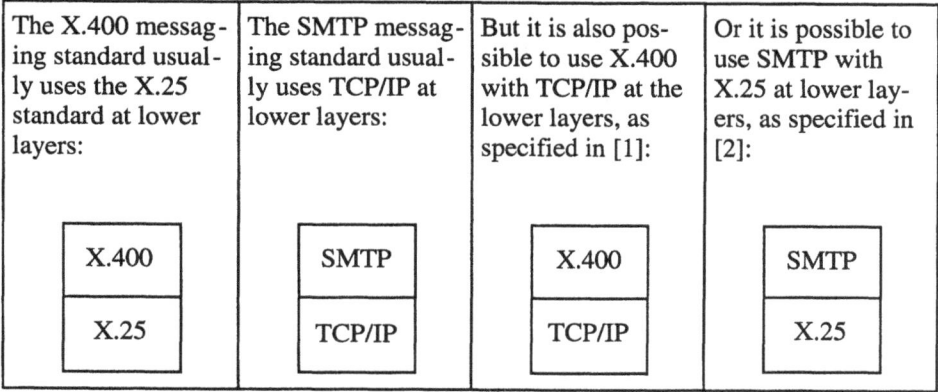

Figure 8.5   Combination of protocols from different layers.

Such combinations are possible in reality, but all possible combinations cannot be achieved without some difficulty. Figure 8.6 shows the combinations of protocol standards on the different layers that are most common for electronic mail. The standard for X.400 on top of TCP/IP is RFC 1006 [1]. Other combinations are possible: for example, SMTP can be run on top of X.25 as specified in RFC 1090 [2]. See Section 8.11.1 for more details.

Protocol / Layer	X.400	X.400	Internet	Phonenet	UUCP	BITNET (original protocol)
7b: Message heading and body	X.420 (P2 or P22)		RFC 822 and MIME		Variant of RFC 822	RFC 822 or NOTE
7a: Message envelope	X.411 (P1)		RFC 821 (SMTP)			BSMTP
4-6: Object transfer	X.214-X.216	TCP		MMDF	UUCP	
1-3: Connection	X.25	IP		Phone calls or X.28		RSCS

Figure 8.6   Common combinations of protocols in different layers.

8.3.2 ASN.1

When transporting data in a computer net, the information in the higher layers appears as a string of bits to the layers below. Therefore there is a need to pack information, which has a complex structure, into a sequence of bits. The recipient must then be able to unpack the sequence of bits and get back the original data structure.

Part of this structuring is done by the layered model itself, as described in Section 8.3.1. But within one layer, there is a need to transport complex data structures. Abstract syntax notation 1 (ASN.1 [27, 29]) is a language for specifying complex data structures. ASN.1 also has encoding rules, ways of coding the data specified by ASN.1 into bit strings. The most common of these are the basic encoding rules (BER [28, 29]).

One important goal of ASN.1 and BER is to provide a machine-independent way of specifying data. Different computer models store data in different ways. For example, floating point numbers can have different number of bits in the mantissa and exponent. Integers can be stored in two-s complement or one-s complement notation. Bit strings can be stored with the first bit first or the last bit first, etc. This means that a binary data structure produced on one computer cannot normally be moved to another type of computer and used by a program there. But an important goal of computer network standards is to allow programs on different computers to work together over the net. They must then be able to exchange data in a machine-independent format.

The main principle of ASN.1 is that new data types can be defined based on simpler types. The example below shows how this is done:

Assume that a meteorological station needs to send a temperature measurement to a meteorological center. The temperature is one single value, it can be encoded in different ways. It can be sent as a **real** value (which in a computer is encoded as a floating-point number, with a mantissa and an exponent) or it can be sent as an **integer** value. It can be given in degrees celsius, kelvin or fahrenheit.

A standard for sending meteorological information must define this. The ASN.1 definition of how temperature information is transferred might look like this:

Temperature ::= REAL - - In degrees Kelvin

This statement just says that the temperature is to be encoded using the ASN.1 rules for encoding floating-point (real) values. **REAL** is a built-in ASN.1 type. ASN.1 has a number of built-in simple data types, like **REAL, INTEGER, BOOLEAN, STRING**, etc. Information which cannot be coded formally in the ASN.1 language can be added as a comment, which is preceded by "- -" as "- - In degrees Kelvin" in the example above.

But how does the recipient know that the value sent is a temperature value and not, for example, the floating-point value of the wind velocity or humidity? One way of doing this is to introduce a *tag*. A tag is a label which is sent before the data value and indicates what kind of information is sent. The ASN.1 definition in that case might be:

Temperature ::= [APPLICATION 0] REAL - - In degrees Kelvin

This statement says that, in this application (the protocol for sending meteorological data), we let the tag "0" indicate that the data which follows is a temperature reading. Wind velocity and humidity might have different tags:

Temperature	**::=**	**[APPLICATION 0] REAL**
WindVelocity	**::=**	**[APPLICATION 1] REAL**
Humidity	**::=**	**[APPLICATION 2] REAL**

The three lines above define three new data types, **Temperature**, **WindVelocity**, and **Humidity**, all encoded using the ASN.1 **REAL** type. Note that it is only in this special application that **0**, **1** and **2** are tags for **Temperature, WindVelocity**, and **Humidity**. In other applications, the tags **0**, **1** and **2** may mean something else.

Sometimes, a new data type requires a combination of several values. A complex number, for example, can be coded as two floating-point values, one for the imaginary and one for the real element of the number. In ASN.1 this might be defined as follows:

```
ComplexNumber      ::=  [APPLICATION 3]   SEQUENCE {
                        imaginaryPart  REAL,
                        realPart              REAL }
```

More complex data types can thus, as in the example, be defined by a combination of more than one element of simpler types.

One type definition may use separately defined types. For example, the type for a record containing temperature, wind velocity, and humidity may be defined as:

```
WeatherReading      ::=  [APPLICATION 4] SEQUENCE {
                        temperatureReading   Temperature,
                        velocityReading            WindVelocity,
                        humidityReading          Humidity }
```

Note that this definition of the new type **WeatherReading** uses the previous definitions of the three types **Temperature**, **WindVelocity**, and **Humidity** as elements. In this way, more-and-more complex data structures which are needed for some applications can be built using previously defined simpler types. For example, we may want to send a series of weather readings from different altitudes in one transmission as an even more complex object:

```
SeriesOfReadings     ::=  [APPLICATION 5] SEQUENCE OF AltituteReading

AltitudeReading      ::=  [APPLICATION 6] SEQUENCE {
                        altitude              Altitude,
                        weatherReading   WeatherReading }

Altitude                  ::=  [APPLICATION 7] REAL - - Meters above sea level
```

This contains three ASN.1 productions, where each production refers to types defined in a later production. ASN.1 productions are usually written in this top-down order, but ASN.1 does not require any particular ordering of the productions.

Using the definitions above, the actual bit string (octet string) sent may be partitioned as shown in Figure 8.7.

ASN.1 is used by many computer network standards, including the X.400 standard for electronic mail. Here is an example of a small part of the ASN.1 used in the X.400 standard:

```
ReportOriginAuthenticationCheck ::= SIGNATURE SEQUENCE {
        algorithm-identifier ReportOriginAuthenticationAlgorithmIdentifier,
        content-identifier ContentIdentifier OPTIONAL,
        message-security-label MessageSecurityLabel OPTIONAL,
        per-recipient SEQUENCE SIZE (1..ub-recipients) OF     PerRecipientReportFields}
```

```
PerRecipientReportFields ::= SEQUENCE {
            actual-recipient-name ActualRecipientName,
            originally-intended-recipient-name
                OriginallyIntendedRecipientName OPTIONAL,
            CHOICE {
                delivery [0] PerRecipientDeliveryReportFields,
                non-delivery [1] PerRecipientNonDeliveryReportFields } }
```

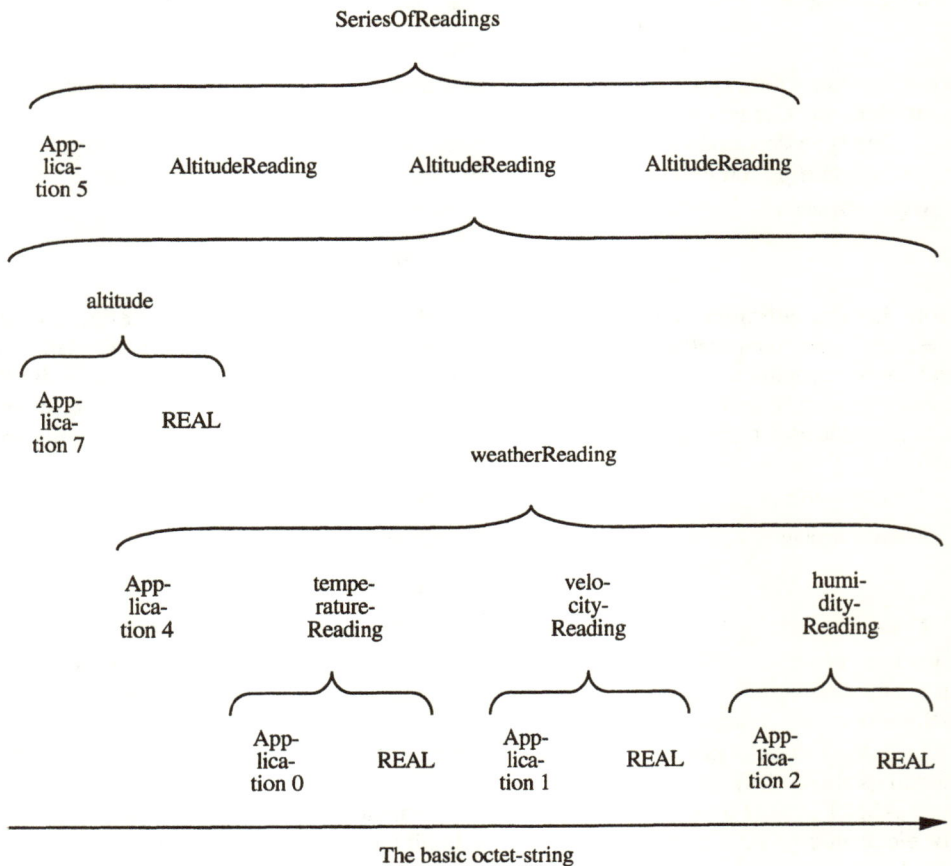

SeriesOfReadings

| Application 5 | AltitudeReading | AltitudeReading | AltitudeReading |

altitude

| Application 7 | REAL |

weatherReading

| Application 4 | temperature-Reading | velocity-Reading | humidity-Reading |

| Application 0 | REAL | Application 1 | REAL | Application 2 | REAL |

The basic octet-string

Figure 8.7   How ASN.1 and BER is used to produce an octet string.

The ASN.1 productions above say that a **ReportOriginAuthenticationCheck** consists of a **SEQUENCE** of four subfields. The fourth of these subfields, is a **SEQUENCE OF** a maximum of **ub-recipients PerREcipientReportFields**. A **PerRecipientReportField** is a **SEQUENCE** of three fields. The third of these three fields can be either a

94

PerRecipientDeliveryReportFields or a **PerRecipientNonDeliveryReportFields**. The word **SIGNATURE** is an ASN.1 macro imported from another standard, the X.522 directory system standard.

8.3.3 Object Identifiers, ANY, EXTERNAL

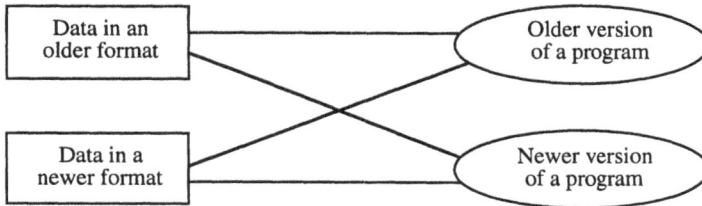

Figure 8.8   Use of object identifiers to allow communication between old and new programs.

Figure 8.8 shows a common problem in distributed systems, where many pieces of software, which have been developed at different times by different people, need to work together. Thus, an older version of a program may receive data from a newer version, in a newer format, which did not even exist when the older version of the program was produced.

ASN.1 contains special constructs to make this possible: constructs for specifying data elements which can be bypassed by older versions of a program and interpreted by newer versions of the same program. These ASN.1 features are used in the 1988 version of X.400 but not in the 1984 version. This means that programs based on the 1984 version cannot always interact with programs based on the 1988 version. But programs based on the 1988 version should be able to interact with programs written in future standards. (In reality, this is not always true, because extensibility is only possible where placeholders for extensions were put into the 1988 standard, and in some places such placeholders were forgotten. For example, the 1988 standard has placeholders for extending ordinary messages, but not for extending notifications. This has been rectified in the 1992 version of X.400.)

Here is an excerpt from the ASN.1 in the 1988 version of X.420, which shows one way of using these extension facilities:

```
ExtensionsField ::= SET OF HeadingExtension

HeadingExtension ::= SEQUENCE {
                    type OBJECT IDENTIFIER,
                    value ANY DEFINED BY type DEFAULT NULL NULL }
                    }
```

```
HEADING-EXTENSION MACRO ::=
            BEGIN
            TYPE NOTATION ::= "VALUE" type I empty
            VALUE NOTATION ::= VALUE (VALUE OBJECT IDENTIFIER)
            END
```

One heading extension, defined in the 1988 version of X.400 using this construct, is:

```
languages HEADING-EXTENSION
            VALUE SET OF Language
            ::= id-hex-languages

Language ::= PrintableString (SIZE (2..2))
```

In the 1992 version of ASN.1, the ANY and MACRO constructs were abolished, and replaced by the new CLASS construct. The above extension facility is instead defined (with the 1994 X.420 syntax) as:

```
ExtensionsField ::= SET OF IPMSExtension

IPMSExtension ::= SEQUENCE {
            type      IPMS-EXTENSION.&id,
            value     IPMS-EXTENSION.&Type DEFAULT NULL:NULL }

IPMS-EXTENSION ::= CLASS {
            &id        OBJECT IDENTIFIER UNIQUE,
            &Type      DEFAULT NULL }
            WITH SYNTAX { [VALUE &Type , ] IDENTIFIED BY &id }
```

The heading extension for languages is with the new 1992 syntax defined as:

```
languages IPMS-EXTENSION ::= {VALUE SET OF Language,
            IDENTIFIED BY id-hex-languages}

Language ::= PrintableString (SIZE (2..5) )
```

As is shown in the example above, a typical such extensible element has two subfields, one field with the name **type** and one field with the name **value**. The type field is particular for every kind of extended field. The value field has a structure which is called **ANY DEFINED BY type** with the 1988 notation and **IPMS-EXTENSION.&Type** with the 1992 notation. This means that, for different values of **type**, different ASN.1 specifications will describe the value. A new extension can then be identified by a new **type** value, and a new ASN.1 specification of the value structure, like **SET OF Language** in the example above.

The **type** field in the example above is specified as an **OBJECT IDENTIFIER**. It can also be specified as an **INTEGER**. The difference between **OBJECT IDENTIFIER** and **INTEGER** is that there are rules defined which allows anyone to obtain a new **OBJECT IDENTIFIER**, which will then be different from any other **OBJECT IDENTIFIER** obtained by anyone else. In the case of **INTEGER**, there is no protection against two different developers using the same integer for two different extensions, which would, of course, create a mess if their systems were connected. Thus, in practice, **INTEGER** only allows extensions made by the international standards organizations, while **OBJECT IDENTIFIER** allows anyone to make his own extension, without risk of a conflict with another extension made by some other person or organization.

The value of an extension can (with the 1988 notation) be either **ANY** or **EXTERNAL**. The difference between the two is that **ANY** refers to an extension specified in ASN.1, while **EXTERNAL** allows an extension specified in some language other than ASN.1.

An implementation, which encounters an extended field, can react to the extended field in four different ways:

(1) The implementation knows about the extension and utilizes it in the way it was intended to be used.
(2) The implementation receives the unknown fields, removes them and continues handling the message as if they had never been there.
(3) The implementation receives the unknown fields, saves them, and transfers them further along with the other data, even though the implementation does not understand and cannot use the information in the extended field.
(4) The implementation recognizes that this is an extended field and then gives an error code saying that it cannot handle the data because it contains an extension it does not understand.

Note that (4) is different from the kind of error that was produced when the incoming data were incorrect. Such errors, called *protocol violations*, carry a risk that a program will crash completely or react in unpredictable ways.

For envelope extensions, the X.400 standard for electronic mail specifies for each extension whether reaction (3) (*noncritical* extension) or (4) (*critical* extension) should be used by an implementation which does not understand the extension. For heading extensions, X.400 states that reaction (3) is suitable.

8.3.4 ROS

Remote operations service (ROS) is a standard for formatting operations which are made by one agent, via the networks, on another agent. ROS specifies how one agent can send an operation to another agent and how the other agent can reply. ROS thus is a way of specifying the dialogue between two agents "talking to each other." X.400 and many other OSI standards use ROS.

For example, here is the template of a ROS operation:

```
.OPERATION
ARGUMENT        <ArgumentDataType>
RESULT          <ResultDataType>
ERRORS          <ErrorOutcomes>
LINKED          <LinkedOperations>
```

Each clause inside <> is a place to insert an ASN.1-type specification when using this template to define a new operation.

8.4   X.400/MHS—THE OSI STANDARD FOR ELECTRONIC MAIL

X.400 is the ITU name of a standard for electronic mail which ISO earlier called message-oriented text interchange systems (MOTIS), and now calls message handling system (MHS)(ISO 10021).

Note: The fact that this book has somewhat more pages on X.400 (Section 8.4) than on the Internet mail standards (Section 8.6) does not indicate that the author considers X.400 more important than the Internet mail standards. But X.400 is more complex and so needs more pages. Also, the consequences of some common features of X.400 and Internet mail are presented in more detail in Section 8.4 and not repeated again in Section 8.6.

8.4.1   Functional Model

The X.400 standards is not a standard for the user interface of electronic mail. (There is one exception: In its 1992 version the standard does recommend a format for showing electronic mail addresses on the screen and for printing them on paper. See Section 8.4.21.) X.400 is also not a standard for the internal structuring of an electronic mail system. X.400 is mainly a standardized protocol for communication between messaging agents. X.400 is built on a model of how message systems are built, but it does not require that connected systems actually be built according to this model. It only requires that, when communicating with other systems, they appear as if they were organized according to this model. This is a very important difference, because it allows message systems which are not built internally according to the X.400 model to communicate with X.400. They use some kind of mapping to map their data and operations on those defined in X.400.

The only requirement when two systems of different manufacture are to work together, is that they can communicate in accordance with one of the interfaces defined in the standard. The standard defines several kinds of agents. Each agent has one or more ports. Some ports in some agents can be connected to some ports in other agents. (An agent need not be a computer: it can be a piece of software talking to another piece of software in the same computer, or it can consist of several computers connected together.)

The basic version of the functional model for electronic mail in X.400 is shown in Figure 8.9. The Figure is simplified. A more complete version is shown in Section 8.4.20.

The model assumes that there are two kinds of agents, MTAs and UAs. Two MTAs can communicate with each other, and an MTA can communicate with an UA, but two UAs cannot connect directly, they can only communicate indirectly via the MTAs.

A message from one UA to another may have to pass several MTAs enroute from the sending UA to the receiving UA.

Each UA represent a user, and it can send and receive messages from one of the MTAs.

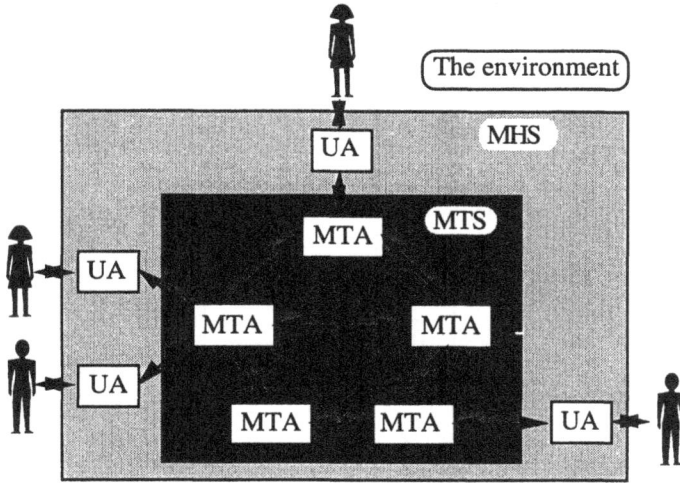

Figure 8.9   Functional model in X.400.

The system of connected MTAs is called the *message transfer system, MTS*. Note that the UAs do not belong to the MTS. There is a wider system, the *message handling system, MHS,* which comprises the MTS plus the UAs which are connected to any of the MTAs in this MTS.

An X.400 message consists of an envelope with information about sender and recipients and a content. The idea is that the MTS will only see the envelope, but that the UAs can open the envelope and look at its content. This idea is not fully adhered to, however, since the standard specifies that an MTA can convert the content, for example, from one character standard to another, if this is needed because a receiving UA cannot handle the character set.

8.4.2   Administration and Private Management Domains

MTAs can belong to different domains (see Section 7.2), with one or more MTAs and none, one, or more UAs in each domain as shown in Figure 8.10.

An administration management domain (ADMD) can include one or more electronic mail systems run by a company providing messaging and other network services. In many countries, this is often a public Telecommunications company. In Britain, for example, ADMD-s are run by British Telecom, but also by other organizations.

A private management domain (PRMD) can include one or more message systems internal to an organization. PRMDs can also provide messaging services to others in the same way as ADMDs do. The difference between ADMD and PRMD is that ADMDs are expected to provide services to PRMDs. They might even, like ADMD 2

99

in Figure 8.10, do nothing except exchange messages for other domains. Probably, much of the international forwarding of messages will be done by the ADMDs, and direct traffic between PRMDs may be mainly between PRMDs who have a large volume of mail to exchange.

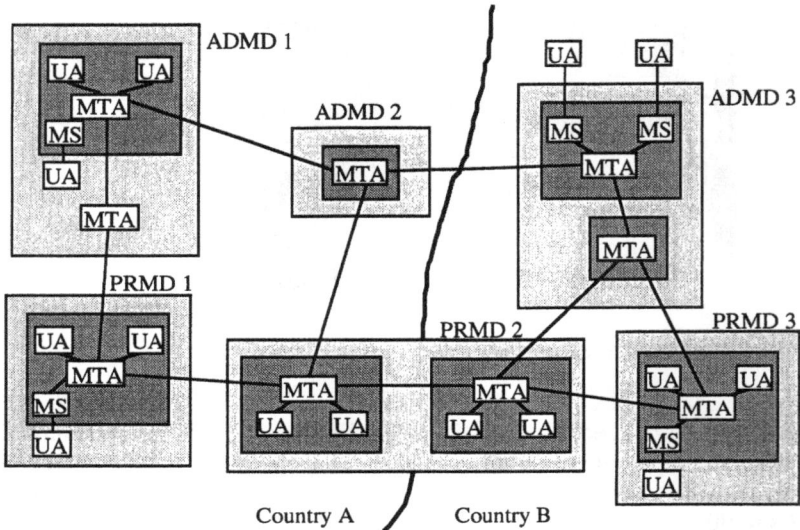

Figure 8.10   Domains in X.400.

This is one point where ITU and ISO might have slightly different viewpoints, since ITU represents the organizations running the ADMDs and thus may expect more traffic to be handled by the ADMDs. One of the few differences between the ITU and ISO versions of the standard is that in Figure 8.10, ITU has no PRMD traffic across country borders (like PRMD 2 in the figure). This, however, is only a difference in the drawings. The actual protocols handle ADMDs and PRMDs in the same ways and do not forbid message routing only via PRMDs.

8.4.3   Configurations of MTA and UA

A message system following the X.400 standard need not have separate units for the different components in Figures 8.9 and 8.10. Many configurations are possible, for example, a system where one single system in one computer handles all the MTA and UA functions and where the users connect via simple terminals like VT100 or IBM 3270. See Figure 8.11.

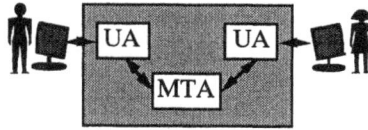

Figure 8.11   Typical minicomputer mail system.

8.4.4 Post Boxes ("Message Store")

Some applications may want to store the contents of a mailbox wholly or partly in a
server computer but still handle the user interface through software in the user's workstation. The X.400 standard supports this (but not in the 1984 version) through a service
called the Message Store (MS). This is a kind of standardized post box. The MS service
may, for example, be provided by the same server as the MTA, while the UA may be in
the user workstation.

The left side of Figure 8.12 shows a computer with a UA, and a single MTA, and
the right side shows an MS and an MTA in one computer, and a personal computer
with the user interface software in the user workstation.

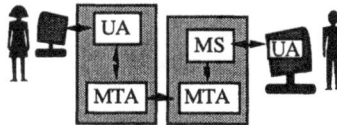

Figure 8.12   Single-computer MTAs.

Note that the MS is a data base of messages belonging to one single recipient. The
MS is not meant to be used as a common archive for several users. All incoming messages to a user of an MS are delivered first to the MS, not to the UA of the recipient.
Delivery notifications are sent (if requested) when the messages have been delivered to
the MS, even if they have not yet been transferred to the user UA.

The intention of the standard is to allow users to buy UA software or services
from one provider and MS software or services from another provider. Because of this,
the protocol for communication between the MS and the MTA is standardized. Some
functions available to the UA via this protocol are the ability to:

- Request a list of seen and/or unseen messages in the MS.
- Request that certain selected messages from the MS are sent to the UA of the
  user. The messages can be selected by giving their numbers or by using certain
  search clauses.
- Request the purging of certain messages from the MS.

- Forward a message which is stored in the MS to other recipients via the MTS. The user thus need not transfer a message to his UA and back again in order to forward it. (See also *forwarding* in Section 8.4.7.)

The P7 protocol in X.400 corresponds to the IMAP protocol in Internet mail. See Section 8.6.8.

8.4.5 Standardized Protocols

A standard is needed if equipment of different manufacture is to be connected. The workstation (terminal, personal computer) of the user is often of different manufacture than the servers it connects to, so a standard is needed for protocols between workstations and servers. (Note that this is more a matter of the software in the workstation and server than the hardware.) Different MTAs may also be of different manufacture, so a standard is needed for the protocol between them. The most important standardized protocols in X.400/MHS are called P1, P2, P3, and P7 (P22 is an extended version of P2). Their functionality is shown in Figure 8.13.

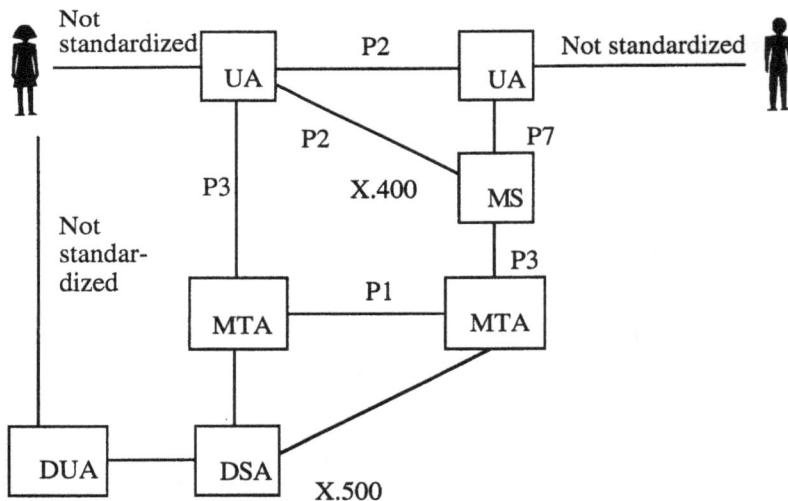

Figure 8.13   Various standardized interfaces in X.400 and X.500.

A brief description of each protocol is given below.

P1   The protocol used between two MTAs, through which they can exchange messages, notifications and probes. This is the most important protocol in the X.400 standard, defined in its part X.411 [37].

P3   The protocol used when an MTA delivers messages to a UA or an MS [37].

P7   The protocol used when a UA communicates with an MS, defined in X.413 [38].

P2   A protocol one sublayer higher, it is used in the indirect communication between UAs which is achieved by sending messages via the MTS. Note that there is no direct connection between the UAs. P2 is also a standard for formatting the contents of messages. Since MTAs only look at the outside of the envelope and the envelope is not normally "opened" until the message is delivered to a UA or an MS, P2 is a protocol between UAs and, to some extent between UAs and MSs.

(There are also other formats for the contents of a message. P22 is the name of an extended variant of P2 which can be used instead of P2 with the 1988 version of X.400 [39]. P35 is a special content type for forwarding of EDI information (see Section 6.5) and P45 [40] is a content type for voice messaging. A content type for file transfer has recently been added to X.400.)

A standardized protocol is only needed to interconnect equipment of different manufacture. The practical experience with X.400 is that there is little interest in implementing P3. Suppliers do not seem very interested in supplying different equipment for UAs and MTAs, and the customers do not seem very interested in buying different equipment for UAs and MTAs. Note that this refers mainly to the software, you can buy the hardware for UAs and MTAs from different manufacturers but still run the same electronic mail software in both of them, and then no ISO/ITU standard is necessary for their interconnection.

When it was found that there was little interest in using the P3 protocol in the 1984 version of X.400, some believed that this was because the P3 protocol was too restricted. For example, the P3 protocol in 1984 assumed that a UA was always, or almost always, connected to its server, and it did not provide a way for a UA to select which messages to download and which not to download from the MTA. It was believed that people used workstations, like MS-DOS PCs, which cannot perform multitasking. This is one reason why the MS and the P7 protocol were added to the standard in 1988. However, there is still little interest in developing systems providing the P7 protocol. The future will show if P7 will ever be widely used.

8.4.6 Envelope, Heading, and Body

Messages following the X.400 standard consist of three main components: the envelope, the heading, and the body, as illustrated in Figure 8.14.

103

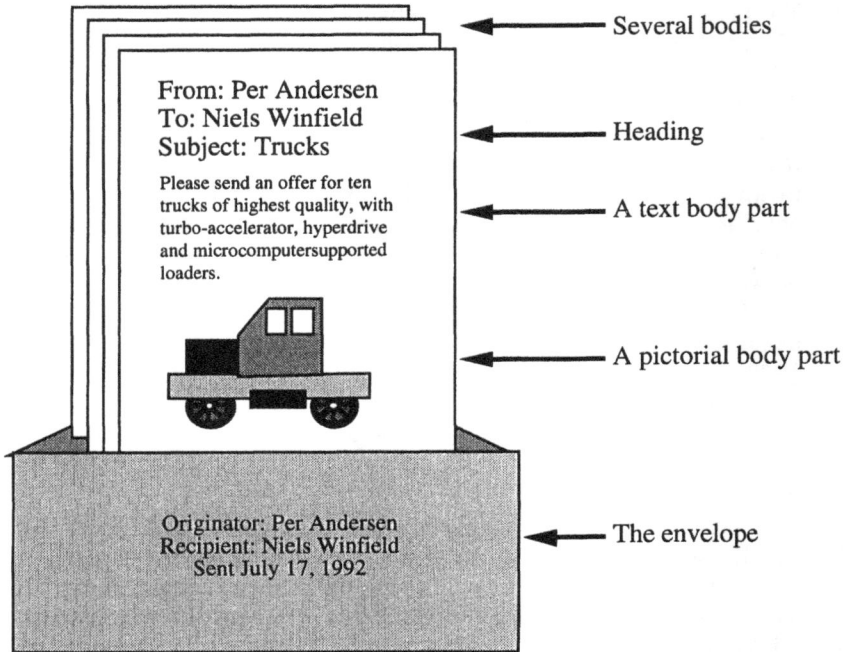

Figure 8.14   Envelope, heading, and body.

The envelope contains P1 information and is in theory the only information handled by MTAs. It contains fields for the originator (sender), recipient, and control information needed for the transfer. The content of an envelope contains information from what in X.400 is called the content protocol, like P2, P22 [39], P35, etc.

The *heading* (within the content) contains information about the originator and recipients, just like the envelope. The list of recipients on the envelope and in the heading need not be the same, however. The list of recipients on the envelope will be modified when the message is redirected via distribution lists and other ways. The list of recipients in the heading is not used in the distribution of the message, so it is possible to include recipients who are not on the envelope, because they have received the message in other ways. You can even include recipients who received the message via media other than electronic mail, and the addresses of the recipients in the heading need not be full X.400 addresses. If one person sends a message on behalf of another person, this can be indicated in the heading.

In the 1988 version of X.400, there is a facility to add additional heading fields and body part types using object identifiers as described in Section 8.3.3. This allows not only standards organizations, but also other developers or organizations to define their own additional heading fields and body parts of different types.

104

The *body* contains the text of the message. It can also contain certain control information related to the format of the text. The same message can contain several body parts with a single common heading. Several body parts can be used if you want to combine texts of different kinds, for example, sound, graphics, text, and binary attachments.

Note the difference between *content type* and *body part type*. Content type is a type for the whole content of a message, everything which is in the envelope, both heading and body parts. A message can in X.400 only have one content type. Body-part type is a type for one of the body parts of a message, and a message can have several body parts of different types. (The word "content" has a different meaning in the Internet e-mail standards, where it is used for what X.400 calls "body.")

New content types are defined when there is a need for new structural information of the kind you would put in the heading. New body part types are defined when you want to transfer different kinds of "text" in a wide sense of that word. The fact that one message can contain several body parts of different types makes new body part types more flexible.

For example, if file transfer is defined as a new body type, then it is possible to send a message with two parts, one a textual comment on the file being sent, and the other the file itself. And a recipient whose UA is not capable of handling the file transfer body part, can still show you the textual comment, since that can be written in one of the basic text types of X.400. This can allow the recipient to see what it is about, and then forward it to some other equipment which can handle the file transfer body part. All this would not be possible if file transfer was defined as a special content type. (ISO/ITU has in reality chosen to standardize both a file transfer body part and a file transfer content type.)

8.4.7 Body Part Types

Each body part is of one particular type. Here is a list of some of the most important body part types in X.400:

- IA5-text (see Section 8.2.1);
- G3 telefacsimile (fax);
- Teletex (T.61) (see Section 8.2.2);
- Videotex according to several different videotex standards;
- Message;
- Bilaterally defined;
- Nationally defined;
- Externally defined (added in the 1988 version of X.400);
- Sound (added in the 1992 version of X.400); and
- File transfer body part (added in the 1992 version of X.400).

In addition to these, there are body part types for encrypted text. The discussion below describes some body-part types of special interest:

Message is a body-part type which allows the insertion of a whole message as a body part within another message. This can, for example, be used if you want to forward a message you have received to additional recipients. You can include the body, the heading, and, if you want, parts of the envelope information for the forwarded message. It is, for example, possible to take an incoming message, add two additional body parts, one before and one after the forwarded message, and then send it all away in the format shown in Figure 8.15. This can be done recursively any number of times, so that a message may, for example, look like the one in Figure 8.16. For a discussion about references between forwarded messages, see Section 8.4.14.

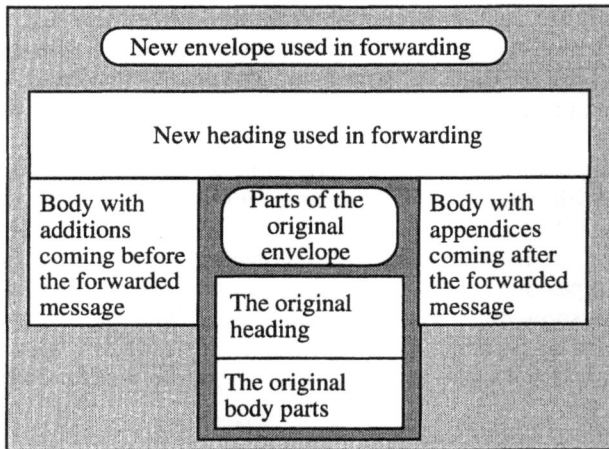

Figure 8.15   Use of the *message* body part.

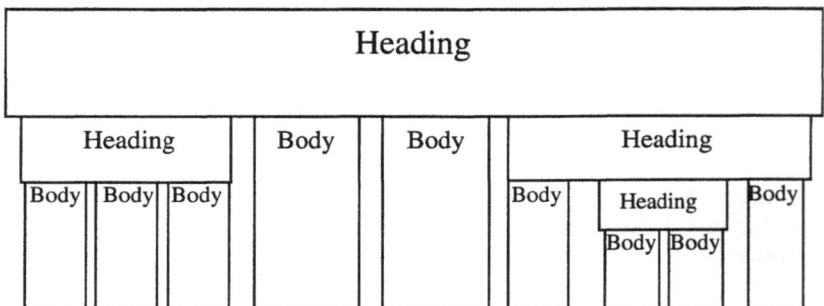

Figure 8.16   Recursively nested messages within body parts.

The externally defined body part uses object identifiers in the way described in Section 8.3.3. This means that not only can international standards organizations define new body part types, but national standards organizations and companies can also. IBM might, for example, choose to register EBCDIC as a body part type, and Microsoft might choose to register CP 850 (the most common character set in MS-DOS) and the rich text format (RTF), which is used for exchange of word processing information between Microsoft's different word processing products.

Bilaterally defined, nationally defined and *encrypted* are body-part types which are not often used. Their purpose is better satisfied by the *externally defined* body part. The most important externally defined body parts as of this writing that have been defined by standards organizations are the *general text body part, Voice* and *File transfer* body parts.

The general text body part contains text which can contain several different character sets within the same body-part type, using ISO 2022 escape sequences (see Section 8.2.1) to switch character set in the middle of a body part.

One interesting thing about the general text body part is the information about the body part types which is included on the envelope. There is a field on the envelope which lists the body-part types used in the message. This field is called *originally encoded information types*. The intention of the field is to allow MTAs to route messages containing special body-part types to terminals capable of handling these body parts, for example, routing messages containing voice to a terminal with a speaker. In the case of the general text body-part type, however, the *originally encoded information types* field in the envelope is expected to list all the different character sets used within the General text body parts.

The *voice body part* contains digital encoding of voice or other sound information. It has a parameter voice-encoding type indicating what algorithm was used to encode voice into a bit string and a parameter indicating the sound duration in seconds of. (Note that X.400 also has a separate content type for voice, see Section 8.4.24.)

The file transfer body part, which was introduced in the 1992 version of X.400, is mapped closely from the functionality of the file transfer and management (FTAM) standard. The difference between file transfer using FTAM and X.400 is that FTAM is based on direct interaction between the sending and the receiving computer, while X.400 is based on store-and-forward transmission of messages.

The file transfer body part can be used to send data in special file formats, such as object programs or binary files readable only by some particular program. A large number of attributes, mostly optional, for the files being sent can be indicated: from which store the file comes, the file name and directory, and whether the file is sent in a compressed form and, if so, what kind of compression algorithm is used. The content type can be indicated using an object identifier to avoid the risk of accidental confusion between two different content types (note that the term "content type" used in a different meaning than elsewhere in X.400). The environment parameter can indicate what operating system or hardware architecture the file is based on. A number of file attributes, which are typically in file stores can be sent with the file, attributes such as creator, creation date, last revision date, etc.

8.4.8 Postmarks, Time Stamps, and Delivery Times

Information about time (calendar date, hours, and minutes) are used in many ways in the X.400 standard. Of particular interest is the timing information which is not available in X.400. There is no information in the heading of messages on the time when they were written or sent. Such times are available in the Internet mail standards and are, of course, common in ordinary postal mail. In X.400, the only information about the sending time is on the envelope. This time stamp is put there by the MTA used by the sender and can be compared to the postmark date on ordinary postal mail. There is also a time stamp on the envelope indicating when the message was delivered to the recipient UA. If the sender requests a delivery notification, these two times will be included in that notification.

The reason why X.400 has chosen to put the time stamp on the envelope and not in the message heading is probably that the times created by the MTS are more reliable and less easy to falsify. However, time stamps created in the MTS *can* be falsified. The closest MTA for senders and recipients is often internal to the organization where they work, and if falsified time stamps are in the interest of this organization, one cannot rely on them as much as on time stamps affixed by public MTAs.

In addition to the time stamps on when a message enters and exits from the MTS, X.400 also allows the sender to indicate an earliest and (in the 1988 version) a latest requested time of delivery. In the message heading, X.400 has fields to indicate a time after which a message expires, and a time before which a reply is requested.

8.4.9 Format Conversion

It is possible to indicate on the envelope which body-part types and character sets are used in the content. If a receiving UA is not capable of handling certain body part types, for example, T.61, it can request the MTS to convert T.61 text in the message content to, for example, IA5 before the letter is delivered.

A disadvantage of this is that conversion usually destroys information, particularly if you convert from a more powerful character set like T.61 into a less powerful set like IA5. It might be better to supply the recipient with the message in its original form, even if the screen used by the recipient cannot display all the characters. Conversion can then instead be done at the time the text is displayed on the user screen. An advantage of this is that a recipient who wishes to see the original text undamaged can resend it to a more powerful printing device. Also, if the recipient forwards the message to a third person, whose screen can show T.61, the forwarded text is not unnecessarily damaged. The sender of a message can request that no such conversion take place for a particular message.

8.4.10 Notifications of Delivery, Nondelivery, Receipt, and Nonreceipt

X.400 has several different types of notifications, as shown in Figure 8.17. In the MTS sublayer, these include:

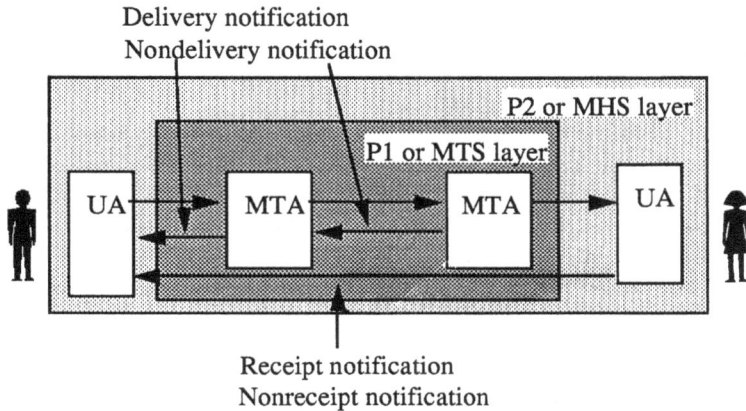

Delivery notification
Nondelivery notification

P2 or MHS layer

P1 or MTS layer

Receipt notification
Nonreceipt notification

Figure 8.17   Transmission of notifications.

- *Nondelivery notification* which indicates that the message could not be delivered to the mailbox of the recipient. This notification is requested by default, but the sender can suppress such notifications.
- *Delivery notification* which indicates that the mailbox of the recipient was found, and that the message has been queued for transferal to that mailbox.[1] By default, no such notification is produced unless the sender explicitly requests it.

In the P2/P22 sublayer, the notifications include:

- *Receipt notification* which indicates that the message has been seen, and probably read or similarly handled by the recipient. X.400 does, however, not dictate when a UA should generate receipt notifications, so it is possible to read a message without producing a receipt notification or to send a receipt notification without reading a message, if the UA software of the recipient allows this.
- *Nonreceipt notification* which indicates that although a message has been delivered to the recipient, it will never be seen. The reason for this may, for example, be that the recipient has canceled his account in his message system without first reading all unseen messages.

---

1   X.400 says that a delivery notification is to be sent when the message has successfully been delivered to the recipient UA or access unit. However, the queue of messages to be delivered to a mailbox is often seen as part of the UA, so that a delivery notification is sent as soon as the message has been put in this queue.

109

In cases of special delivery, which notification and when to send it, is a complex issue and not fully clear from the present standards.

In the case of postal delivery, notifications and nondelivery notifications can be generated both when the message was transferred from the MTS to the postal delivery access unit (PDAU) and when it was physically delivered to the ultimate recipient. In the latter case, a delivery notification indicates that the postman has actually a signed document from the ultimate recipient that the recipient received the message.

Note that this means that a mail system may not be designed with the assumption that there will be at most one delivery or nondelivery notification for each recipient. In addition to the case described above, distribution list and other forwarding can also cause more than one delivery notification for each originally intended recipient.

In the case of voice mail, delivery and nondelivery notifications are delivered when the message is transferred from the MTS to the voice mail access unit (VMAU).

In the case of EDI, delivery and nondelivery notifications are generated when the message is delivered to the electronic data interchange access unit (EDIAU), and a new special kind of EDI notification is produced at delivery to the EDI object.

In the case of telex delivery, delivery and nondelivery notifications should, if possible, be produced at delivery to the recipient telex machine. The same principle is recommended for fax delivery. However, when MTS is used to deliver messages from one fax distribution service to another, then notifications should be produced at the delivery to the fax AU.

See Section 8.4.18 for information about notifications for distribution lists.

8.4.11 Probe

Probes can be used by senders to check in advance which electronic mail addresses are correct and possible to reach. Probes are also useful for administrators of message systems in checking out their systems. A probe is sent exactly the same way as a normal message until delivery to the mailbox of the recipient but is not delivered. Instead, a delivery notification is sent back if the probe would have been deliverable, and a nondelivery notification is sent if it would not have been deliverable. The increasing use of directory systems (see Sections 6.11 and 8.5) might reduce the need for probes.

8.4.12 MTS Recipient Indication

A UA can deliver a message to the MTS with a list of recipients, to whom the message is to be delivered. If the message goes to a distribution list, this list of recipients will be extended by the expansion in the distribution list.

If a message is sent to several recipients on the same MTA, only one copy of the message is sent to this MTA. The MTA will copy the message for the different recipients before delivering it.

The sender can indicate that the recipient is to be told of all the other MTS recipients of the message. It is not technically possible, however, to ensure that the recipient is told of all recipients created by distribution list expansion and other methods of resending. If the sender makes such a request, then no names are removed on the envelope when the message is turned into separate copies for separate groups of recipients. Instead, for every recipient there is a flag called the *responsibility flag*. If this flag has the value "responsible," then the receiving MTA is expected to deliver to this recipient. If the flag has the value "nonresponsible," then the MTA will only forward the information about the recipient, but will not try to deliver the message to this recipient. See Figure 8.18.

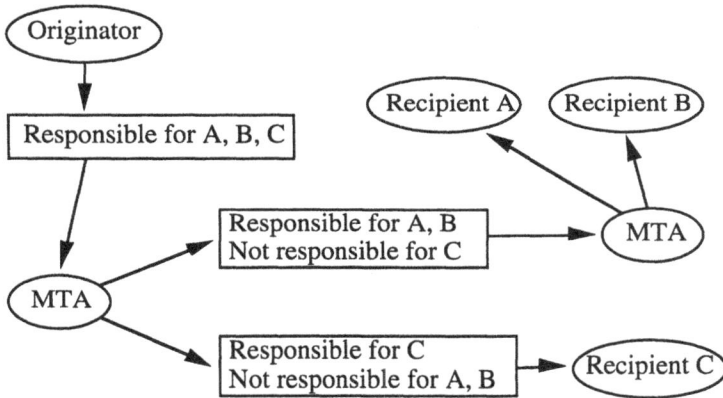

Figure 8.18   Use of responsibility flag in X.400.

If, however, the originator does not request that the recipient be told about other recipients of the message, then forwarding MTAs can remove the nonresponsible recipients from the envelope. This can save transmission cost, especially for messages with many geographically distributed recipients. Note that the sender can also indicate information about other recipients in the message heading. See Section 8.4.13.

The functionality of separating recipients to which a message is delivered and recipients whose name are mentioned but to whom delivery is not expected by the MTA to which a message is passed, is essential for a smooth-running electronic mail system. Most systems for electronic mail have such a facility.

8.4.13   Primary Recipients, Copy Recipients, and BlindCopy Recipients

The message heading can also contain a list of recipients. This list, however, is optional and is not used to control delivery. Delivery is solely controlled by the list of recipients on the envelope. The list of recipients in the message heading allows three types of

111

recipients: *primary, copy* and *blind-copy recipients*. A blind-copy recipient is a recipient whose existence will not be divulged to other recipients of the same message. Whether the blind-copy recipients are told of each other's names is not mandated by the standard.

Note that by introducing the blind-copy recipient heading field, the heading of the same message can be different for different recipients. This also means that a recipient who gets the same message via different routes (for example, forwarded by two different people) can receive copies of the message which are not identical. There are also other reasons why two copies of the same message need not be identical. One may have its text converted (see Section 8.4.9) and one may be sent with only envelope and heading but no body parts. The fact that two copies of the same message may not always be identical is important because an important quality of good UA software is the ability to stop the recipient from getting the same message twice. Since, however, copies of the same message may sometimes appear not to be identical, the implementation of such a facility in a UA is not easy!

Note that there are two ways of creating the effect of recipients whose name are kept secret from other recipients. One way is to use the blind-copy recipient facility. The other way is first to send the message to the nonblind recipients and then to forward the message (including the original heading and body) to the secret recipients. In my personal opinion, this would have been a neater way of implementing a blind-copy recipient facility, since it would avoid the problem of a small difference in the heading between two copies of the same message.

The corresponding features in Internet mail are described in Section 8.6.4.

8.4.14 References between Messages and Global Message IDs

There is often a need to let a message refer to previously sent messages: for example, in replies. It is an important facility for a recipient of a reply to be able to easily ask his electronic mail system for the message to which the reply replies. It is also useful for users of electronic mail systems to be able to browse through whole conversations (see also Section 6.7). In order to be able to transfer a reply link between two messages which are sent at different times, it is useful if every message has a globally unique identifying code. This is a code which no other message has or is going to get.

X.400 has some kinds of identifying codes on the envelope and in the heading. The code on the envelope, however, is shortlived, and long-lived references between messages are handled using the identifying code in the heading. A globally unique identifying code in the heading is produced by combining two subfields. One subfield is a valid electronic mail name (usually of the originator, but some other valid name can also be used) plus an identifying code which is unique relative to this electronic mail name. Since electronic mail names and addresses must be unique (otherwise it would not be possible to deliver a message to its recipient), this will then produce a globally unique identifying code for the message itself.

The electronic mail name component of this message identifier is formally optional, but the standard says that "its omission is discouraged."

In the 1988 version of X.400, the name of this globally unique identifying code in the message heading is *IPM Identifier*. In the 1984 version, the same field is called *IPMessageID*. (In Internet mail standards, it is called *Message-ID*.)

X.400 supports three different kinds of references between messages, all indicated by use of the IPM Identifier:

- *Replied-To* for ordinary replies.
- *Related-To* for other kind of references. (This field was called *cross-references* in the 1984 version of X.400.)
- *Obsoletes* when the new message is a replacement of an old message, for example, a new version of a text under development or containing a copy of the original message with an error corrected.

A message cannot have a *replied-to* reference to more than one previous message, while the number of messages it is *related-to* or *obsoletes* can be more than one. A consequence of this is that a conversation which is created using the *replied-to* field will always have a tree structure, something which is not true for conversations created by *related-to* and *obsoletes*. Another consequence is that two different conversations can be merged into one if the *related-to* and *obsoletes* fields are used to create conversations. Such merging is not possible if only the *replied-to* field is used.

Figure 8.19 shows how the IPM Identifier can be used to connect a reply to the original message, using a data base of IPM Identifiers with pointers to the messages they refer to in the mailbox data base of both the sender and the recipient.

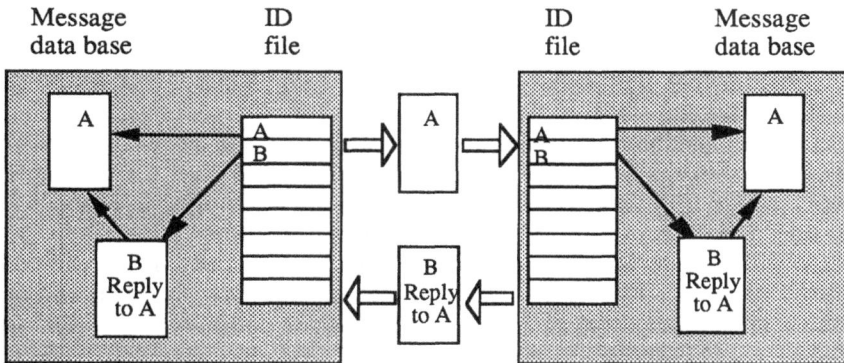

Figure 8.19   Use of IPM Identifier to correlate replies with the original message.

When you create a reply link on a message which contains forwarded body parts, you should carefully consider to which heading the reply link should refer. This is illustrated in Figure 8.20.

113

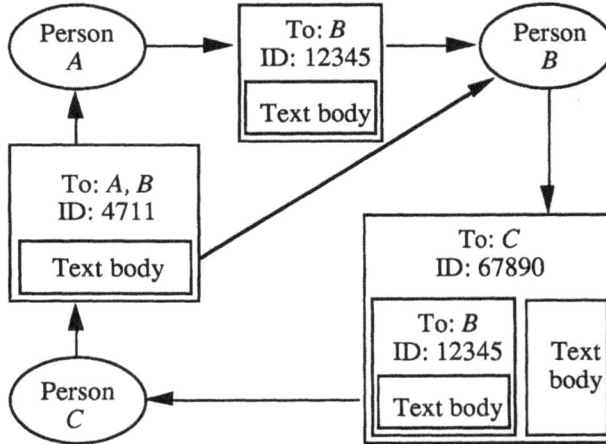

Figure 8.20   Problem with references to the wrong IPM Identifier.

Person *A* writes a message to person *B*. *B* forwards the message to *C*, using the forwarding mechanism of including the whole text of the original message as a body part of the forwarded message. *C* then writes a reply to the original message and sends the reply to both *A* and *B*. It is very important for *C* to think carefully of whether to use the ID of the original message (12345, in the example) or the ID of the forwarding message (67890, in the example) in the *Replied-to-IPM* field. This is important because *A* has never seen the forwarding message. This means that a reference in the reply, saying that it is a reply to 67890, will not be understood by *A*. Good message systems should be designed to protect users from such mistakes.

Of course, the intention of *C* may be to reply also or mainly to the text body which *B* added when the message was forwarded to *C*. But if that is the case, *C* should either send the reply only to *B* or forward the whole message on to *A*, since a reply sent to *A* on the forwarded body part in 67890 will otherwise not be understood by *A*.

A person will often get several copies of the same message, forwarded by different users and distribution lists. It is an important service to the user that his electronic mail system be able to correlate these copies, so that the person will not have to read the texts more than once and so that the person can find all comments, appendices, and recipients of the message. Such correlation should also be done when the recipient receives the same message both directly and included as forwarded body parts in other messages. The globally unique IPM Identifier is the code which is used to provide such correlations. Note the use of the word "correlate," not the word "merge." Since all copies of the same message are not always identical (see Section 8.4.13), information can be destroyed if they are merged carelessly.

The corresponding features in Internet mail are described in Section 8.6.4.

8.4.15 Reply Requests

X.400 allows the sender of a message to indicate in the message heading where they want replies sent. This can, for example, be used if someone other than the sender the processes the replies, or when you want replies sent to a group of people. The latest time for replies can also be indicated. It is also possible to indicate for each recipient whether you want a reply from that recipient.

Note the difference between the first two attributes above (where and when replies are to be sent) and the third attribute (if a reply is requested). The first two are attributes of the whole message, while the third is an attribute of each recipient. These are called *per-message* attributes and *per-recipient* attributes. Per-recipient attributes are useful if you want to set different attributes for different recipients.

8.4.16 Automatic Forwarding

There are several different facilities for the automatic forwarding of messages in X.400. On the P1 level, both the sender and the recipient can request that a message be sent to someone else if the original recipient cannot be reached:

- Originator requested alternate recipient, and
- Recipient assigned alternate recipient.

Many message systems forward incoming messages with incomplete recipient addresses to a person usually called *postmaster*. This person checks the message and, if necessary, the content of the message to find out to whom the message should go. If the originator does not want anyone but the intended recipient to see a message, and thus prefers a nondelivery report to having the message seen by a postmaster, the originator can indicate this in an envelope field called *alternate-recipient-allowed*.

As described in Section 8.4.7, at the IPM level there is also a way of indicating in the message heading that a message has been forwarded: by including the new message as a body part within a new message with a new heading. On the IPM level, there is also, a heading field to indicate whether or not a message has been automatically resent (*auto-forwarded*).

8.4.17 Other Message Heading Fields

In addition to what has been described above, X.420 includes some additional P22 message heading fields. Some examples are described below:

The *importance* heading field indicates whether the importance of a message is *low, normal* or *high*.

The *sensitivity* heading field indicates whether a message is *personal*, *private,* or *company-confidential*. The field is omitted if neither of these sensitivity classes apply.

The *incomplete-copy* heading field (added in 1988) is used if a message is sent without its body parts. This is useful if you are sending a message to someone who already has the message, because you can avoid the cost of sending the whole body again. You would need to send a message to someone who already has it, if, for example, you want to tell that person you have forwarded his message to someone else.

The *languages* heading field (added in 1988) can indicate which human languages are used in a message. Languages are coded using two character-language codes taken from an ISO standard [30]. This field can, for example, be used to control the translation of messages written in languages a recipient would not otherwise understand.

The *autosubmitted* heading field (added in 1992) indicates that a message was sent automatically by either a machine or computer program, without human intervention. This can be used for sorting incoming messages and also to avoid loops where two computer programs endlessly send automatic replies to each other.

8.4.18 Distribution Lists

Technically, one might envisage introducing distribution lists into an electronic mail standard like X.400 at either the P1 or P2 level. If distribution lists are implemented at the P1 level, MTS resends the message using the information on the envelope. If distribution lists are implemented at the P2 level, each list is represented by some kind of UA, which receives the message and forwards to the list members it using the P2 forwarding facilities. The tools for preventing a message from endlessly going back and forward between two lists that are members of each other directly or indirectly (see Section 7.4) will then also use either envelope or heading information for storing trace lists or IPM Identifiers to recognize loops.

In X.400, the distribution list is implemented on the P1 level, because this allows distribution lists to be used independently of the content type.

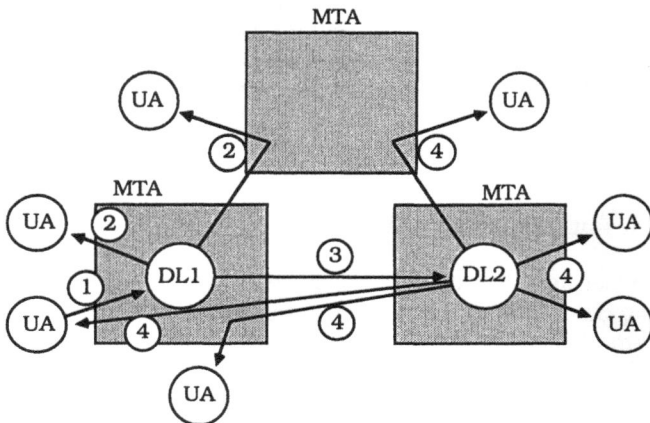

Figure 8.21   Use of nested distribution lists in X.400.

116

Figure 8.21 shows the basic features of the X.400 distribution list facility:

(1)   The originator sends the message to the first list;
(2)   Some recipients get the message directly from the first list;
(3)   The message is forwarded from the first to the second list; and
(4)   Some recipients receive the message from the second list.

An interesting issue is how to handle notifications for distribution lists. Shall the delivery and nondelivery notifications be sent to the originator, the list maintainer, or to both? X.400 allows both alternatives. Delivery- and nondelivery notifications are always sent back the same way the message was initially distributed, stepping back from list to list, as is shown in Figure 8.22.

The sending of a message via distribution lists:

The return of delivery or nondelivery notifications:

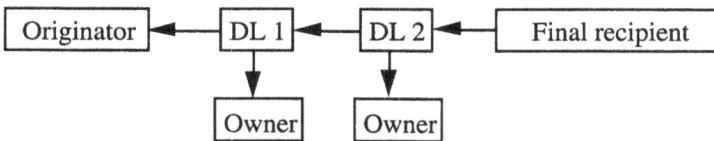

Figure 8.22   Notification propagation via distribution lists.

The owner of a distribution list decides whether the list is set up so that delivery and nondelivery notifications are sent to the list maintainer, the sender, or both. For a message coming from a distribution list, note that "sender" means the previous list and not the message originator. Thus, in Figure 8.22 the message originator will get delivery and nondelivery notifications only if both lists are set up to send notifications to the sender.

For large lists, it is more common to request notifications to the list maintainer, since the maintainer can use them to keep the list up-to-date. For small lists, it may be more common for the originator to get delivery notifications so that he can ensure that the message has reached its intended recipients.

An important function in the standard for distribution lists is that a recipient, who gets a message via one or more distribution lists, is always told on the envelope of the delivered message whether this message comes via a list and if so which list. This allows the recipient UA software to sort messages from different lists into different folders or even to totally reject undesirable messages. Some countries have laws that

117

allow people to have their addresses deleted from postal mail advertising mailing lists, and this is the corresponding feature in electronic mail (see Section 10.5).

8.4.19 Avoiding Loops

There is an obvious risk that a message can circulate endlessly back and forth between two MTAs if each believes that the other is most capable to deliver the message to its recipient. To stop this, X.400 puts a *trace* list on the envelope of the MTAs that a message has passed through. This means that when a message returns to the same MTA, it can recognize its own name in the trace list and stop the loop.

X.400 is designed so that this trace list is normally thrown away when a message passes from one PRMD or ADMD to another. Instead, a separate trace list of the PRMDs and ADMDs which the message has passed through is used to stop loops between management domains. An effect of this feature is that it is not possible to route a message back to another MTA in a domain which the message has left. (Presumably the reason for this is to cut down on the size of the trace list, but is this advantage really worth the complexity introduced?)

If a message has passed through a distribution list, it is, however, allowed to come back to an MD or an MTA which it has previously passed as shown in Figure 8.21. Thus, the normal trace list is inhibited by distribution list expansion. However, the names of the distribution lists are kept on the trace list to stop endless message loops.

Similar features are used to stop loops caused by certain kinds of automatic forwarding (redirection) of messages.

8.4.20 Messages to Other Media

In the 1988 version of X.400, electronic mail an be sent automatically to a telex, teletex, fax or printer (to be sent as ordinary postal mail), as shown in Figure 8.23. These features are accessed via AUs such as PDAUs for postal mail. In the opposite direction, incoming telexes and teletex messages can be converted and resent as X.400 messages.

Delivery notifications can be produced, if requested and possible, upon delivery to the AU and to the final recipient (see Section 8.4.10).

To support these features, in 1988 the electronic mail address format of X.400 was extended to include a number of postal-delivery fields like zip code, post box number, and so forth.

8.4.21 Addressing in X.400

An electronic mail address in X.400 (*originator/recipient-name, O/R-name* or *O R-name*) is based on the domain naming principle described in Section 7.2, but with some added complexity. First, the OR-name has two main subfields, a *directory name* and an *OR-address*. The directory name describes the recipient in logical organizational terms such as country, organization, department, etc. The directory name cannot always be

118

used directly for routing a message to its recipient. Because of this, the directory name must be looked up in the *directory* (see Section 8.5) before routing the message from one MTA to another MTA. The directory will then return the *OR-address*. This look-up can be done by the sender's UA or by the MTA to which the message is first submitted.

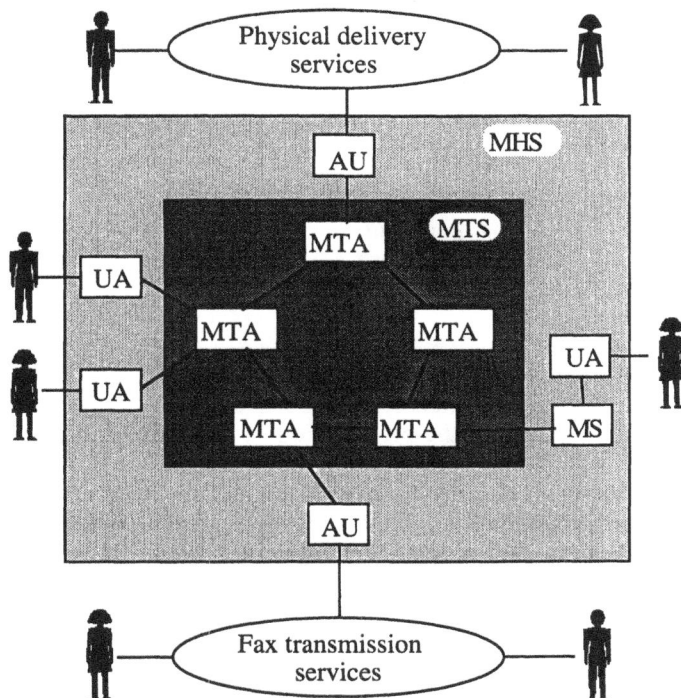

Figure 8.23   Communication between X.400 and other media.

The OR-address also has a complex format. Only the most common variant of OR-addresses is described below:

- *Country name;*
- *Administration domain name (ADMD name);*
- *Private domain name (PRMD name);*
- *Organization name;*
- *Organizational unit names*(four sublevels allowed);
- *Personal name*, split into:
  - *Surname,*
  - *Given name,*
  - *Middle initials, and*
  - *Generation qualifier;* and

119

- *Common name* (Added in the 1988 version. It is an alternative to the personal name for objects like distribution lists and organizations whose names are not naturally split into surnames and given names.).

A typical X.400 OR-address might look like this:

Given name (G)	John
Surname (S)	Smith
Organization (O)	A Bank Ltd
Org. Unit (OU1)	IT Dept
Org. Unit (OU2)	MSG Group
PRMD (P)	A Bank Ltd
ADMD (A)	Snomail
Country (C)	AQ

Observe that PRMD and organization happens to be identical, since the organization to which this person belongs also runs his PRMD. (An unsolved controversial issue is whether it is permitted to omit the organization in cases where it is identical to the PRMD.)

Note that all the fields described above are not mandatory. If you send an electronic mail message to the A Bank Ltd., wanting the message to be handled by A Bank Ltd. as a company, and not to any particular employee of A Bank Ltd., then you might, for example, use only the following fields in the OR-address:

Organization (O)	A Bank Ltd
PRMD (P)	A Bank Ltd
ADMD (A)	Snomail
Country (C)	AQ

X.400 does not standardize the user interface of messaging systems. There is, however, one exception to this. The 1992 version adds, an annex which indicates a format for showing OR-addresses when they are shown on screen or printed. This allows people to put their electronic mail address on business cards, postal-mail headings, etc., in a format which the recipient of the business card can use in sending electronic mail to the card owner, even though they use systems of different manufacture.

According to this standard, the OR-address can be shown in the format used in the example above. If this format is used, the text before the parenthesizes can be printed in languages other than English, but the text inside the parenthesizes should always be the English abbreviation given in the example above. For example, in Norwegian the address above might be printed like this:

Fornavn (G)	John
Etternavn (S)	Smith
Organisasjon (O)	A Bank Ltd
Organisasjonsenhet (OU1)	IT Dept
Organisasjonsenhet (OU2)	MSG Group
Privat domene (P)	A Bank Ltd
Admininstrasjonsdomene (A)	Snomail
Land (C)	AQ

There is also a shorter format for printing OR-addresses as a single string, which in the example above can look like this:

```
X.400: G=John; S=Smith; O=A Bank Ltd; OU1=IT Dept; OU2=MSG Group;
PRMD=A Bank Ltd; A=Snomail; C=AQ
```

(The delimiter between the fields above can be either the ";" or the "/" character, a typical compromise to attain consensus in a standards committee.)

Note that even in this short form, the OR-address is quite complex and difficult to type in accurately. Users of X.400 systems cannot be expected to enjoy typing this long string every time they want to send a message to someone. Because of this, most good X.400 systems are associated with some kind of directory that contains lists of the people you commonly communicate with. You can then input an abbreviation, and the directory translates the abbreviation to the full name.

Psychological experiments show that it is easier for a user to input an X.400 OR-address if it is done by filling in a form with different fields for given name, surname, organization, etc., than if the user has to type a string like the one above.

See Section 8.2.3 for more information about character sets and national characters in names.

Single Space ADMD Convention

The original version of X.400 required that ADMD be a mandatory component of each OR-address. From a user point of view, however, it would be an advantage if the user did not have to specify the ADMD. Omitting the ADMD component is reasonable only if the following two conditions are fulfilled:

(a) All ADMDs in a country are willing to and capable of handling messages to other ADMDs in the country than their own. Usually, they would route such messages to the recipient ADMD.

(b) All PRMD names in a country are unique, that is, PRMD names are not relative to the ADMD name.

Since the X.400 standard formally specifies that the ADMD component must be present, the X.400 standardization body has agreed that an omitted ADMD is indicated by making the ADMD component equal to a one-character string containing only a space character. Often, in the user interfaces, the user can omit the ADMD, and the user interface will automatically translate this omitted ADMD into a single-space ADMD.

Whether or not to allow single space ADMDs or not is decided individually by each country. Thus some countries allow it, but others do not. For example, Great Britain has decided to allow single-space ADMDs.

8.4.22 Extensibility

Section 8.3.3 described a method for making standards extensible. These features are used in X.400 (the 1988 version) in the following ways:

- Critical envelope extensions: systems which receive such extensions and do not understand them should reject the message;
- Noncritical envelope extensions: systems which receive such extensions and do not understand them should ignore them, but, if possible, forward the extension information unchanged;
- On the envelope: new content types can be added;
- IPM content type: new attributes can be added to the heading;
- IPM content type: new body types can be added, for example for new character sets or file types.
- IPM notifications: Extended attributes can be added (in the 1992 version of X.400).

Most of these extensions use *object identifiers* to label extensions (see Section 8.3.3), so that anyone can add extensions without risk of confusion with extensions added by others. However, the critical and noncritical envelope extensions use *integers*. In this way, the standards organizations have chosen to indicate that only extensions made by major standards organizations in cooperation are to be accepted. The reason for this is to reduce the risk of the standard diverging through extensions into different incompatible paths.

8.4.23 The EDI Content Type

The EDI content type (P35, added in 1990 in the X.435 standard) is used to forward EDI information (see Sections 6.5 and 8.2.5), that is, information forwarded between computer applications. The format of the EDI content type is modeled after the IPM (interpersonal messaging) content type (P22) but modified to be more suitable for EDI messaging. Some of the differences between the P35 (EDI) and P22 (IPM) content type include:

- The EDIMIdentifier has the same format as the IPMIdentifier, which allows EDI and IPM messages to refer to each other. However, stricter requirements for EDI ensure that the identifier will always be globally unique.
- In EDI, there is one primary body part, the rest are additional body parts.
- A system can transfer the responsibility for handling an EDI message between EDI user agents.
- Additional notification types, indicate how a recipient has disposed of an EDI message.
- An extension mechanism more powerful than in IPM, allows for critical and noncritical extensions.

8.4.24 The Voice Content Type

In 1992, X.400 was extended with X.440 on voice messaging. It is intended primarily for the interconnection of voice mail systems. When voice is sent together with other text, then the voice body part is used and not the voice content type.

Some of the differences between the IPM content type and the voice content type are:

- There is a *spoken name* attribute for the spoken name of the originator and/or recipient, and a *spoken subject* field containing the subject of the message in spoken format.
- As in the EDI content type, there is an extension mechanism with a criticality flag.

8.4.25 Security in X.400

The original 1984 version of the X.400 standard had the following security features:

- Weak authentication (see Section 7.6.2) between UA and MTA and between MTAs;
- Delivery, nondelivery, receipt and nonreceipt notifications (see Sections 6.13.3 and 8.4.10); and
- Probes (see Section 8.4.11).

In the 1988 version of X.400, a large number of new security features were added, most of them based on combinations of checksums, encryption, and public-key-encryption (as described in Section 7.6.1 through 7.6.3). All these functions are optional. Examples of the new security features are:

Message origin authentication	Tools for checking that the original sender of messages is not falsified.
Report origin authentication	Tools for checking that notifications are not falsified.
Probe origin authentication	Tools for checking that probes are not falsified.
Proof of delivery	A more secure variant of delivery notifications.
Proof of submission	Tools to ensure that a message has been submitted.
Secure access management	Strong authentication between UA and MTA and between MTAs.
Content integrity	Protection against illegal modification (that is, electronic seals).
Content confidentiality	Protection against unauthorized reading of electronic mail.
Message flow confidentiality	Protection against showing the recipient by which route a message arrived.
Message sequence integrity	Protection against getting a sequence of messages in the wrong order or missing one of the messages in a sequence.
Nonrepudiation of origin	Protection against claims by original sender that they never sent a certain message (that is, electronic signatures).
Nonrepudiation of delivery	Protection against claims by recipients that they never received a certain message.
Nonrepudiation of submission	Protection against claims that a message was never submitted.
Message security labeling	Ability to indicate the security category of a message and ensure that it is processed in accordance with its security category.

As an example, according to X.400 an originator can first encrypt a message with a symmetric encryption algorithm. The symmetric encryption algorithm and key can then be encoded with the public key of the recipient (this must be done once for each recipient) and included with the message.

Data origin authentication and integrity are provided by computing a hash of the message content and encrypting this with the secret component of the public key pair for the sender. Public keys are certified using X.500 certification methods (see Section 7.6.4).

8.4.26 Different Versions of the X.400/MHS Standard

The first version of X.400 was established by CCITT (as ITU-T was then known) in 1984. In 1988 a second version, common to both CCITT and ISO, was developed. ISO called its version MOTIS at first, but has changed its name of the standard to MHS. In 1992, ISO and ITU jointly put forward a third version of the standard. Between these two versions, CCITT established an additional standards part on EDI messaging in 1990. Not all implementations support more than the 1984 version. Some of the most important differences between the 1984 and the 1988 version are that in the 1988 version:

- A UA can supply the name of the recipient as either a directory name or an OR-address. In 1984, only the OR-address format was allowed. When a user supplies the name as a directory name, the first MTA is expected to use the directory to translate this to an OR-address. It is thus not permitted to route a message from MTA to MTA or from domain to domain (P1 protocol) without an OR-address.
- The use the T.61 character set instead of the printable string character set is allowed in most fields in the OR-name. Since many message systems, especially in English-speaking countries, which use only the basic A through Z character sets, may not be capable of handling the additional character sets from other languages, it is, recommended that both a printable string and a T.61 version of OR-addresses sent to these countries be included.
- Distribution lists were added (see Section 8.4.18).
- A standard for outgoing messages to be printed on paper and forwarded by postal mail to their recipients was introduced (see Section 8.4.20).
- The message store facility was introduced (see Section 8.4.4).
- There is a more strongly worded requirement that IPM Identifiers should be globally unique, that is, include an OR-name field (see Section 8.4.14).
- New heading attribute was added to indicate the language in which a message is written (See Section 8.4.17).
- More security functionality was added (see Section 8.4.25).
- Extensibility, using the mechanisms for extensibility in ASN.1 (see Section 8.3.3), was added for additional envelope fields, additional heading fields, and additional body part types.

The most important new facilities added between 1988 and 1992 were:

- New content types for EDI and voice messaging.
- New body part types for general string (ISO already had this in 1988) and file transfer, and a more fully defined voice body part format.
- A standardized format for writing OR-addresses on business cards, postal mail headings and on computer screens. This is the only case where the standard says anything about the user interface of electronic mail systems.
- Extension facility for IPM notifications.

The ISO and ITU versions of the standard are almost identical. The differences are mostly of a political nature and will not influence the technical working of the standard.

8.5 X.500—THE OSI STANDARD FOR DIRECTORY SYSTEMS

8.5.1 General Structure and Schema

ITU X.500 and ISO 9594 are the joint ITU/ISO standard for directory systems (see Section 6.11). This standard makes it possible to build a globally distributed directory system of all electronic mail users across the world. (The same directory system might also be used for other kinds of directories, for example, of phone numbers.)

The directory system sees its data base as a hierarchical structure, part of which might look as shown in Figure 8.24.

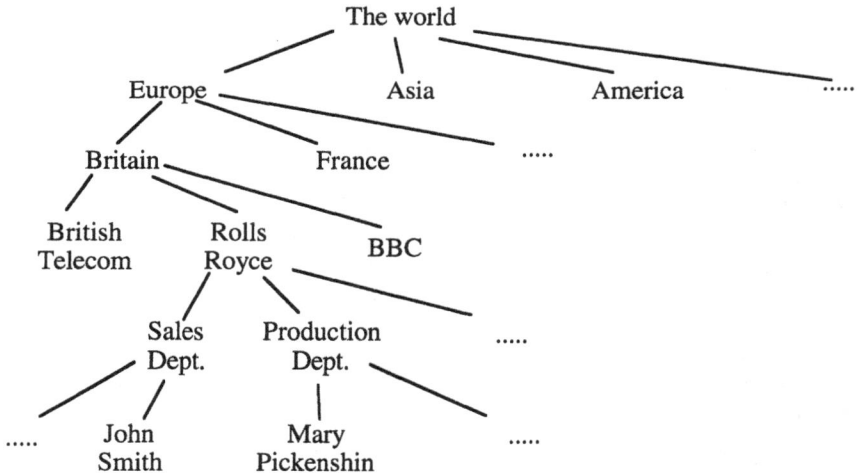

Figure 8.24   X.500 hierarchical world view.

So it will be general and useful for many different directory applications, the directory system has a *schema*, a logical description of the structure of its data base. Different schemas can be used for different directory applications. The schema indicates which attributes are to be stored on the directory entries. It also indicates which of the directory entries are part of the name of the distinguished name (DN) of the entry. A distinguished name (DN) is a globally unique name of an object and thus might be used for various applications where such a name is needed, for example, for sorting, merging, look-up, finding duplicates, etc.

The distinguished name of a directory item is actually made up of subnames of the nodes from the top of the tree to the named node. Thus, for example, in Figure 8.24, the distinguished name of "John Smith" might be "Europe.Britain.Rolls Royce.Sales Dept.John Smith." Each of the subcomponents of such a name, such as "Rolls Royce" or "John Smith," are called *relative distinguished names (RDN)*, since they give a name to their node in relation to other nodes in that subbranch of the directory tree.

The directory system also allows aliases. In the example above, UK, GB, United Kingdom and Great Britain might be aliases for Britain. As this example demonstrates, aliases are possible not only for leaves of the directory tree, but also for branches in the middle of the tree. If aliases are use, however, one of the names of a branch or leaf is always the distinguished name, and the other names are alternate alias names.

Note the difference between directory entries and domain addresses (see Section 7.2). If a person, Jaques Dupont, lives in France, but has a mailbox in an American message system, then his directory entry might be *Jaques Dupont.Citroen.France.Europe,* while his domain address might be *Jaques Dupont.Dialcom.US.*

8.5.2 Distributed Data Base and Query Forwarding

The directory system can be distributed, so that one computer stores the public British directory, another the internal directory within Rolls Royce, etc. Each such system, which manages its subtree within the global directory tree, is called a directory service agent (DSA). A user who makes a search in the directory will do so through a system unit called a directory user agent (DUA). In practice, a DUA may, of course, often be combined with an X.400 user agent (called only UA, not MUA, messaging user agent, since X.400 was first) to provide a coherent combined user interface.

Suppose that a person in France wants to find the electronic mail address of a person employed by Rolls Royce in Britain. His search query may then be transferred as shown in Figure 8.25.

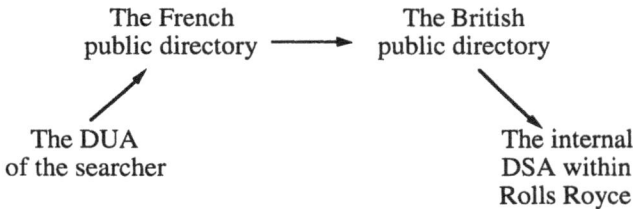

The French
public directory ⟶ The British
public directory

The DUA
of the searcher

The internal
DSA within
Rolls Royce

Figure 8.25   Chaining.

Handling a search in the directory system, by forwarding a query from DSA to DSA until the reply is found and then returning the reply the same way is called *chaining*. Chaining is only one of three ways in which queries in the directory system can be forwarded from DSA to DSA. The other two are *referral* and *multicasting*. See Figure 8.26. All three methods are supported by the X.500 standard.

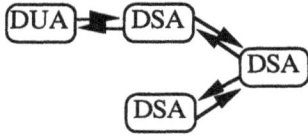

This diagram shows *chaining*, where a query is forwarded from DSA to DSA and the reply is returned the same way.

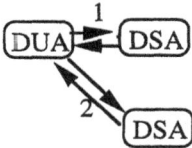

This diagram shows *referral*, where the DUA which sends a query is referred, by the initial DSA, to another DSA which is able to answer the query.

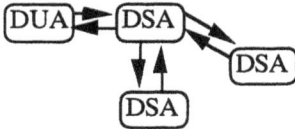

This diagram shows *multicasting*, where the first DSA will simultaneously send the query to several other DSAs and collect the replies.

Figure 8.26   Chaining, referral and multicasting.

For every directory entry, one-and-only-one DSA has the main responsibility. The version of the directory entry in this DSA is called the *Master Copy*. This does not mean that every directory entry must always be taken from the DSA which manages the master copy. In order to make directory searches more efficient, one DSA can store copies of entries belonging to other DSAs. There are two ways of handling such copies of entries at nonmaster locations: *caching* and *shadowing*.

In *caching* that a DSA, which via chaining or multicasting has received a copy of a directory entry mastered by another DSA, will keep a copy of this directory entry for a certain time. Any new query looking for the same entry during the time the copy is kept will be answered directly. This, of course, means that there is a risk that the entry is outofdate. To reduce this risk, cached copies are kept only for a limited time. (Note that with chaining, more information passes the DSA closest to the user, and thus the opportunities for caching are better for DSAs using *chaining* than for DSAs using *referral*.)

In *shadowing* two DSAs agree that one will to keep shadow copies of some of the entries mastered by the other DSA. The mastering DSA knows which DSAs have shadow copies of which entries, so that it can automatically forward any changes in the master copy. This reduces the risk of incorrect shadow copies.

8.6   INTERNET MAIL STANDARDS

8.6.1   Internet Overview

The first and largest network of connected electronic mail systems is called the *Internet*. Internet was originally an American network for universities and research organizations. It consists of a large number of smaller nets (like nets within a certain university or company), nets for certain kinds of computers (like *BITNET* for IBM VM computers), or nets within a certain country (like the American research net *NSFnet* or the Swedish university net *Sunet*). Even though these nets have different names, they operate together as if they were one large global net, and it is this large global net which is called Internet. Individual nets all use the same network standard, TCP/IP, and have a common naming and addressing scheme for the network nodes.

In addition to this global net, many of the individual nets are based on other standards. The standard BITNET uses, for example, is partly TCP/IP and partly an IBM special protocol called remote spooling control system (RSCS). In fact, a majority of the nodes within BITNET are actually non-IBM computers, but they often still use the RSCS protocols. Mainly in European countries, there are academic nets based on the X.400 standard. Mail can also be transferred between mail servers by dial-up phone lines using usually one of two protocols: Unix-to-Unix-copy (UUCP, See Section 8.8) and Phonenet, and between servers and clients using either the POP or IMAP protocols (See Section 8.6.8).

Internet has its own standards for electronic mail. The first version of these standards was developed long before X.400 and are still the most used electronic mail standard in the world. No one knows whether either the X.400 or the Internet mail standards will eventually overtake the other or whether both standards will be merged or replaced by some new standard in the future.

See Section 9.3.10 on gateways between Internet and other nets.

8.6.2   The Simple Mail Transfer Protocol

The simple mail transfer protocol (SMTP) is used to forward mail from one host (MTA) to another on the Internet. It is also used by UAs to submit messages to MTAs. It is described in RFC 821 [16]. The transfer of the message is done by a series of operations, performed by the SMTP sender on the SMTP receiver. The operations and the data belonging to them are coded as more-or-less readable text strings. Each operation begins with a short sequence of characters containing the name of the operation. After this name, some commands contain a space character followed by a parameter to the command. The main operations are:

MAIL FROM: This is the first operation undertaken when sending a message. It contains as a parameter a path (electronic mail address) back to the sender of the message. Note that the sender need not be the same as the author. The name given here is usually called the SMTP sender. When a message is forwarded from a distribution list, the name of the manager of the list is given, not the name of the original sender.

When, for example, a nondelivery notification is sent back, it should be sent to the SMTP sender of the message causing the notification to be produced.

The sender field in notifications themselves should be empty. This avoids loops of mail servers sending notifications back and forward between each other.

RCPT TO: Here, the electronic mail address of one recipient at a time is sent. If the same message is to be delivered to multiple recipients through the same SMTP connection, the RCPT TO operation is repeated once for each such recipient.

In its reply the receiving host will indicate whether or not it is willing to deliver mail to this recipient. In the beginning, the intention was that a receiving host would only indicate such willingness for mail recipients local to the host. Today, however, most hosts also accept mail for nonlocal recipients. The host will then send the mail along to the host of the recipient, using SMTP or some other protocol (like X.400, if the host is a gateway from SMTP to X.400).

If the receiving host always verified that the e-mail address referred to a reachable mailbox before giving a positive response to a RCPT TO operation, then to some extent this could replace the lack of a defined format for delivery notifications in Internet mail standards (work on developing such a format is in progress). However, since many hosts now accept mail for forwarding, without verifying that the e-mail address refers to an existing and reachable mailbox, a positive response to an RCPT TO operation is not any more a promise that this mailbox is reachable.

This procedure of routing messages via intermediate hosts can be used to reduce the load on the network when, for example, a message is transmitted from far away to many recipients at hosts close to each other (see Figure 7.4). The procedure can also be used when direct connections from sender host to receiver host is forbidden or impossible.

When all the recipients have been listed with the RCPT TO operation, the next operation is DATA.

DATA This operation forwards the body of the message, both heading and text. In the original version of RFC 821, only 7-bit ASCII text was allowed. See section 8.6.6 on how to handle other kinds of data.

SMTP also has some additional operations that are used for special purposes. The two most important of them are:

VRFY   This receives a user name and returns the user's e-mail address, if found.

EXPN   This receives the name of a distribution list and returns a list of all the members of the list.

In addition to the operations described above, of course, SMTP also has operations to open (HELO) and close (QUIT) connections. There is also an operation called TURN to switch status between sender and recipient, so that mail can be sent in both directions during the same session. Table 8.1 gives an example of the dialogue between two agents communicating via the SMTP protocol in order to send a message from one sender to two recipients. SMTP responses start with a three-digit response code. The text after this response code is optional and not handled by the software of the sending agent to which it is sent.

Table 8.1
Example of an SMTP dialogue

Sending agent command	Responding agent response
HELO dsv.su.se	250 nexor.co.uk
MAIL FROM: jpalme@dsv.su.se	250 OK
RCPT TO: <j.onions@nexor.co.uk>	250 OK
RCPT TO: <seb@nexor.co.uk>	250 OK
DATA	354 Start mail input; end with <CRLF>.<CRLF>
... the lines of text in the message ...	
	250 OK
QUIT	221 nexor.co.uk service closing transmission channel

Applications in the Internet are assigned particular port numbers, for example, the port number for SMTP is 25. When an application accesses an Internet host, it indicates that it wants to talk SMTP to the host by giving this port number.

A number of proposals for extensions to SMTP are being developed. These extensions allow the sending of delivery-report requests, binary and 8-bit data, and an SMTP sender can check if a very large message can be received before sending it. These extensions are only to be used by extended SMTP servers, so there is also a protocol for two SMTP servers to query each other's capabilities at the start of an SMTP session. This protocol thus provides an extension mechanism to SMTP and is called ESTMP (extended simple mail transfer protocol).

8.6.3 Routing and Use of Name Servers in Internet

The methods for routing mail messages using name servers in Internet is described in RFC 974 [18], RFC 1101 [23], RFC 1123 [20], and RFC 1348 [24]. Section 7.2 describes the general principles of routing and the use of name servers. An introduction to the Domain Naming system (DNS) is also given in [12].

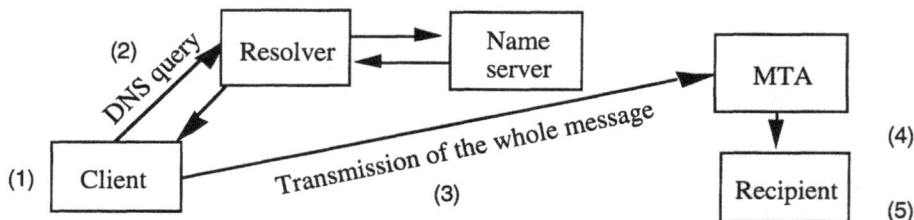

Figure 8.27   Use of name servers for Internet mail routing.

E-mail handling in the Internet is usually done in the following stages. (The numbers refers to numbers in Figure 8.27.)

(1)   The originator edits and submits his message for mailing. The mail consists of a heading and a text body. The heading is in a format which is readable by both humans and computers. This format is usually called RFC 822 [17] after the standard which specifies the primary part of it (see Section 8.6.4).

(2)   For each recipient, the name server facility is used to find the IP-address of the host which is most suitable for delivering mail to the recipient (see Section 8.6.3 for more information on how the name server facility is used.)

(3)   The mail is then forwarded to the hosts serving each recipient. The SMTP protocol is used for this (see Section 8.6.2).

(4)   The host described in (3) can be the host closest to the recipient or an intermediate host which forwards the message, for example, a gateway to another network with a different mail standard. If it is an intermediate host, this host will then use SMTP or some other protocol (like X.400 P1) to forward the message to the next host in a chain leading to the recipient. If the message is sent to a distribution list, the host handling the list will expand the list and forward the message to the members of the list.

(5)   Finally, the recipient reads the mail. The mail system of the recipient can use the machine-readable information in the message heading to aid the user in providing facilities like:
   (a)   Finding the message to which the current message is a reply.
   (b)   Finding messages from a certain sender, or messages which arrived via a certain distribution list.
   (c)   Finding messages written between certain dates.

132

Name servers for routing in the internet are called DNS servers. A DNS server takes as input an Internet domain address, such as EIES2.NJIT.EDU. There are many DNS name servers, all responsible for only part of the DNS tree. This means that sometimes the first name server contacted by a resolver may not have the information requested. The information can then be found by using either *chaining* or *referral*. These terms are more fully described in Section 8.5.2. The Internet DNS allows both chaining and referral. Every DNS server must support referral. Support for chaining is optional.

A DNS server may store the response to queries for some time, so that if it soon gets a new query for the same information, it can return the answer without having to use another name server through chaining or referral. Such storage is called *caching*.

The DNS can be used to translate domain-addresses to the physical address of the computer on the Internet which has this domain address. This is used, for example, when the DNS is invoked in order to find where to connect to a particular computer on the Internet.

In the case of e-mail, however, the messages should not always be sent to the host which has a particular domain address. There need not be a direct correspondence between e-mail domain names and host domain names. Also, many companies want all their e-mail to be routed first to a particular mail-sorting computer. Some e-mail domain addresses refer to gateways, which route messages to some other net.

Thus, the DNS contains separate data bases for Internet hosts and for e-mail addresses. The e-mail address data base consists of records in the DNS called MX-records (Mail eXchange). An MX record will return two attributes for an input domain name. One attribute is the DNS name of the host which handles mail for this e-mail domain name. The other attribute is a priority integer, where zero is the highest priority.

A search of the DNS will sometimes return more than one MX record. The one with the highest priority (lowest priority integer value) is to be used first.

The DNS can also store more than one alias name for the same mail domain. In such a case, one of the alias names is the canonical name, and the other names are converted to the canonical name before being used.

A serious problem with mail routing is the risk of loops. To avoid them, a host, which is itself on the MX record list for a particular domain, should only route a message to other hosts which have a higher priority (lower priority integer value) than itself. This is more fully described in RFC 974 [18].

If a DNS search does not return any MX record for a particular domain, an error message is normally sent to the user saying that the e-mail address used is invalid.

8.6.4 The Internet Message Format

The format of the messages themselves (corresponding to the P2/P22 protocols of X.400) is specified in RFC 822 [17], RFC 1036 [19], RFC 1123 [20], and the multi-purpose Internet mail extension (MIME) standards [21, 22].

Figure 8.28 shows an example of a message heading according to the RFC 822 standard. Note that what is shown is not some legible print-out of the heading, but the actual contents, since RFC 822 uses readable IA5 characters in the heading.

```
From comp.protocols.iso.x400-outbound-request@ics.uci.edu Wed Nov  4 04:16 MET
             1992
Received:    from sunic.sunet.se by heron.dafa.se (16.6/SiteCap-3.0)
             id AA09605; Wed, 4 Nov 92 04:16:24 +0100
Received:    from ics.uci.edu by sunic.sunet.se (5.65c8/1.28)
             id AA25221; Wed, 4 Nov 1992 04:15:03 +0100
Received:    from ics.uci.edu by q2.ics.uci.edu id aa14794; 3 Nov 92 13:47 PST
Received:    from USENET by q2.ics.uci.edu id aa14789; 3 Nov 92 13:46 PST
From:        "Paul.Rarey" <Paul.Rarey@ssf-sys.dhl.com>
Subject:     Re: X400 address
Message-ID:  <921103134349.16483@maverick.ssf-sys.DHL.COM>
Encoding:    35 TEXT, 12 TEXT SIGNATURE
X-Mailer:    Poste 2.0
Date:        3 Nov 92 21:46:13 GMT
To:          mhsnews@ics.uci.edu,
             Piet Beertema <mcvax!cwi.nl!piet@uunet.uu.net>
cc:          ifip65@ics.uci.edu

... Text of the message ...
```

Figure 8.28   Example of an RFC 822 message heading.

Note the difference between the coding techniques used in X.400 and those in the Internet mail standards. X.400 uses a binary format, ASN.1 (see Section 8.3.2) while Internet mostly encodes information as more-or-less readable text.

The names of e-mail users in RFC 822 headings can have two parts. One part is the address, and one is an informational part for the end user. In SMTP, only the e-mail address part is used. This is similar to X.400, where the user names in P2 can also contain an informational part in addition to the OR-address. The "From" line in Figure 8.28 is parsed in Figure 8.29.

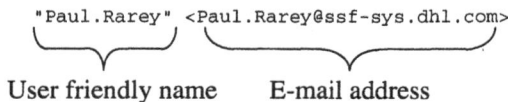

Figure 8.29   Name and address part.

RFC 822 specifies a heading format, which is intended to be readable for both humans and computers. It is used for communication between the sender and the recipient and is not used during transmission. The most important fields in Internet mail headings are:

Received:	Contains a trace of the hosts through which a message has passed. It is mainly used when investigating problems with the mail transfer. Such a trace could be used for loop control (as in X.400) but in practice usually is not. Many UA softwares suppress these lines when showing the header to their users.
From:	The e-mail address of the author of the message.
To:, Cc: and Bcc:	The recipient(s). Note that this is not the recipient(s) to be used when delivering the mail (those are given in the SMTP protocol). This is information to be read by the recipient(s) or their mail program. It can even contain names which are not proper e-mail addresses. Compare with X.400 in Section 8.4.13.
Message-ID:	A globally unique identity code for the current message, which can be used in the "Reply-To" field to eliminate duplicates of the same message arriving via different routes. (Compare with X.400 in Section 8.4.14).
Reply-To:	Used to indicate that personal replies to a message are to be sent to someone else than the name in the "From" field. Note that the name in this field should not be used for "group replies," that is, replies intended for the group of recipients or the mailing list that received the replied-to message.
Followup-To:	Similar to "Reply-To" but used for group replies. (This is not part of RFC 822 it is defined in the Usenet News standard, RFC 1036 [19].)
In-Reply-To:	Used to coordinate replies with the original message. An intelligent mail software can use this field to help the user find the original message of a reply.
References:	Similar to "In-Reply-To." It is used mainly in Usenet News to indicate references between postings to newsgroups.
Date:	The date, time, and time zone when the message was sent.
Subject:	A title line describing the topic of the message.

Note: Most of the discussion about references between messages ("In-Reply-To," "References" etc.) in X.400 in Section 8.4.14 is also valid for similar references in the Internet mail standards.

The RFC 822 heading often contains additional fields not defined in the RFC 822 standard. Some of them may be defined in other standards, while others are not standardized at all. In the heading shown in Figure 8.28, the fields "Encoding" and "X-Mailer" are not part of RFC 822.

The RFC 822 heading ends with a blank line, which marks the beginning of the text of the message.

8.6.5 Distribution Lists in Internet Mail

Internet does not (as of this writing) have any complete standards for distribution lists. Some general principles are, however, agreed on for distribution lists in the Internet, although they are not yet fully described in Internet standards documents:

- Distribution lists can be nested, but there is usually no loop control, so the list maintainer must ensure that there are no loops. Some software provides loop control by saving checksums of messages passing through the list expander.
- By adding "-request" to the part of the distribution list name before "@," you get an e-mail address which can be used to send mail to the list manager.
- When expanding a distribution list, the SMTP sender should be the address of the list maintainer, while the RFC 822 "From" field should indicate the original author of the message.
- Nondelivery reports should be sent to the SMTP sender, not to the RFC 822 "From" author, which means that they are sent to the list manager, not to the original author.
- To subscribe to Internet distribution lists, see Section 6.7.2.

8.6.6 The MIME Standard for Additional Body Types in Internet Mail

MIME Introduction

The Internet mail standards used before 1992 could handle only text in the 7-bit ASCII alphabet and did not allow the additional body-part type facilities available in X.400. However, in 1992, the Internet mail standards added facilities in an extension called MIME. MIME is defined in RFC 1521 [21] and RFC 1522 [22]. A good tutorial on MIME is given in [25]. There is an FAQ[2] on MIME [44] which includes a list of known MIME implementations.

MIME allows Internet mail to contain the following

- Multiple objects in one message.
- Unlimited line length and message length.
- Character sets other than IA5 (7-bit ASCII). In particular, the ISO 8859-1 character set is important (see Section 8.2 for more on character sets).
- Binary and application-specific files.

---

[2] A FAQ (frequently asked question) is a document containing answers to questions frequently encountered in Internet discussion groups. There are many FAQs on various topics, and they often contain a lot of useful information.

- Diagrams, pictures, voice, video, and multimedia in messages.
- References to files, which can be retrieved automatically through the net when the recipient wants to read the message. The contents of the file is thus not transported with the message.

With MIME, it is possible to have several content parts representing the same information in different formats. The recipient or his client software can then choose the version which it is best capable of displaying. For example, a recipient with an IA5-terminal can see a message in this format, while a recipient with an ISO 8859-1 terminal can see a better version of the message. (For example, with IA5, no distinction can be made between "Å" and "]"on screen , if they both occur in the same text, but ISO 8859 can show the two characters correctly. Thus, the string "[Åström 1993]" will look like "[]strlm 1993]" on an IA5 screen set to the US version of IA5, and as "ÄÅström 1993Å" on an IA5 screen set to the Swedish version of IA5.)

MIME Encoding of Data

There was a problem when MIME was defined: it was essential that existing e-mail systems be able to handle MIME messages in a reasonable way without modification. However, some previous Internet e-mail systems could not handle messages with 8-bit characters in the text or with unlimited line length, binary information, etc. in the body.

Because of this, MIME encodes the new body parts in a format which looks like 7-bit ASCII to old mail software. This is not a very neat solution, but it was necessary since no extension facility for body parts was included in the old Internet mail standards. MIME encodes additional information in either of two ways so that it looks like 7-bit ASCII. These two methods are called *base64* and *quoted-printable*.

Base64 uses four ASCII characters to represent three 8-bit bytes. The 24 bits of the three 8-bit bytes are split into four groups of 6 bits, and each such bit is encoded in a character set which has 64 different values. These 64 values are those characters in 7-bit ASCII which are least likely to be corrupted.

Quoted-Printable represents those bytes, which have an exact correspondences in 7-bit ASCII, with their 7-bit ASCII values. Other characters are encoded as an "=" character, followed by two digits with the hexadecimal value of the byte. An exception is the "=" character itself, which is coded as "=3D."

Example of a Complete MIME-Encoded Message

Figure 8.30 shows a complete example of a MIME message as it is transmitted (not as it is shown to the user). This message contains two body parts. Each of the body parts contains the same text in ISO 8859-1.

```
Test message containing 8-bit characters.
AE=Ä, OE=Ö.
```

The two lines above are transmitted in both body parts in the MIME message below, but the text is encoded as quoted-printable in the first body part and as base64 in the second body part.

```
Return-Path: <jpalme@ester.dsv.su.se>
Date: Sun, 26 Sep 1993 18:49:01 +0100 (MET)
From: Jacob Palme DSV <jpalme@dsv.su.se>
Subject: A pine message
To: Lars Enderin <larse@dialog.se>
Message-Id: <3.85.9309261822.A27024-0200000@ester>
Mime-Version: 1.0
Content-Type: MULTIPART/MIXED; BOUNDARY="1430317162"

--1430317162
Content-Type: TEXT/PLAIN; CHARSET=ISO 8859-1
Content-Transfer-Encoding: QUOTED-PRINTABLE

Test message containing 8-bit characters.
AE=3D=80, OE=3D=85.

--1430317162
Content-Type: TEXT/PLAIN; CHARSET=ISO 8859-1
Content-Transfer-Encoding: BASE64

VGVzdCBtZXNzYWdlIGNvbnRhaW5pbmcgOCliaXQgY2hhcmFjdGVycy4KQUU9
gCwgT0U9hS4K
--1430317162--
```

Figure 8.30   A complete MIME message.

As can be seen from the example in Figure 8.30, quoted-printable has an advantage over base64 because a recipient whose mail system is not MIME compatible will still be able to understand much of the content, especially the ordinary English text. In the example, quoted-printable is also shorter: only 61 characters are required compared to 73 characters for base64. Base64 is, however, more suitable for pure binary text, such as a graphic bit image or an encoded sound.

In addition to base64 and quoted-printable, MIME also allows the encodings *7bit*, *8bit* and *binary*. These are not really encodings, since they represent uncoded data. Because of this, 8bit and binary should not be transmitted via mailers which are not MIME-compatible. To transport such data uncoded, extensions to the SMTP standard for message transport are also needed.

MIME Heading Extensions

MIME defines the following extended fields to the RFC 822 heading:

`Content-Type`	Specifies the type and subtype of the data in the body.
`Content-Type: TEXT`	Specifies textual information in several different character sets.
`Content-Type: MULTIPART`	Specifies that the body contains more than one body part. Each body part can have additional heading fields at the beginning of the body part.
`Content-Type:APPLICATION`	For application-specific or binary data. Of special importance is `APPLICATION/POSTSCRIPT`.
`Content-Type: MESSAGE`	For an encapsulated mail message.
`Content-Type: IMAGE`	For a bitmapped picture using, for example, the graphics interchange format (GIF) or joint photographic experts group (JPEG) formats.
`Content-Type: AUDIO`	For sound. (Note that the word "voice" is used in X.400. However, X.400 voice is probably not intended to be restricted only to spoken sounds.)
`Content-Type: VIDEO`	For video using, for example, the motion picture experts group (MPEG) format. The video may, but need not, contain a sound track.
`Content-Transfer-Encoding:`	Specifies how the data is encoded. Encoding type may also be given in the content-type heading field.
`MIME-Version:`	To indicate that MIME is used and which MIME version is used.
`Content-ID:`	ID code for the content. Can be used to allow one body part to refer to another body part in another message or for references between the body parts in a message.
`Content-Description:`	Contains a textual description of the content.

Note: Much confusion has been caused by the fact that the word "content" has different meanings in MIME and in X.400. The MIME word "content" corresponds to the X.400 word "body," and the X.400 word "content" corresponds to the "RFC 822 message."

IANA (Internet Assigned Numbers Authority), the internet global registration authority, maintains a register of MIME content types. A difference from X.400, where anyone can register a new body part by just buying an object identifier, is that IANA requires a publicly available description of the new format, or, alternatively, that public domain viewers for the new format are available. A consequence of this is that some commercial companies have been unwilling to to register the formats of their products. In such cases, a Content-Type EIGHTBIT has to be used instead. The disadvantage with this is that the receiving client software cannot automatically start a viewer for the new format when messages in that format arrives.

Multipart Messages in MIME

The MULTIPART attribute in a MIME heading specifies that the body contains more than one body type. Each body part can have additional heading fields at the beginning of the body part, including recursive use of the multipart attribute to include MULTIPARTs as parts in higher level MULTIPARTs.

Of special interest are

- MULTIPART/MIXED for several parts of different types;
- MULTIPART/ALTERNATIVE for the same information in more than one encoding;
- MULTIPART/PARALLEL as mixed, but to be viewed at the same time (for example, voice in parallel with a drawing);
- MULTIPART/DIGEST to indicate that each part is a digested message; and
- MULTIPART/EXTERNAL to include a file reference instead of the actual file. The client software will have to retrieve the file when the user wants to view it.

Mime Heading Character Sets

MIME allows extended character sets also in message headings. The encoding is rather ugly and some implementations do not support it.

8.6.7 Privacy Enhanced Mail

Privacy enhanced mail (PEM) is the name for the Internet standard for cryptography used to increase security in messaging. All PEM information is encoded in the body of messages (this is different from X.400 security features) which means that messages, previously transformed by PEM, may be transferred using X.400 messaging. PEM creates the body of a message in two parts: parameters and letter text.

PEM provides facilities to:

- Control who may read messages;
- Ensure that the message content has not been modified or corrupted;
- Ensure that a message comes from the stated sender; and
- Eliminate the possibility that the sender can repudiate sending a message.

PEM provides security services: confidentiality, integrity, sender authentication, recipient authentication and sender's nonrepudiation. It may be implemented using either secret key or public-key cryptography.

An alternative standard for crypthographic security functions also used in Internet is called PGP (pretty good privacy). A difference between PEM and PGP is that PEM uses a system of registration authorities to assign certificates, while PGP lets any user provide certificates for any other user. This means that PEM is more suited for secure handling of a large number of certificates, while PGP is easier to start using when no certificate authorities are yet available.

8.6.8 Client-Server Protocols on the Internet

When a user runs an e-mail client package on his personal computer, this client needs a protocol to talk to a server, corresponding to the P3 and P7 protocols in X.400 (See Section 8.4.4). In the Internet, the most important such protocols are:

- Post Office Protocol (POP) [9], a protocol for fast downloading of mail to client software, where the client stores and handles the mail, corresponding to P3 in X.400.
- Interactive Mail Access Protocol (IMAP) [8], a protocol for cases where the user wants to store his messages in the server, and wants to be able to manipulate this storage from client software on his personal computer. IMAP is a more complex protocol than POP.

8.6.9 Comparison of X.400 and the Internet Mail Standards

SMTP roughly corresponds to the P1 protocol in X.400, and RFC 822 roughly corresponds to the P2 protocol. Thus, SMTP controls the interaction between message systems in forwarding messages, and RFC 822 controls the format of the message heading which is shown to the recipient.

Here are some important differences between the Internet and the X.400 message standards:

- The existence of the DNS means that Internet does not require any ADMDs. This is one of the major reasons why Internet e-mail is often less expensive than X.400 e-mail.
- RFC 822 is a pure textual format. You can thus produce a message formatted according to RFC 822 using an ordinary text editor. The X.400 formats are binary formats coded using the ASN.1 BER (see Section 8.3.2). This means that RFC 822 uses English-like words in its syntax, while X.400 is not dependent on any particular "natural" language. Internet mail features that are not fully standardized may appear in any language; this is a disadvantage for a recipient who does not understand the language used.
- The fact that RFC 822 uses a simple text format makes it much easier to make heading extensions, and such extensions will be understandable to other people, while X.400 extensions often cannot be understood without knowledge of the particular extension. A consequence of this is that it is much more common to add extra heading fields in RFC 822 than in X.400. They vary from natural extensions like *phone-number* and *postal-address* to rather funny ones like *phase-of-the-moon*.
- Although store-and-forward handling of mail is an important property of Internet mail handling, the protocols are oriented more towards direct connections between the electronic mail systems of the sender and recipient. Both standards, however, allow for sending a message through both direct connections and relaying.
- Networks based on the Internet mail standards often have better connectivity and, by using the Domain Naming System, can route without the costly need of ADMDs.
- Internet electronic mail addresses are much simpler than X.400 addresses. A typical Internet electronic mail address might look like this:

```
jpalme@dsv.su.se
```

(see Section 7.2 for a fuller description of such names) the corresponding X.400 address might be:

```
S=jpalme;O=dsv;PRMD=su;ADMD=sunet;C=se
```

- The Internet mail protocols are not fully defined by their defining documents, that is, there are deviations between standard and reality, as discussed in Section 8.12. There are probably such deviations for X.400 too, but not necessarily the same deviations.
- X.400 has dynamic loop controls to avoid the same message circulating endlessly. The Internet mail standards have loop controls built into the routing protocol (see Section 8.6.3).
- The division of tasks between SMTP and RFC 822 is mostly the same as the division between P1 and P2 in X.400. However, there are some differences. RFC 822 has a field for the time and date when a message was written, X.420 has no such field. Trace information about the hosts passed during the transmission of a message is put in the envelope in X.400, while they are with the

Internet mail standards, put at the top of the RFC 822 heading as a sequence of "Received" fields.

Here are some functions which X.400 has but which Internet mail does not feature yet: ·

- A standardized format for delivery and nondelivery notifications. Internet has a limited facility for nondelivery notifications in direct SMTP connections between two hosts, but this feature does not work in practice, since a large number of hosts accept mail to anyone, try to forward it, and thus never produce nondeliveries of this kind. Most Internet MTAs do produce nondelivery notifications, but there is no standard format for them, so that they can be handled in an intelligent way by the mailer receiving them. You might even get a non-delivery message in a foreign language which you cannot read. Work is in progress to define such facilities also for Internet mail, so they may be defined when you read this book. Note however that there is often several years between the definition of a new feature in a standard and this facility becoming common in implementations.
- A facility for receipt notifications, but this is not widely used.
- Standards for how to request and suppress notifications.
- Rules for how distribution lists should work. (Internet uses distribution lists a lot, and there is some agreement on how they should work, but this agreement is not used by all systems.)
- The ability to send out corrections to incorrect messages using the *obsoletes* feature of X.400. ("Obsoletes" is defined, in Internet mail, as gatewaying to X.400, but this is probably not meant to be used internally within Internet mail. Usenet News often uses a not-yet-standardized heading field, Supersedes, for a similar facility.)

Here are some functions which Internet mail standards have but not X.400; these features are new in Internet mail and not yet often implemented:

- The ability to send only a reference to where the body part is stored. The receiving message-reading client will then have to retrieve the body part through the net when the recipient wants to read it. This is useful for bulky appendices, which not all recipients of a message may want to read.
- The use of *parallel* body parts (for example a picture and a sound), which are to be transmitted to the recipient simultaneously. In X.400 all body parts are expected to be shown after each other in a sequence.

- The use of *alternate* body parts, which means that the same message is sent in more than one encoding and the recipient can choose to read either, depending on the capabilities of his software to interpret the encodings.

For discussions about the pros and cons of OSI versus TCP/IP standards, see [13 and 42].

8.6.10   Attributes in X.400 and in Internet Mail

Below is a list of some important attributes of messages in X.400 and in Internet mail. The list is not complete, obscure and seldom-used attributes are not included, nor are security-related attributes.

Addressing Information

Description	Attribute Name in Internet	Internet Standard	Attribute Name in X.400	Where in X.400
Original sender. Should be empty when sending notifications over the Internet, and be the list administrator when forwarding from a distribution list	MAIL FROM	RFC 821	Originator-name	X.411
Relative address to the original sender along the reverse path through which the message was sent	Return-Path:	RFC 822	Trace	X.411
Similar to "Return-Path:," also sometimes used as message separator in files with lists of messages	"From " (Note: From followed by a space, *not* the same as "From:") Variants: ">From ", "From_."	RFC 976		
Recipient to which message is to be delivered	RCPT TO	RFC 821	Recipient-name	X.411

Envelope and Format Information

Description	Attribute Name in Internet	Internet Standard	Attribute Name in X.400	Where in X.400
Precedes what is inside the envelope	DATA	RFC 821	Content	X.411

Description	Attribute Name in Internet	Internet Standard	Attribute Name in X.400	Where in X.400
Trace of MTAs which a message has passed	Received:	RFC 822: 4.3.2	Trace	X.411
Version of MIME protocol used	MIME-Version:	RFC 1521: 3	Mapped into body part	RFC 1496
Format of content (character set, etc.)	Content-Type:	RFC 1521: 4	Mapped into body part	RFC 1496
Coding method used in content	Content-Transfer-Encoding:	RFC 1521: 5		
List of MTAs passed	Path:	RFC 1036: 2.1.6	Trace	X.411
Special Usenet News actions	Control	RFC 1036: 2.2.6		
Trace of distribution lists passed	DL-Expansion-History:	RFC 1327	DL Expansion History Indication	X.411
Which body part-types occur in this message	Original-Encoded-Information-Types:	RFC 1327	Original-encoded-information-types	X.411
Special distribution list controls in X.400	Not available		DL Expansion Prohibited	X.411
Special informational message	Message-Type: Delivery Report	RFC 1327	Notification	X.411
Controls whether this message may be forwarded to a postmaster if delivery is not possible to the intended recipient. Default: Allowed	Alternate-recipient:	RFC 1327	Alternate-recipient-allowed	X.411
Whether nondelivery report is wanted at delivery error. Default is to want such a report	Prevent-NonDelivery-Report:	RFC 1327	OriginatorReport Request	X.411
Whether a delivery report is wanted at successful delivery. Default is not to generate such a report	Generate-Delivery-Report:	RFC 1327	OriginatorReport Request	X.411
Whether recipients are to be told the names of other recipients of the same message. This is primarily an X.400 facility, such disclosure is done in Internet mail via the To:, Cc: and Bcc: heading fields	Disclose-Recipients:	RFC 1327	Disclosure-of-recipients	X.411
Indicates whether the content of a message is to be returned with nondelivery notifications	Content-Return:	RFC 1327	Content-return-request	X.411

Header Fields Containing Mailbox Names and Other Usually Addressable Entitities

Description	Attribute Name in Internet	Internet Standard	Attribute Name in X.400	Where in X.400
Replacement for "From:" to which replies are to be sent	Reply-To:	RFC 822: 4.4.3	Reply-recipients	X.420
Author, approver	From:	RFC 822: 4.4.1	Authorizing-users	X.420
Moderator	Approved:	RFC 1036: 2.2.11	Authorizing-users	X.420
Sender information inside the envelope	Sender:	RFC 822: 4.4.2	Originator	X.420
Main recipients	To:	RFC 822: 4.5.1	Primary-recipients	X.420
Additional recipients	Cc:	RFC 822: 4.5.2	Copy-recipients	X.420
Recipients not shown to other recipients	Bcc:	RFC 822: 4.5.3	Blind-copy-recipients	X.420
Group to which article was posted	Newsgroups:	RFC 1036: 2.1.3	Primary-Recipient	X.420
Where group replies to this message are to be sent	Followup-To:	RFC 1036: 2.2.3		
Limitation on where this message can be distributed	Distribution:	RFC 1036: 2.2.7		

Message Identification and Referral Attributes

Description	Attribute Name in Internet	Internet Standard	Attribute Name in X.400	Where in X.400
Unique ID of this message	Message-ID:	RFC 822: 4.6.1	IPM Identifier	X.420
Unique ID of one body part of the content of a message	Content-ID:	RFC 1521: 6.1		
Reference to message to which this message is a reply	In-Reply-To:	RFC 822: 4.6.2	Replied-to-IPM	X.420
Reference to other related messages	References:	RFC 822: 4.6.3	Related-IPMs	X.420
Reference to previous message being corrected and replaced	Obsoletes:	RFC 1327	Obsoleting	X.420

Other Textual Attributes

Description	Attribute Name in Internet	Internet Standard	Attribute Name in X.400	Where in X.400
Search keys for data base retrieval	Keywords:	RFC 822: 4.6.4	Heading extension	RFC 1327
Title, heading, subject	Subject:	RFC 822: 4.7.1	Subject	X.420
Comments on a message	Comments:	RFC 822: 4.7.2	Extra body part	X.420

Description	Attribute Name in Internet	Internet Standard	Attribute Name in X.400	Where in X.400
Description of a particular body part of a message	Content-description:	RFC 1521: 6.2	Heading extension	RFC 1327
Organization to which the sender of this message belongs	Organization:	RFC 1036: 2.2.8	Organization-name	X.520
Short text describing a longer message	Summary:	RFC 1036: 2.2.10	Heading extension	RFC 1327
A text string which identifies the content of a message	Content-identifier:	RFC 1327	Content-identifier	X.411

Attributes Containing Dates and Times

Description	Attribute Name in Internet	Internet Standard	Attribute Name in X.400	Where in X.400
The time when a message was delivered to its recipient	Delivery-Date:	RFC 1327	Message-delivery-time	X.411
On the Internet, the date when a message was written; in X.400, the time a message was submitted	Date:	RFC 822: 5.1	Message-submission-time	X.411
A suggested expiration date. Can be used both to limit the time of an article which is not meaningful after a certain date and to extend the storage of important articles	Expires:	RFC 1036: 2.2.4	Expiry Date Indication	X.420
Time at which a message loses its validity	Expiry-Date:	RFC 1327	Expiry Date Indication	X.420
Latest time at which a reply is requested (not demanded)	Reply-By:	RFC 1327	ReplyTimeField	X.420

Attributes Containing other Types of Information

Description	Attribute Name in Internet	Internet Standard	Attribute Name in X.400	Where in X.400
Can be normal, urgent, or nonurgent and can influence transmission speed and delivery	Priority:	RFC 1327	Priority	X.411
Size of the message	Lines:	RFC 1036: 2.2.12	Heading extension	RFC 1327
Has been automatically forwarded	Auto-Forwarded: TRUE	RFC 1327	Auto-Forwarded Indication	X.420

Description	Attribute Name in Internet	Internet Standard	Attribute Name in X.400	Where in X.400
Can be high, normal or low and is only used in the recipient client (UA)	Importance:	RFC 1327	Importance	X.420
Body parts are missing	Incomplete-Copy:	RFC 1327	Incomplete Copy	X.420
Can include character codes for the natural language used in a message (for example "en" for English)	Language:	RFC 1327	Language	X.420. ISO 639
Can be personal, private, company-confidential or absent	Sensitivity:	RFC 1327	Sensitivity	X.420
The body of this message may not be converted from one character set to another	Conversion: prohibited	RFC 1327	Implicit-conversion-prohibited	X.411
The body of this message may not be converted from one character set to another if information will be lost	Conversion-With-Loss: prohibited	RFC 1327	Conversion-with-loss-prohibited	X.411
Can be used in Internet mail to indicate X.400 extensions which could not be mapped to Internet mail format	Discarded-X400-IPMS-Extensions:	RFC 1327	ExtensionsField	X.420
	Discarded-X400-MTS-Extensions:	RFC 1327	ExtensionsField	X.411

Resent-Attributes

Description	Attribute Name in Internet	Internet Standard	Attribute Name in X.400	Where in X.400
When forwarding a message, attributes referring to the forwarding, not to the original message	Resent-Reply-To:, Resent-From:, Resent-Sender:, Resent-From:, Resent-Date:, Resent-To:, Resent-cc:, Resent-bcc:, Resent-Message-ID:	RFC 822, C.3.3	Embedded message bodies should be used for forwarding	X.420

Sometimes Occurring Heading Fields in Internet Mail not According to Standard

This list is by no means complete. There are hundreds of nonstandard heading fields which sometimes occur in Internet mail.

Description	Attribute Name in Internet	Internet Standard	Attribute Name in X.400	Where in X.400
Inserted by Sendmail (a common Internet MTA software) when recipients are missing in RFC822 heading. This behavior of Sendmail is not proper MTAs should not modify RFC822 headers except inserting Received lines	Apparently-to:	RFC 1211		
Pre-MIME way of indicating special encoding of text	Encoding:	RFC 1154		
Address to which notifications are to be sent. Internet standards recommend, however, the use of RCPT TO and Return-Path, not Errors-To, for this	Errors-To:, Return-Receipt-To:			
Fax number of the originator	Fax:, Telefax:			X.520
Name of file in which a copy of this message is stored	Fcc:			
Information about the client software of the originator	Mail-System-Version:, Mailer:			
Same as "Organization"	Organisation:		Organization-name	X.520
Phone number of the originator	Phone:		O/R Descriptor, telephone-number	X.420, X.500
Same as "References:"	Xref:		Related-to	

Terminology Comparison between X.400 and Internet Mail

Description	Term in Internet	Internet Standard	Term in X.400	Where in X.400
Protocol for forwarding messages between MTAs	SMTP	RFC 821	P1, MTS	X.411
Protocol for submitting messages from a UA to an MTA	SMTP	RFC 821	P3	X.411
Protocol for batch downloading of messages to a UA from an MTA	POP	RFC 1460	P3	X.411
Protocol for selective retrieval of messages from a remote mailbox store	IMAP	RFC 1203	P7	X.413
Message heading format for interpersonal mail	RFC 822	RFC 822	P2, P22	X.420

149

Description	Term in Internet	Internet Standard	Term in X.400	Where in X.400
Format for including various text and other data types in messages	MIME	RFC 1521	P2, P22	X.420
The combination of a heading and one or more bodies into a message	Message	RFC 822, RFC 1521	Content	X.420, X.435, X.445, etc.
Encoding of text and other information	Content-Transfer-Encoding	RFC 1521	ASN.1, Body part type	X.208, X.209, X.420, etc.

8.7 BITNET FORMAT

More and more BITNET is changing to TCP/IP connections and the full Internet mail standards as described in Section 8.6. Some BITNET systems still use the old BITNET mail formats. There are four such older formats:

(1) BSMTP + RFC 822: BITNET Simple Mail Transfer Protocol (BSMTP) is a variant of SMTP. It differs from SMTP in that SMTP is an interactive protocol, where two connected systems send a number of statements back and forth, while in BSMTP, the sender puts all the envelope information into a BSMTP heading which precedes the RFC 822 heading.

(2) Only RFC 822: in this format, if the recipient, is an MTA, it is expected to deliver to all the recipients in the RFC 822 heading which are within the responsibility domain of that MTA. (In normal usage of Internet standards, all delivery control is done by SMTP information, and the RFC 822 heading information, like in X.400/IPM, is used only by the recipient.)

(3) Note format. This is a format which is similar but not identical to RFC822.

(4) Neither envelope nor heading, the message is just deposited as a file in the incoming file area of the recipient.

Here is an example of a BSMTP envelope:

```
HELO CUNYVM.BITNET
TICK 3077
MAIL FROM:<stef@nma.com>
RCPT TO:<JPALME@QZCOM>
DATA
```

8.8 UUCP FORMAT AND USENET NEWS

UUCP has two formats, one for conference messages (Usenet News or Netnews) and one for personally addressed letters (UNIX mail). Both formats are variants of the SMTP/RFC 822 formats. A special format for relative addresses is sometimes used with "!" between the MTA names (see section 7.2) and some additions to RFC 822 are commonly used, including a format for requesting delivery notifications. A difference from Internet usage in general is that Message-IDs are mandatory and that In-Reply-To and References links are used in a more consistent manner, which will make them more useful (see Section 8.4.14 for information about these functions in X.400).

Usenet News is a distributed computer conferencing system. Conferences in Usenet News are called newsgroups, and messages are called articles.

The basic principle of Usenet News is that a local server handles most of the functionality. The Usenet News standard mainly specifies the protocol for the interaction between adjacent servers in the net. Each server can download as much as it wants of what is available on any of the adjacent servers. Loop control is handled both by both a trace list and a list of the Message-IDs of received messages stored by each server, so that the server can reject the same message coming back again. The procedure for distribution of news can be likened to pouring water onto a flat surface; the water flows out in all directions (see Figure 8.31).

There are many different user-interface softwares for Usenet News, Some of them, of course, do not provide all the available functions.

In addition, Usenet News provides an interesting functionality which restricts communication to only those members of a newsgroup who work in the same organization or live in the same area or country. This functionality, however, is not used very much, and its existence is controversial, since it means that different users will get different views of the same newsgroup.

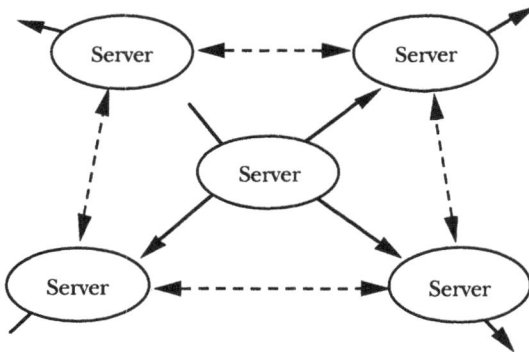

Figure 8.31   "Pouring water" principle of Usenet News distribution.

Usenet news has a *cancel* command, which can delete messages already sent out. Obsoletes in X.400 can be used to get an effect similar to the cancel command, by obsoleting a message with an empty message. However, cancel in Usenet News really deletes messages, while obsoletes sends information to the recipient UA, which need not cause deletion. Many UAs store both the new and the old version so that the recipient can choose to see the obsoleted version if he so wishes.

The most important restriction of Usenet News is that closed groups are not well supported. The Usenet News protocol is called network news transfer protocol (NNTP) and is specified in RFC 1036 [19].

8.9 VMSMAIL

Mail11 or VMSmail (virtual memory system mail) is a proprietary mail standard Digital Equipment Corporation (DEC) to buyers of their computers. I would, however strongly recommend those who purchase DEC computers to use mail systems based on X.400 or SMTP, not on VMSmail, since gateways from VMSmail to other mail standards often cause problems.

8.10 APPLICATION PROGRAMMING INTERFACES

When designing large and complex software, it is often useful to split the software into several layers with a well-defined interface between the layers. One of the most common such layers is the interface between applications and the operating system. This interface provides application programs with standardized operations for asking the operating system to perform various tasks, such as opening a file, getting the current date and time, sending a file to a printer, etc. These interfaces are often called *application programming interfaces* (APIs).

There can obviously be several such layers below each other, where each higher layer accesses the functions of the next lower layer through a separate programming interface. There is no concrete definition of what an application is and what an "operating system" is, and the boundaries between them are coming more fluid. Modern operating systems, like Apple's Macintosh operating system and IBM OS/2, offer many functions which had been performed by applications. In the case of Microsoft Windows, it is open to discussion whether it is an operating system or an application program. The borderline between applications and underlying infrastructure is fluid with more and more functionality moving from application programs to the underlying infrastructure. Because of this, ISO recommends using the term "programming interface" instead of API. API is however the common term used for such interfaces.

APIs for e-mail are particularly advantageous if people designing application programs (word processing, data base, etc.) want to add the functionality of sending and receiving e-mail (just as it is already common for such applications to communicate with printers and file systems). This is especially useful for EDI and work-flow applications (see Section 6.5).

As of this writing there is no general agreement on such APIs in the e-mail area. A number of proposals are being worked on by standards organizations and companies. Some of these APIs are:

- XDS for access to X.500 directory systems.
- X.400 gateway API for passing messages to X.400 nets.
- Common mail calls (CMC) is a proposal for an interface between applications and the X.400 MTS.
- Microsoft messaging application program interface (MAPI), a Microsoft standard for the access to the mail infrastructure from Windows applications.
- Vendor independent messaging interface (VIM), an alternative proposal to MAPI developed by Lotus, Apple, Novell, IBM, and Borland.

A design difference between MAPI and VIM is that VIM defines a direct interface between application and the underlying messaging infrastructure, while MAPI defines two interfaces, one between the application and the Windows messaging subsystem and another between the Windows messaging subsystem and the message transport services. Communication between the application and the message transport services is thus direct with VIM and indirect through Windows with MAPI. Another difference is that MAPI provides operations which cause the underlying system to open dialogue boxes to the users. With VIM, the idea is that such functions should be part of another standard, called the open collaborative environment (OCE) developed by Apple. VIM plus OCE thus provides the facility of predefined dialogue boxes as in MAPI. Both VIM and MAPI contain between fifty and a hundred defined operations, such as creating a message, adding a recipient to a message, sending a message, searching for incoming messages, etc.

The confusion and competition between different standards proposals is an obstacle to development in this area, and it is hoped that ISO standards work will lead to a commonly accepted API for electronic mail.

8.11 GATEWAYING STANDARDS

This section presents protocols and standards for gateways in the mail area. The actual gatewaying services are discussed in Section 9.3.10.

8.11.1 Tunneling and Gatewaying

Sending X.400 across TCP/IP-like networks such as the Internet, or sending Internet mail across OSI networks, such as X.25/X.75, can be done in two ways: *tunneling* and *gatewaying*.

When tunneling is used, the lower layers in the OSI model are replaced by corresponding layers in the other network, while the higher layers are unchanged. This means that the application information (the formatting of envelope and content according to X.400 or Internet mail) is the same as if the information had been transported in its original network before tunneling. Consequences of this are:

(a) No information is lost.
(b) End-user systems must comply with the tunneling standard, for example, an end user system used when X.400 is tunneled through the Internet must comply with the X.400 standard.

Gatewaying, on the other hand, means that a gateway agent translates the message from the format according to one standard to the format according to another standard.

Table 8.2 compares these two models.

8.11.2 Gatewaying Standards Document

Since there are many different standards for electronic mail, and since everyone wants to be able to send mail to everyone else, gateways are needed between networks using different standards. Standards are also needed for how the gateways should translate between the formats of the different standards. The most important such gatewaying standard is RFC 1327 [3]. An addition to this are RFC 1494 through RFC 1496 [4, 5, 6], which describe how MIME body parts are handled in gateways between Internet mail and X.400 mail.

Table 8.2

Four Modes of Gatewaying between Internet and OSI

Function	Tunneling		Gatewaying	
	X.400 through TCP/IP-based Networks	**TCP/IP through X.25/X.75 Networks**	**X.400 to Internet**	**Internet to X.400**
Envelope and heading infor- mation	X.400 format	Internet format	Translated at gateway from X.400 to Internet format	Translated at gateway from Internet to X.400 format
Loss of infor- mation	No application information is lost, since messages are still in their original format		Information may be lost if full translation is not possible because of differences in the standards. Current gatewaying standards try to minimize such loss.	
End-user software	Must comply with X.400 functionality, even if used on the Internet	Must comply with Internet mail functionality, even if used on X.25/X.75 networks	Complies with Internet format for TCP/IP recipients, even if the message was originally sent in X.400 format	Complies with X.400 format for X.400 recipients, even if the message was originally sent in Internet mail format
Standard used	RFC 1006 [1]	RFC 1090 [2]	RFC 1327 [3]	RFC 1327 [3]

The most difficult task in a gateway between Internet and X.400 mail standards is the handling of e-mail addresses. There are two main ways of mapping e-mail addresses between the two mail standards: standard attribute address (SAA) and non-SAA mapping. They are easiest explained by example, as in Table 8.3.

The advantage of the SAA mapping is that it is simple and logical; the disadvantage is that some information has to be added, for example, ADMD=sunet in the Table 8.3. This means that this mapping requires translation tables, tables which will, for example, indicate that su.se belongs to the *Sunet* ADMD, as seen from X.400. These translation tables should contain the same translation rules for all gateways throughout the world, which means that a mechanism for establishing and distributing these tables is necessary.

If all gateways between X.400 and Internet mail use the same translation tables, then a user address will be translated in the same way in all the gateways, and it can pass gateways many times without trouble. (See also [31].)

With the non-SAA method, the whole Internet address is embedded in an attribute DDA.RFC-822 in X.400, and the rest of the X.400 address is the address of the gateway. In the other direction, the whole X.400 address is embedded in the user name. This method resembles the use of the "%" character for source routing, as described in Section 7.2. This method is less neat but is sometimes necessary when domains are not covered by the translation tables guiding the gateways.

Table 8.3

Mapping of E-Mail Addresses between X.400 and Internet Mail

Mapping Direction	Original E-Mail Address	SAA Mapping	Non-SAA Mapping
From SMTP to X.400	`Jacob.Palme@` `su-kom.su.se`	`G=Jacob;S=Palme;` `O=su-kom;P=su;` `A=sunet;` `C=se`	`DDA.RFC-822=` `Jacob.Palme(a)` `su-kom.su.se;` `P=chalmers;` `A=sunet;C=se`
From X.400 to SMTP	`G=Jacob;S=Palme;` `O=su-kom;P=su;` `A=sunet;C=se`	`Jacob.Palme@` `su-kom.su.se`	`/G=Jacob/S=Palme` `/O=su-kom/P=su/` `A=sunet/C=se@` `chalmers.se`

Even when the SAA method is used, some gateways map addresses onto constructs where the name of the net is part of the new address. For example, members of the Swedish parliament have X.400 names of the format:

    G=given-name; S=surname; P=riksdagen[3] ; A=400NET; C=se

These names are converted by the present Internet gateway run by the Swedish PTT into names of the format:

    Given-name.Surname@riksdagen.400net.tip.net

Here `400net.tip.net` is the name of the X.400 network used by the Swedish parliament. Other such names are names ending with `.bit.net` or `.bitnet`, or `.arpanet` or `.uucp`. A more normal internet address for a member of the Swedish parliament should with more concise gatewaying be:

    Given-name.Surname@riksdagen.se

The advantage of name translations containing network names, like `.400net.tip.net` in the example above, is that they make it very easy for a name server in the Internet to address mail to such recipients to the proper gateway. The disadvantage is that the name contains routing information, with all the problems which such names will cause (see Section 7.2), and that the name is more complex and not as simple and logical as the normal Internet address. With proper name server information (see Section 8.6.3), it should be possible to use more normal Internet addresses and avoid these kinds of source routings through gateways.

---

3   "Riksdagen" is the Swedish-language name for the Swedish parliament.

8.12 DEVIATIONS BETWEEN STANDARDS AND REALITY

With most complex standards, the part that is really implemented is different than the standard itself (see Figure 8.32). The real implementations may implement only a subset of the standard's facilities. They may also implement additional functionality so that the real implementations and the standard only partially overlap. Two different implementations can usually only work together with that part of the functionality which is common to both implementations. This means that the user functionality may often be much less than what is described in the standards.

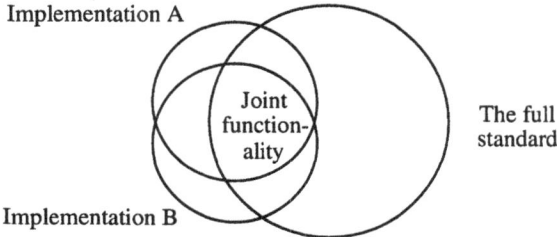

Figure 8.32   Overlapping functionality between different implementation of a real standard.

A common view on this is held by people who might be called "standards fundamentalists." They take the words of the full standard as gospel and criticize every deviation from it. This is in reality impractical, since it that is not how standards work in the real world.

A variant of the fundamentalist viewpoint is the "liberal-conservative" viewpoint, which can be expressed in the statement "be liberal in what you accept, and conservative in what you send" [43]. According to the liberal-conservatives, a good implementation should react intelligently, or at least not in problematic ways, to many kinds of input which may not quite agree with the standard, but the implementation itself should produce only data which strictly agrees with the standard. The problem with this view is that it does not explicitly state what should be accept and what should be produced. The idea is that there are two "virtual standards." One is the "liberal view" which includes as much as possible of the full standard plus common deviations. The other is the "conservative view" which includes only a subset of the full standard accepted by most systems. But the statement is meaningful only if these two variants, the liberal and the conservative, are defined. People who adhere to the liberal-conservative view often have extensive experience in standards implementations, so that they "know" what is conservative and what is liberal. It would be better if they specified this in writing and not let it remain an unspoken assumption which implementors should adhere to, even though it is not stated in any official standards document.

Here are some examples of common deviations between standards and the reality of their implementation in the case of Internet mail:

- The standards officially allow any ASCII character in e-mail addresses as long as these characters are *quoted*. Two methods of quoting are allowed, surrounding an item with double apostrophes """" or preceding the problem character with the "\" character. Thus, the e-mail address

```
"John Müller"@host.net
```

is legal according to the official standards. But everyone "knows" that quoting does not always work, and is thus not part of the conservative view, and that a good implementation of Internet mail should never for its own users provide e-mail addresses which require quoting. But how should an implementor know this, when the standards writers refuse to define the conservative and liberal "virtual" standards view?

All use of the "space" character in e-mail addresses should be strictly avoided, and spaces in names should be replaced preferably by periods. (Some systems replace spaces with the underscore character, but this causes problems with some mail systems, so the period is preferable.) The e-mail address above should preferably be changed to either

```
John.Muller@host.net
```
or
```
John.Mueller@host.net
```

- The "%" convention for relative addressing is officially disallowed but is so commonly used in reality that a good implementation should recognize it to at least some extent. For example, a user command to "find the last letter from

```
jpalme@dsv.su.se
```

should in most cases also find letters from

```
jpalme%dsv.su.se@searn.bitnet
```
or any other letters from a recipient whose name begins with `jpalme%dsv.su.se@`

Implementors would be greatly aided if a document was developed that which specified these and other important deviations between standards and reality, that is, specifies the conservative and the liberal virtual standards to which implementors are expected to adhere. There is an attempt to do this in the OSI world with the so-called functional standards and implementors' guide, see Section 8.13. Corresponding documents for Internet mail would be very welcome. The work begun in [43] is a start, but much more is needed.

8.13   FUNCTIONAL STANDARDS AND IMPLEMENTORS' GUIDE

As you can see from the description of X.400 in this book, it is a rather large and complex standard with many special features. An implementation of X.400, however, need not include all these features. Some of the features are *mandatory*, but many are *optional*. There is then a risk that different implementations of X.400 will choose different sets of optional features. This may reduce the common functionality to a very small subset of common features, which, in the worst case, would make interworking between systems formally adhering to the same standard impossible in reality.

To avoid these risks, there are special kinds of standards called *functional standards*. These standards are based on an existing standard called the *base standard*. They split the features of the base standard into one or more classes, where a *class* is a collection of features which must be supported by systems adhering to that class.

158

A functional standard may also include in its classes, for example, the data definitions to be used for a particular application of a standard like X.500, whose schema allows different data definitions for different directory applications.

Functional standards for both X.400 and X.500 are important reading for anyone who intends to implement or buy an electronic mail system. They are available in several different versions from different standards organizations, but fortunately the different versions are similar in content. One of them is found in [7].

Since ISO/IEC and ITU do not test the implement of their standards before publishing them, new standards will often contain a large number of bugs. *The Implementors' Guide* [41] is an ITU publication which lists official corrections to such bugs in X.400.

8.14 PICS PROFORMA

A standardized list of questions and answers on which functionalities are provided by which software packages can greatly aid anyone who is buying an e-mail system. To make it easier to produce such lists, ITU has published detailed a list of questions which a supplier can answer in order to indicate how well his software agrees with the X.400 messaging standards. These lists are called protocol implementation conformance statements (PICS Proforma) and are published in ITU recommendations X.481 to X.485 [32-36].

REFERENCES

[1] Cass, D. and Rose, Marshall T., *ISO transport services on top of the TCP*, Internet RFC 1006.

[2] Ullman, R. *SMTP on X.25*. Internet RFC 1090.

[3] Hardcastle-Kille, S., *Mapping between X.400(1988) / ISO 10021 and RFC 822*, Internet RFC 1327.

[4] Alvestrand, Harald Tveit and Thompson, S., *Equivalence between 1988 X.400 and RFC-822 Message Bodies*, Internet RFC 1494.

[5] Alvestrand, Harald Tveit et al., *Mapping between X.400 and RFC-822 message bodies*, RFC 1495.

[6] Alvestrand, Harald Tveit et al., *Rules for downgrading messages from X.400/88 to X.400/84 when MIME content-types are present in the messages*, Internet RFC 1496.

[7] ISO/IEC, *Information technology—international standardized profiles—AMH2n—message handling systems*, ISO/IEC ISP 12062.

[8] Crispin, M., *Interactive mail access protocol - Version 2*, Internet RFC 1176.

[9] Rose, Marshall T., *Post office protocol - version 3*, Internet RFC 1460.

[10] Radicati, Sara, *Electronic Mail: An Introduction to the x.400 Message Handling Standards*, New York, McGraw-Hill, 1992.

[11] Betanov, Cemil, *Introduction to X.400*. Norwood, Ma: Artech House 1993.

[12] Rose, Marshall T., *The Internet Message: Closing the Book with Electronic Mail*. Englewood Cliffs, NJ: Prentice-Hall 1993.

[13]   Kuhn, Markus, *Frequently asked questions about OSI with answers*. Available from URL ftp://ftp.uni-padeborn.de/FAQ/comp.protocols-iso/comp.protocols-iso_FAQ.

[14]   Alvestrand, Harald Tveit, *Frequently asked questions on comp.protocols.iso.X.400,* available from URL ftp://aun.uninett.no/pub/mail/x400faq/FAQ-mhsnews.text.

[15]   ISO, *Code for the representation of names of languages*, ISO International Standard 639.

[16]   Postel, J., *Simple mail transfer protocol*, Internet RFC 821, 1982.

[17]   Crocker, D., *Standard for the format of ARPA Internet text messages*, Internet RFC 822, 1982.

[18]   Partridge, C., *Mail routing and the domain system,* Internet RFC 974.

[19]   Horton, M. and Adams, Ric, *Standard for the interchange of USENET messages*, Internet RFC 1036.

[20]   Braden, R., *Requirements for Internet hosts—application and support,* Internet RFC 1123.

[21]   Borenstein, M. and Freed, N., *MIME (multipurpose Internet mail extensions) part one: mechanisms for specifying and describing the format of internet message bodies*, Internet RFC 1521.

[22]   Moore, K., *MIME (multipurpose internet mail extensions) part two: message header extensions for non-ascii text*, Internet RFC 1522.

[23]   Mockapetris, P., *DNS encoding of network names and other types,* Internet RFC 1101.

[24]   Manning, B., *DNS NSAP RRs*, Internet RFC 1348.

[25]   Grand, Mark, *Mime overview*, available from url ftp://ftp.netcom.com/pub/mdg/mime.ps and pub/mdg/mime.txt.

[26]   ISO, *Reports on application program interfaces (APIs)*, ISO/IEC JTC 1/SC 18 document N 2836.

[27]   ISO, *Specification of abstract syntax notation one (ASN.1)*, ISO/IEC IS 8824.

[28]   ISO, *Specification of basic encoding rules for abstract syntax notation one (ASN.1).* ISO/IEC IS 8825.

[29]   Steedman, Douglas, *ASN.1: the tutorial and reference*, Technology Appraisals, 1990.

[30]   ISO, *Code for the representation of names of languages*, ISO IS 639.

[31]   Grimm, Ruediger, *A minimum profile for RFC-987: mapping between addresses in RFC-822 format and X.400 standard attributes*, GMD, 1987.

[32]   CCITT, *P2 Protocol - protocol implementation conformance statements (PICS) proforma*, ITU recommendation X.481.

[33]   CCITT, *P1 Protocol - protocol implementation conformance statements (PICS) proforma*, ITU recommendation X.482.

[34]   CCITT, *P3 Protocol - protocol implementation conformance statements (PICS) proforma*, ITU recommendation X.483.

[35]   CCITT, *P7 Protocol - protocol implementation conformance statements (PICS) proforma*, ITU recommendation X.484.

[36]   CCITT, *Voice messaging protocol implementation conformance statements (PICS) proforma*, ITU recommendation X.485.

[37]   CCITT Recommendation X.411, *Message handling: message transfer system: abstract service definition and procedures*, 1992. [Almost identical to ISO/IEC 10021-4.]

[38]   CCITT Recommendation X.413, *Message handling: message store: abstract service definitions*, 1992. [Almost identical to ISO/IEC 10021-5.]

[39]   CCITT Recommendation X.420, *Message handling: interpersonal messaging system*, 1992. [Almost identical to ISO/IEC 10021-7.]

[40]   CCITT Recommendation X.440, *Message handling systems: voice messaging system*, 1992.

[41]   CCITT, *MHS implementors' guide*, CCITT Group on Message Handling Systems. Available from URL gopher://mars.dsv.su.se/11/iso-mess/impg.

[42]   Rose, Marshall T., The future of OSI: A Modest Prediction, in [12].

160

[43] Braden, R. (ed.), Requirements for internet hosts—application and support. Internet RFC 1123, 1989.

[44] Vielmetti, Ed, Sweet, Jerry, and Goodwin, Tim, Frequently asked questions about MIME, available from URL ftp://relay.cs.toronto.edu/pub/usenet/comp.answers/mailmime-faq.Z.

[45] MacPherson, Andrew, *International Telecommunications Standards Organizations*. Norwood, MA: Artech Books, 1990.

Chapter 9

The Market for Electronic Mail

Figure 9.1 shows the three most important components in the market for electronic mail. These three components are:

- The provision of *public electronic mail services*. Users dial up or connect to the public electronic mail services and use these systems to read and write their messages.
- The provision of *software for internal company electronic mail systems*. This is thus the marketing of software, rather than marketing of services.
- The provision of *networks* which can transfer messages between various internal company and public electronic mail systems.

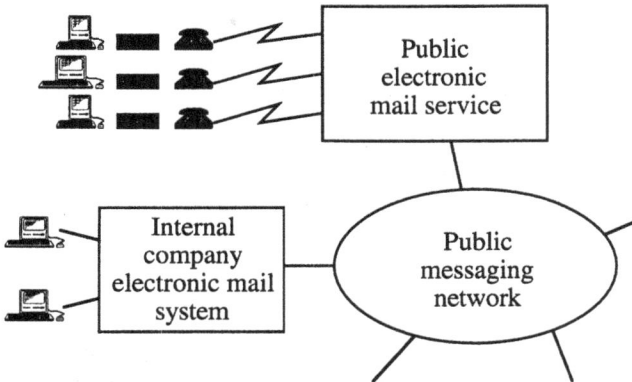

Figure 9.1   Three marketing areas for e-mail services and products.

In addition to these three market components, there is also a market for the sale of the general hardware and operating system software used by electronic mail systems.

9.1 HISTORY

The first electronic mail systems were software on interactive, multiuser computers (time-sharing computers) which allowed users on the same computer to send mail to each other. Such systems existed by the end of the 1960s on the early time-sharing computers like MULTICS, PDP-10, etc.

At the beginning of the 1970s, a number of computers, mainly used at research laboratories in the United States, were connected through a network called ARPAnet. It was expected that this network would be used mostly for file transfer and running programs on remote computers. However, electronic mail soon became the largest volume application on the ARPAnet. Electronic mail on the ARPAnet started with users simply sending files to each other. They found that it was practical to have a similar heading on files containing electronic mail. Thus, a common format grew through existing usage, and this common format was written down as RFC 733, a precursor to RFC 822. The present Internet mail standards are a further development of the early ARPAnet and its electronic mail conventions.

In the early 1970s, another development occurred independently of the ARPAnet. Two groups, one lead by Murray Turoff in the Washington D.C.-based Office of Emergency Preparedness, and the other by Jaques Valee at the Institute of the Future in California, were initially working to computerize the Delphi method for futurology: the process of collecting information from a number of professional experts and the subsequent discussion of this information. As a result, they developed the two earliest computer conferencing systems, Turoff's EMISARI and Valee's FORUM/PLANET.

Turoff later developed a new system, EIES, which has played an important part as a generator of ideas and experimental laboratory in the area of computer conferencing and electronic mail. In the mid 1970s, Turoff visited Sweden and talked about his ideas. His visits generated enthusiasm for the ideas and led to the development of the COM[1] and PortaCOM conferencing systems. The Commission of the European Community first used COM and later PortaCOM as a central information exchange hub for several multibillion dollar European cooperation projects. This system, run at the University College of Dublin, is known as EuroKOM.

During the 1980s, new networks made up mainly of research computers grew in most of the industrialized countries. The most important of these networks, next to ARPAnet, were UUCP and BITNET. They used variants of the ARPAnet mail protocols. Usenet News was especially important. It is the world's largest distributed computer-conferencing system, with users on thousands of computers in hundreds of countries.

Researchers, mainly in Europe, also started to use X.400 in the mid 1980s, and an informal X.400 network was developed under the name R&D MHS.

---

[1] COM is not an acronym. It can be seen as an abbreviation of either "communication system" or "come together."

Around 1980, VolvoData, the computer center of the multinational automobile manufacturer, began developing a messaging system for IBM/MVS (multiple virtual storage operating system) computers called Memo. Memo has been a marketing success and versions for other host environments have been developed.

The growing use of local area networks (LANs) towards the end of the 1980s encouraged the development of a number of electronic messaging systems for such networks. Many systems came from personal computer software companies. Examples include Word Perfect Office, Lotus Notes, CCmail, Microsoft Mail, etc.

In the computer conferencing area, a number of second-generation systems were developed during the 1980s, for example, Cosy, Participate, Confer, Caucus.

The third generation of conferencing systems are the distributed systems, where users do not need to use one central host. The first of these was Usenet News. Later systems include Lotus Notes, EIES 2, First Class, and SuperKOM.

Commercial electronic mail services began as mail systems but later supplied networks to internal company electronic mail systems They also grew in the 1980s, for example, TELEMAIL, Dialcom, and MCI Mail in the U.S.A. and Telecom Gold in the United Kingdom.

Public computer conferencing services also grew during the 1980s, mainly in the United States. Well-known services include BIX, America Online, CompuServe, Prodigy, GEnie, etc. These services usually combine computer conferencing and electronic mail with access to data bases of texts and of public domain software.

The big personal computer software suppliers, Microsoft, Lotus, Borland, Word-Perfect, etc. can be expected to increase their offerings in the electronic mail area in the future.

Note: The rest of this chapter is more technical. If you are not interested, skip to Chapter 10.

9.2 SOFTWARE

Some electronic mail systems are described below.

9.2.1 Memo

Memo is a typical internal company electronic mail system. It was originally written for computers of IBM architecture running under the MVS operating system. Memo is well adjusted to the MVS environment and 3270 terminals. Users of Memo can sort messages into folders. Personal distribution lists (stored in the mailbox data base of the sender) are available. An example of a user interaction with Memo is given in Section 12.4 below). Memo has a Memo-specific protocol for sending mail between Memo systems on different MVS computers, but Memo has also recently developed an X.400 interface.

The success of Memo has meant that versions have been developed for the VM (virtual machine) and VSE (virtual storage extended) operating systems and for MS-DOS, Windows, and LANs. Memo is marketed by the company Verimation.

9.2.2 EAN/Envoy 400 and other X.400 systems

At the University of British Columbia in Canada, the first electronic mail system in the world based on the X.400 standard was developed in 1984. It is named EAN and was widely used in academia in the second half of the 1980s, mainly in Europe and Canada.

EAN was marketed commercially under the name Envoy 400. Many computer manufacturers bought original equipment manufacturers (OEM) versions of EAN[2]. Some of them substantially developed it, so that many manufacturers sold systems which were more-or-less developed versions of EAN. An example of the original user interface of EAN is shown in Section 12.3.

There are many other X.400 products available on the market. Many are developed in Europe, because the European Community requires X.400 to be used for public e-mail usage. For a list of X.400 software products, see [6]. X.400 software products fall into the following categories:

- X.400 P3 protocol user agents;
- X.400 P7 protocol user agents;
- X.400 MTAs with P1 and possibly P3 and P7 support; and
- X.400 gateways to Internet e-mail and to proprietary e-mail products like Microsoft Mail, Lotus CC-Mail, etc.

9.2.3 Conference Systems

The most well-known computer conferencing systems are:

- The EIES family, developed by Murray Turoff, Roxanne Hiltz, and their coworkers at the New Jersey Institute of Technology. The EIES family has supported a large amount of new ideas and experimentation, which have stimulated to other systems.
- The *KOM* family, including *COM, PortaCOM, SuperKOM* and *LysKOM*. Systems in this family exhibit high integration of personally addressed electronic mail with computer conferencing and strong support for conversations. An example of SuperKOM is given in Section 12.2.
- *Usenet News* is a worldwide network of connected conference systems. The functionality is somewhat limited compared to other systems; for example,

---

2   OEM is used when a company develops hardware or software and sells it to another company to sell under its own brand name instead of the brand name of the original developer.

private (closed) conferences are not well supported. There are many different Usenet News products available, many of them freeware or shareware.

- *Caucus* is a simple and well-functioning system available with user interfaces in many natural languages.
- *Lotus Notes* is a combination of data base and computer conferencing. See Section 9.2.4.
- *First Class* is a system that has become very popular in the last few years because of good functionality, an excellent user interface and a low price.

Usenet News, Lotus Notes, First Class, SuperKOM, and EIES 2 are distributed systems, and do not require one central host to which all users connect.

Other well-known American systems are *Cosy* (developed at the University of Guelph in Canada) and *Confer* (developed at the University of Michigan), a precursor to *Caucus*.

9.2.4 Lotus Notes

Lotus Notes has become popular recently because it combines computer conferencing and a data base in the same system. An application in Lotus Notes combines features of both a computer conference and a data base. As in computer conferencing, news control aids users in finding new entries they have not yet read. Like a data base, the entries in a conference can have a specified format with defined subfields. Each entry in the conference corresponds to a record in a data base. In each application, built-in report generators can produce lists of the entries in different formats. Lotus Notes uses a replicated data base between several servers: the manager of an application decides to which servers his application will be replicated.

9.2.5 FidoNet and Other Personal Computer Systems

There are many combined electronic mail and computer conferencing systems for personal computers. These systems are often called bulletin board systems (BBSs). The earliest such systems were based on one dedicated personal computer. Users dialed in or connected to this personal computer to leave and fetch messages. A limitation of these systems in the beginning were that they could handle only one user at a time, which reduced the number of users sharply because too often the line was busy when you tried to connect.

Later systems have been designed to avoid this. They either use equipment which can multiplex several user lines to one personal computer (like Galacticom and First Class) or run a multiuser operating system on the personal computer (like UNIX for SuperKOM). A third solution is to develop software that allows the BBSs to connect to each other. Thus, even if each BBS can only handle one user at a time, a network of several BBSs can provide a common message-exchange service to larger user groups.

The most well-known system based on this principle is known as Fido its net is FidoNet.

There has been some controversy over such BBSs, since a few of them have developed an "underground" which spreads secret passwords between crackers (criminally inclined hackers), pirate copies of software, illegal obscene pictures, or engages in other more-or-less illegal conduct.

9.2.6 Systems from Computer Manufacturers

Most of the large computer manufacturers today supply their own electronic mail systems, often integrated with their office information systems. Examples of this include *PROFS* from IBM, *All-in-One* from DEC, etc. These systems usually use their own internal protocols, but provide gateways to X.400 and/or Internet mail for connection to other systems from other manufacturers.

9.2.7 Public Domain Software

Some software products mentioned below appear in both public domain and non-public-domain versions.

ISODE is a public domain package that aids in the implementation of OSI applications on top of X.25 or TCP/IP nets.

Sendmail is a central mail sorter (MTA) for Internet mail and UUCP mail which is almost universally used. Sendmail has a powerful alias macro facility which is not easy to use. It is controlled by complex tables, and it can be difficult to know how to modify these tables to get the desired effect. No one seems to be very fond of Sendmail, but almost everyone uses it. Many people claim that MMDF and PP do a better job, but sendmail is still the software mostly used.

MMDF (multi-channel memo distribution facility) is an alternative Internet mail MTA software which is liked by its users but still not as much used as Sendmail.

PP is a software for MTAs which can handle both the X.400 and the Internet mail formats and the gatewaying of messages between them. It was developed by Janet, the British University net, based on ideas from MMDF. PP is also available as a commercial product.

Listserv is a distribution list software initially written for IBM/VM computers. Even though it was initially meant to be used only within BITNET, it is used more and more for handling distribution lists in the Internet environment. A special feature of Listserv is that by writing e-mail messages to Listserv itself users can subscribe and unsubscribe to lists and control the format in which the lists' entries are sent to them. If you want Listserv to send entries to a non-Listserv distribution list or computer conference system, then you have to send a fake message with the list or conference as a fictitious sender of the fake message in order to subscribe or unsubscribe. Listserv can handle nested list with automatic routing of subscribe/unsubscribe request to the most suitable sublist in the hierarchy.

The normal format of sending out messages from Listserv has most of the original heading information removed. The reason for this is that many mail system misuse heading information, so the Listserv designer thought it best not to provide information which can be misused. You can, however, ask Listserv to send full headers. If you ask for full headers you will get the Message-ID, which is important for eliminating duplicates and correlating conversational chains.

Note: Newer versions of Listserv will no longer be in the public domain. For more information about Listserv see Sections 6.7.1, 6.7.2 and 6.10.

9.3 PUBLIC SERVICES

This section describes several of the public services available for electronic mail.

9.3.1 Internet

Internet is a collection of many different nets (NSFnet, CSNET, etc.), which logically works as one single large net. It began as a network of research contractors and universities financed by the U.S. defense Department and was called ARPAnet. But ARPAnet grew rapidly by adding new servers and merging with other nets, eventually creating the present Internet. Its main basis is still in the American university and research nets, but today many other nets are part of the Internet. Many nets which do not use the Internet standards have gateways to it so that the Internet works as a world-wide interconnected electronic mail network. The basis of the net is noncommercial messaging, but there are a growing number of commercial users who also connect to the net. The Internet mainly uses leased lines between packet net nodes and a packet net protocol called TCP/IP. Note that this is not the same as the packet net protocol, X.25, which many nets provided by the public Telecom companies use. There are several leased lines across the Atlantic Ocean providing Internet service also to a growing regional European net.

As of 1993, it was estimated that more than three million individual e-mail mailboxes could be reached through the Internet, and this number is increasing by about 15 % a month.

The Internet is not a commercial enterprise, and not all of the different nets that make up the Internet have commercial agreements with each other. The Internet is, too a large extent, made up of individual organizations which voluntarily place some services at the disposal of the Internet. Usually, none of the participating organizations pay each other for these services.

In practice the Internet is works as a kind of global backbone for electronic mail, with gateways to most other nets. Thus, the largest and most comprehensive net for global forwarding of e-mail is the Internet, and not, as the Public Telephone and Telegraph companies (PTTs) would have preferred, the X.400-based nets that they provide.

Many books about the Internet have been published lately. Two of the most complete are [4 and 5].

9.3.2 UUCP/EUNET

UUCP and its European branch European UNIX network (EUNET) are one of the largest nets of electronic mail systems in the world, encompassing tens of thousands of hosts in almost all industrialized countries. UUCP started as a UNIX net based on dial-up lines. However, it is moving towards greater usage of leased lines and away from its own protocols to the Internet mail protocols. One important application which started in UCCP is its world-wide distributed conferencing system, Usenet News. Today, the Usenet News network has largely migrated to the Internet and is therefore often called Netnews.

9.3.3 BITNET/EARN

BITNET and its European branch, the European academic research network (EARN) is also a very large net, encompassing many thousands of hosts. BITNET started as a net using proprietary IBM protocols, although it was often implemented on non-IBM equipment. BITNET is based on using leased lines between the hosts. BITNET is moving towards use of TCP/IP and the other Internet mail protocols. In the fall of 1994 EARN will merge into the RARE (reseaux associes pour la recherche Europeene) organization.

9.3.4 R&D MHS/National Academic Nets/RARE/TERENA

The academic nets in Europe have a cooperative organization called *TERENA* (Trans-European Research and Education Networking Association). TERENA publishes recommendations for building a European mail network based on the X.400 standard. Most European countries have nets which participate in TERENA. TERENA was previously known under the name *RARE*, but merged in the autumn of 1994 with *EARN* (European Academic Research Network), under the new joint name TERENA.

European academic nets include Janet in the United Kingdom, DFN (Deutsches Forschungsnetz) in Germany, Danet in Denmark, Uninett in Norway, Funet in Finland, and Sunet in Sweden.

9.3.5 Commercial Nets

Several companies provide public electronic mail systems. Some of them connect several systems through nets, and some of them allow internal company systems to connect to the nets. Well-known nets of this kind are IBM (Screenmail), General Electric (QUIKCOMM), MCI Mail, Dialcom, and Telenet. Some of them provide nodes in many different countries, so that they can provide global mail networking for their customers.

9.3.6 DASNET

The academic nets have reasonably well-working gateways. The situation for the commercial nets is more chaotic. Because of this, a market has opened for a particular company called DASNET. DASNET provides gateways between different nets, which otherwise would not be connected. For a fee, DASNET customers can send messages between these nets. DASNET does this is by emulating a mailbox in the nets it interconnects. In this way, no change in the nets themselves is necessary in order to use DASNET.

9.3.7 The Telecom Companies (PTTs)

The telecom companies (PTTs) in most industrialized countries have set up electronic mail exchanges, based on the X.400 standard. They want this to be a regular telecom service. They also want people to use a worldwide PTT-run electronic mail net in much the way as people today use the telephone nets. In many countries, the PTTs more-or-less have a monopoly on running telephone services, and some expect the same for electronic mail. The PTT services usually provide both public electronic mail systems and nets for interconnecting company's internal mail systems.

In the United States, there is no single dominate telecom company. Electronic mail services are provided by several companies, some of them connected to telecom companies. Some of the largest are Telenet, Dialcom, GE-Quik-COMM, and MCI Mail. Many of the PTTs in other countries have bought software from some of the three large American systems, Dialcom, GE and Telemail. *Dialcom* software is used in Australia, Denmark, Finland, Hong Kong, Ireland, Israel, Italy, Japan, Mexico, Holland, New Zealand, Puerto Rico, Singapore, South Korea, and Germany. *GE* software is used in Bahrain, Bermuda, The Philippines, Liechtenstein, Luxembourg, Monaco, Saudi Arabia, Venezuela and Austria. *Telemail* software is used in Belgium, Chile, Italy, Japan, Norway, Sweden and Taiwan.

The efforts of the PTTs to establish themselves as the dominate e-mail network providers have not been very successful. In spite of their efforts, the largest usage of e-mail is in the Internet and not in the PTT-provided nets.

9.3.8 The Future of Electronic Mail

It is not possible today to predict very much about the future of electronic mail services. Maybe the PTTs will monopolize e-mail as they have with phone services in many countries. But there seem to be market forces moving towards more competition in this and other telecommunications areas, so it seems more probable that in the future public electronic mail services will be provided by competing companies.

One interesting aspect of the issue is that the academic, mainly noncommercial nets are in fact larger and better interconnected than the commercial nets. Many of the academic nets use standards based on TCP/IP and Internet mail protocols, while the commercial nets more often use standards based on X.25 and X.400. By the end of the 1980s, many people expected that the commercial nets and their interconnected X.400 services would soon dominate. This has not happened. Instead, Internet and the TCP/IP-based nets have grown, and many commercial nets today offer TCP/IP based services in addition to or as a replacement for X.25 based nets. One reason for the success of the TCP/IP-based nets is that their standards are simpler, less advanced but easier to implement, and that much reasonably good public domain software is available for them. However, many organizations, including important government organizations, are pushing for OSI, the X.25-based standards, and today it is not possible to predict which will ultimately succeed. Academic organizations in some countries, especially Germany and the United Kingdom, have been pushing for the OSI standards. Large companies with multiple e-mail systems often choose X.400 in preference of Internet mail standards for internal company messaging, while Internet mail standards are used for external messaging.

In general, many of the so-called OSI standards have had problems in being accepted. People seem to find that they are too complex, too advanced, and not tested well enough. Internet requires a standard to be implemented and tested before it is accepted, but ISO has no such requirements. It is much easier to gain access to Internet standards documents, since they can be downloaded from the nets. ISO standards can only be bought at high cost, and even then you will only get a paper copy. The advantage of being able to browse the document electronically is not available. A discussion of these issues can be found in [2].

9.3.9 Registration Authorities

As more and more electronic mail networks are interconnected, it is essential for good service to agree on electronic mail addresses so that every mailbox can have a globally unique address and that confusion over addresses can be avoided. In order to achieve this goal, there needs to be a system to register new names, which ensures that no two different mailboxes get the same name. Registration authorities are used for this. A user who wants a new name sends this request to the registration authority, and the registration authority ensures that the new name is unique.

Most registration authorities work on the principle of delegation based on domain names. An example of this is shown in Figure 9.2. My e-mail address is jpalme@dsv.su.se, where "se" represents the country of Sweden, "su.se" represents the organization Stockholm University, and "dsv.su.se" represent my university department. The central Internet registration authority, IANA, registers country names (usually using ISO two-letter standard country designations like "se" for Sweden [3]). For each country, this registration authority delegates further registration within that country to a submanager, which in Sweden is the technical manager of the Swedish University Network, Sunet. This means that when a Swedish organization wants to register a subdomain to "se," it need not go to the central Internet registration authority, IANA. It will instead go to the manager of the subdomain "se." In the same way, the manager of this subdomain will delegate responsibility for names within the "su.se" domain to Stockholm University. Thus, if a department within Stockholm University needs a new domain, it need not ask the manager of the "se" domain, it can ask the manger of the subdomain "su.se" to register the new department. The assignment of "jpalme@dsv.su.se" can then be done locally within the "dsv.su.se" department.

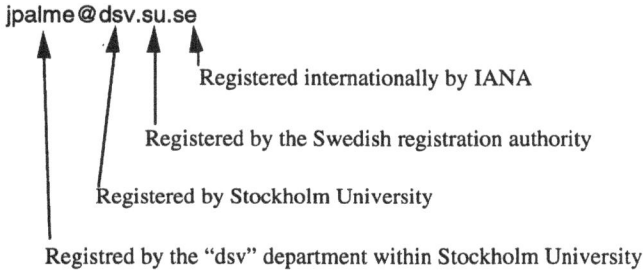

jpalme@dsv.su.se

Registered internationally by IANA

Registered by the Swedish registration authority

Registered by Stockholm University

Registred by the "dsv" department within Stockholm University

Figure 9.2   Example of delegation of responsibility between registration authorities.

Registration authorities are needed for several different kinds of entitities used in e-mail; as cam be seen below

Internet domains (see Section 7.2) are registered as described above.

Internet e-mail-addresses (see Section 8.6.4) are registered in similar ways.

Internet port numbers (see Section 8.6.2) are registered by IANA, no subdomain system is used for port numbers.

Object identifiers (see Section 8.3.3) are registered using a domain naming system which allows subdelegation of naming for different branches of the object identifier tree. There are three top level domains, one for subregistering by ISO, one for subregistering by ITU, and one for subregistering jointly by ISO and ITU.

Directory names (see Section 8.5.1) are registered using a domain naming system where the top level domains are the countries of the world.

X.400 e-mail addresses and *OR-addresses* (see Section 8.4.21) need the registration of different elements of the OR-address, such as ADMD name, PRMD name, and organization name. The registration of these names are delegated to each country. A country can choose to make PRMD names relative to ADMDs (which means that their registration can be delegated to the ADMDs) and organization names relative to ADMD and PRMD. The registration of these names in that country can then be delegated to the particular ADMD or PRMD. A country can also choose to require that these names are nationally unique. They must then be registered with a central registration authority for each country. More information about this can be found in Section 8.4.21.

Conversion tables between X.400 e-mail addresses and Internet e-mail addresses also need registration. For more information see Section 8.11.2.

Public keys for use as described in Section 7.6.1 are registered by certification authorities (see Section 7.6.4).

Most registration is done nationally in a way that each country decides for itself. Some registration is done internationally, such as top-level domains, port numbers in Internet, and object identifiers in standards developed by ISO and/or ITU. Central international registration authority within the Internet is IANA. For X.400 and other ISO/ITU standards, ISO and ITU are central international registration authorities, and national registration is delegated by ISO and ITU to the national members of ISO and ITU in different countries.

9.3.10 Gateways

For Internet electronic mail, there are usually gateways between nets based on different standards, so that mail can be sent from any user of any node in any academic net to any other user in any other academic net. There are also sometimes, but not always, gateways between the academic nets and commercial nets. For example, in Britain there is a gateway between the academic net (Janet) and Telecom Gold, and in the U.S. there is a gateway between Internet and CompuServe. Standards for such gateways are discussed in Section 8.11.

When sending mail from the Internet to other nets, you can sometimes address the user by an Internet e-mail address whose highest domain is "net." For example, BITNET e-mail addresses belong to the domain "bit.net" and when you send a message to a recipient within this domain, the Internet name servers (DNS) will automatically direct the message to a suitable gateway from Internet to BITNET.

A neater alternative to such ".net" domain addresses is to use logical domain addresses showing the organizational location of the user, combined with storing of the information in the DNS that mail to certain domains are to be forwarded to gateways between the Internet and other nets (see also Section 8.11.2).

One particular problematic issue is that of gateways between X.400 and the Internet. The problem is that there are a large number of different X.400 subnets, and many gateways are only willing to forward messages from the Internet to their own subnet. This means that when you want to send e-mail from Internet mail to X.400, you must find the particular gateway to the subnet of your recipient. This is not always easy, and some better way of handling this will have to be found in the future. The mhsnews FAQ [1] discusses this problem.

9.4 PUBLIC MESSAGING SYSTEMS AND CONFERENCE SYSTEMS

A user of electronic mail can either use an company's internal electronic mail system or connect via phone or computer nets to public systems. Those companies which provide network services (see Section 9.3) often provide public systems for those customers who do not have internal company electronic mail systems. There are also systems which provide public mailbox systems more than network services.

Many of these systems also provide other data base services. For example, they may have data bases of news, public domain software, etc. They also often provide computer conferencing services that allow people in many specialized areas to exchange experiences and information. Examples of such companies in the United States are *BIX* (Byte Information eXchange, owned by *Byte* magazine), *CompuServe, America Online, Prodigy, GEnie,* etc. Some of these American services also have dial-in lines in European countries. In Europe, *EuroKOM* has a strong position because of its European Community support. In some European companies, especially France, the public *Videotex* systems (*Minitel* in France) partly fill a similar role.

9.5   FEES AND CHARGING

The costs of electronic mail are:

- Getting a terminal or a personal computer. Most electronic mail users purchase them for other applications and do not regard this as a separate cost for electronic mail.
- A terminal emulator or an electronic mail client program to install in the personal computer. Good terminal emulators are available as public domain software (for example Kermit), while electronic mail software for personal computers are usually purchased.
- A leased line to a computer network or a modem to use with a phone line. This cost may vary from about $ 100 per year to $ 1000 dollars or more.
- The mailbox system or mail exchange services used. This can be either an internal company system or a public one. Public systems usually charge approximately half a dollar per message or a flat monthly/hourly fee.
- Transferring the message from the sender to the recipient. This cost is also maybe half a dollar per message or a flat monthly/hourly fee in commercial nets.

In the case of Internet connections, users often only pay a fixed fee for the connection to the Internet, and then no volume charge dependent on the size and number of messages sent or received.

An interesting question is who should pay: the sender or the recipient. Many nets split the charge between the sender and the recipient. Some nets, for example, charge per minute of connection time, whether you are sending or receiving messages. Some nets, which are based on leased lines, charge for the line, sometimes varying with line speed, but independent of usage.

One requirement of a good accounting system is that those who benefit from the communication and those who can influence the usage of resources should pay. Following this principle, it is not obvious that the sender should always pay the whole cost. For public distribution lists and conferences, it is usually the recipient who decides whether to participate or not. Subscribing to such a list is somewhat similar to subscribing to a newspaper, which is a service the recipient pays for.

In certain cases, for closed distribution lists it may be desirable that neither the sender nor the recipient but rather the owner of the list pays.

A further problem with charging for electronic mail is the existence of gateways. A message will sometimes pass several gateways between nets on its way from the sender to the recipient. Ideally, the cost should be split according to the services the gateway provide. But the cost of such ideal charges may be unreasonably high. Because of this, bulk agreements are often made between the nets, in much the same way as postal companies do for international postal mail. A common such agreement is that each net pays all costs within the net, and that the cost of running the gateway itself is split halfway between the connected nets. Thus, no payment is actually made from one net to the other for using services of the other net.

Problems with agreeing and charging is one reason for the difficulty in establishing gateways between commercial electronic mail networks. The largest problem occurs with a gateway between one network, which charges per message and bills all costs to the sender (let us call this net Commercialnet), and another network, which charges for the line to the network and nothing more (let us call this net Internet). Commercialnet wants to bill Internet for all messages which Internet forwards to it. But Internet has no method of paying such costs, since it has no method of billing the original sender. This is especially troublesome when a user in Commercialnet subscribes to an active Internet distribution list. The user in Commercialnet then gets a lot of messages, and neither the owner of the list nor the ultimate sender is willing to pay for delivering the message to the members of the list.

REFERENCES

[1] Alvestrand, Harald Tveit, *X400/Internet gateways FAQ,* available from URL
     ftp://aun.uninett.no/pub/mail/x400faq/FAQ-gateways.text.
[2] Rose, Marshall T., *The Internet Message: closing the book with electronic mail.* Englewood
     Cliffs, NJ: Prentice-Hall, 1993.
[3] ISO, *Codes for the representation of names of countries.* ISO International Standard 3166.
[4] Hahn, Harley, *The Internet Complete Reference,* Berkeley, CA: Osborne McGraw-Hill, 1993.
[5] Hahn, Harley, *The Internet Yellow Pages,* Berkeley, CA: Osborne McGraw-Hill 1993.
[6] Alvestrand, Harald Tveit, *Currently known X.400 implementations,* available from URL
     ftp://aun.uninett.no/pub/mail/x400faq/FAQ-products.text.

Chapter 10

Law and Order

An earlier version of this chapter has previously been published in [9].

10.1 ETHICS AND ETIQUETTE

10.1.1 Is There a Need for Electronic Mail Ethics?

As in other areas of human interchange, there is a need in electronic mail for:

- Ethics, principles for suitable and unsuitable uses of the medium; and
- Etiquette, forms for handling communication so that users know that certain types of communication are handled in certain ways.

Ethics and etiquette often consist of unwritten rules. Sometimes, people try to write them down in more or less formal collections. Breaking these rules is usually sanctioned by social pressure—if someone breaks the rules, other people complain, which often gets the person to change his behavior. More formal organizational forms for sanctions, include ethics boards and rules that, for example, close the account for those who regularly break the rules.

There are few laws, specifically controlling electronic mail. When the use of electronic mail is more widespread there may be more control of the medium through legislation. It is dangerous, however, to try to make laws controlling a technology under development—the laws will easily be antiquated and can even cause more harm than benefit.

Not everyone agrees on the proper ethics and etiquette in electronic mail. One community of users may have ethical rules which are in direct contradiction with those in another community. As an example, some electronic communities (for example EARN) forbid political discussions, while the constitution of many countries, allow unrestricted discussions of political issues.

When two communities with different written or unwritten views on ethics and etiquette are connected, cultural collisions sometimes occur. People from one community act according to their ethics, and people in the other community may then find that these people are, for example, nasty, ill-mannered, ruthless, arrogant, lofty, stupidly careless, muddled, and vague. Strong emotional reactions and serious misunderstandings sometimes occur. Each group may try to use social pressure to get the other group to change their behavior.

New users of electronic mail will often begin by trying to apply ethics and etiquette learned in other communication media like postal mail, telephone, or face-to-face meetings. The need for special ethical rules for electronic mail is especially important in cases where such ordinary ethics and etiquette are *not* suitable. The principles common to all human communication are often felt to be so obvious that they need not be included in the ethics of electronic mail.

The reason why different kinds of ethics and etiquette may be needed for electronic mail is that it works differently than other media, and this causes different kinds of communication problems. Important differences between electronic mail and other media are that electronic mail makes it so easy, fast, and relatively inexpensive to distribute information to many recipients and that this information can be saved and forwarded in more ways than is possible with voice communication. Because of this, many ethical rules for electronic mail are primarily concerned with the use of electronic mail for group communication.

Different electronic mail systems are designed in different ways, and this influences the need for ethical rules. As an example, a common rule of etiquette is that you should not send the same message to more than one distribution list. This rule is needed, because otherwise people who are members of several lists will get the same message several times. However, good mail systems are capable of recognizing such duplicates so that their users will only see one of the duplicate messages, even though they get the messages via different routes. In such systems, it may sometimes be suitable to send a message to more than one group.

Another example is that some systems have a rule that says that you should delay sending a message, to see if someone else has already sent a message with similar content. Some systems even have a rule that you should not reply to everyone on a list, but only to the author of a message (this author is then expected to summarize the replies he gets for the whole list). These rules arise partly because of by delays in the distribution of messages, so that you cannot always be sure that you have seen all comments already written on an issue when you write your own entry. With shorter delays in the nets, these problems become less serious.

When you read collections of ethical rules for electronic mail, you sometimes wonder if these problems could not be solved by better design of the systems instead of by regulating their users. A rule saying that people should not write long messages can be avoided if the system makes it easy for recipients to skip reading the rest of one message. A rule, that discussions should not branch off outside their initial topic may be avoided if it is easy for participants to unsubscribe only from the branch of a discussion which they are not interested in.

Some people try to write ethical rules into the computer software, by designing electronic mail programs so that they stop users from behaving in ways the program designer finds unethical. Doing this, however, can be dangerous. It is difficult to teach a computer to judge correctly whether certain behavior is ethical or unethical. A behavior which in some cases may be unsuitable, may in other circumstances be necessary and suitable. It might be better to let the computer recommend and guide users towards good behavior but not to make it impossible for the users to knowingly break rules when necessary.

Another form of control is to have one or more people whose task is similar to the chairman at a meeting. Their special task is to control what is written in a computerized group discussion. Some systems are designed so that these moderators must read every contribution, before it is sent to the group (*premoderation*). In other systems, the moderators have the power to remove entries which are not suitable to the topic of a group, move them to another group, or start a new subgroup (*postmoderation*). If a system gives the moderator such facilities, it is important that moving an entry automatically moves the whole branch of the discussion tree to which the entry belongs—including future, not yet written entries.

Premoderated groups, which require the moderator to read all messages before they are sent out, give the strongest control but slow down the interaction in the group. While the typical time between an entry and a reply is normally less than a day in groups which are not premoderated, it is usually about a week in premoderated groups.

There are several reasons why organizers make certain groups premoderated. The first is that you can avoid messages which have no relevance to the subjects which the group is to discuss. The second is that you can avoid duplicates, where the same idea is put forward by different people. The third reason occurs when recipients get the messages via distribution lists, which send the messages to the personal mailboxes of the recipients. With the premoderated lists, the moderator collects all messages on a certain topic once or twice a week, so that the recipients get these messages together and not mixed up with other messages. This problem does not occur with good systems, since such systems will automatically sort incoming messages by topic so that the recipient can read messages by topic. This is another example of how human rules can circumvent technical shortcomings in the design of some message systems.

My experience is that premoderation seems to be necessary for very large groups, with hundreds of participants, while postmoderation is more suitable for smaller groups.

10.1.2   Some Common Ethical Rules

This collection is based on ethical rules for Usenet News [1, 8], for CSNET [2], for EARN [3], for KOM [4], and a collection made by Anne-Marie Eklund [5].

One property of electronic mail is that it is so easy to disseminate a message to so many people. Many ethical rules try to avoid the problems which this may cause. Such rules say that you should *think* before you write, *keep to the topic* of a group discussion, *begin with the most important thing* you have to say (so that those not interested can skip the rest), *never write a message when you are angry,* etc. The fact that you can wait a few hours to calm down before you write a message is an advantage electronic mail compared to face-to-face meetings.

The more work an author puts into his message, the more time is saved for the recipients. This means that there is reason to spend more time writing a message if it is to be read by many people. Most people intuitively understand this principle. A problem with electronic mail is that you are not always aware of how many people are going to read what you write. A function which tells the authors of messages how many people will see their message might be useful. A person who writes a message usually sits alone in front of a computer screen. This intimate environment may tempt one to write something suitable for a group that is smaller than the group that will actually read the message. These kinds of experiences lead to ethical rules that personal assessments of other people should not be sent via electronic mail, or at least only to a very small closed group.

Electronic mail is more often used as a replacement for spoken than for written communication. An important difference is, however, that you do not have the same fast and direct interaction with electronic mail. This means that behavior patterns which are suitable in spoken communication may not work in electronic mail. An example of this is *booking time for a meeting.* People new to electronic mail try to do this the way you normally do in a face-to-face situation: you propose one possible time, and if this is not acceptable, you propose another possible time until you have found a time acceptable to everyone. This method is not always suitable in electronic mail. A better method in electronic mail is to begin by indicating a series of possible times, and asking each participant which time they prefer. The participants then say which times are not suitable for each of them, so that a time suitable to all can be found.

General courtesy rules of *friendliness* and *consideration* may be more important in electronic mail than in face-to-face communication, since you cannot, for example, immediately see a negative reaction and correct and clarify what you mean.

A question can be answered by a message to the author only or to everyone who got the question. As an example, a question sent to a group of people asking at which time their flight will arrive is usually best answered personally to the author only. It is valuable if the electronic mail system allows the author to indicate where replies should be sent. However, many systems have a *reply-to* field but do not clarify what is meant by this field. It might mean:

- Always reply to this address,
- Use this address for personal replies to the author, or
- Use this address for replies meant for all who read the answered message.

Because of this, such reply-to fields often cause more problems than they solve. The general agreement in the Internet, however, seems to be that such reply-to fields are to be used only as substitutes for the originator, not as substitute for the group. Not all software is designed in that way, however. Usenet News has another field, called Followup-To, that indicates where group replies are to be sent. This field, however, is not available in ordinary electronic mail.

In some messaging communities, there is more-or-less a rule that if someone asks a question to a group of people, the reply should be sent to the author, and the author is then expected to *summarize the answers* to the whole group, if he feels that they are of general interest. This is of special importance in nets with long time delays, because otherwise there is a risk that several people, independently of each other, will write the same reply.

Some systems even allow the recipient of a message to choose whether to see all replies to a question or only the summary of the replies composed by the author of the original question.

Now and then, it happens that a message written to a small group is forwarded without permission from the author to a much larger group. Sometimes, the author of the message does not like this. Because of this, a common ethical rule is that you *should not resend texts to larger and more open groups without permission from the author*. This, like most ethical rules, should not be absolute. It is easy to see that in a particular case, the forwarding of a message will not be controversial: or that there may be a large common interest in something which has occurred in a small group that should be known by a larger group. Copying texts written by others is also controlled by copyright laws: see Section 10.6.

The rules on *advertising* in electronic mail vary between nets. American nets usually have stronger restrictions against advertising than European nets, something which sometimes causes clashes when the two are connected. However, both European and American nets find it valuable that people representing hardware and software suppliers can participate in technical meetings on their product, and the border between desirable technical information and undesirable advertising is not always easy to define. One solution may be to have separate discussion groups and distribution lists for information from the suppliers and for general discussion of hardware and software products.

It is important that recipients should be allowed to control what lists they subscribe to, and be allowed to unsubscribe to lists when they want. This can be compared to the laws in some countries, that allow recipients to ask that their names be removed from direct-mail address lists (see Section 10.5).

10.1.3   Ethics and Language

Face-to-face communication involves body language, facial inflections, and nuances of voice. Such tools give important emotional signals in association with what you are explicitly saying—for example, to clarify that you were ironic. Because written communication lacks these tools, serious misunderstandings can occur. To avoid this, special punctuation (so-called "smileys") is sometimes used in electronic mail to indicate that what you are saying is not to be interpreted at face value. Common punctuation is, for example, ":-)" (which looks like a smiling face if you turn it 90 degrees:" ☺ ").

There are also other special syntactical conventions used in electronic mail. Many electronic mail networks are not capable of forwarding underscored, **bold,** or *italic* text. Because of this, a common convention is to write one or more asterisks around a word you want to stress. Another common convention is to put ">" in front of quotations, usually at the beginning of a line. For example,

```
Andersen writes something very **important**:
> Body language can sometimes be replaced by special symbols,
> but sometimes people may overstep the mark.
```

Some e-mail communities also adopt a modified language for use in e-mail. Such language can, of course, be a barrier to new e-mail users. Here are some examples of special terms in such a modified language:

BTW   by the way

IOW   in other words

FYI   for your information

IMHO   in my humble opinion

RSN   real soon now (which may be a long time coming)

FAQ   frequently asked question

OBO   our best offer

2   "to." For example, "F2F" or "face2face" as abbreviations for "face to face"

:-)   this is a joke, not to be taken seriously

:-(I am unhappy

;-)   winking, teasing, flirting

Several books have been published with collections of such acronyms and smileys [6, 7]. You can also easily find more complete lists by, for example, using the Internet Veronica.

10.1.4   Private Usage of Office Mail Systems

One controversial issue is whether employees in companies and government departments should be allowed to use the electronic mail system for private messages, and if not, how to stop this. The problem can be compared to using your office phone for private phone calls or talking to your coworkers during office hours about personal problems. For some reason, perhaps because it is a new medium, some people are more troubled by such behavior in the case of electronic mail than in the case of phone and face-to-face misuse of office resources.

It is important to be aware that the borderline between private and official usage of electronic mail is not always easy to define. An important usage of electronic mail is to

exchange information and learn. The borderline between what you are learning privately and what you are learning to be able to do your job better is also not easy to define.
For example: if an employee of the defense research institute discusses computer security or nuclear power security, is this private communication or part of his job? Even if
the employee is not at that moment working on security issues in these areas, knowledge in such areas are important in defense planning.

There are not many statistics available on the extent of private usage of electronic
mail. In the KOM system, I found that about 10 percent of the usage was obviously private, like Bridge playing or computer games.

These issues might be easier to solve if they are split into issues of *economics,
ethics,* and *power/influence.*

- From an *economic* viewpoint, the benefits of electronic mail (see Chapter 5)
  are so large, that even if 10 percent of the usage of the system is private, it still
  benefits the employer. This is even more so if you take into account that phone
  and face-to-face communication in the office are sometimes used for private
  purposes.
  One should also note that computers, like electricity, cost very little during low
  usage times of day. Because of this, some companies have issued rules that
  their employees may use the electronic mail system privately, but only outside
  office hours.
- From a *moral* and *ethical* point of view, many people feel that private usage of
  an office electronic mail system is to be condemned even though the costs to
  the employer are not large.
- From a *power/influence* point of view, management may sometimes feel that
  the introduction of electronic mail reduces their ability to control what is happening in their company. They sometime try to rectify this by instituting ethical
  rules against private usage of the system.

10.1.5 Anonymous Messages

It is not surprising that the ability to send anonymous messages (see Section 6.9) causes
ethical problems. Some people claim that such messages should not be allowed, because the misuse this facility can produce like slander, defamatory statements, and libel
or other illegal communication. Other people say that anonymity is valuable since it
allows people to make public valuable information which they dare not divulge
otherwise because of pressure from powerful people.

The real fact is however that anonymity exists, whether we like it or not and will
continue to be available unless very stringent measures are used to stop it. Anyone, in
any country, who believes in anonymity can set up an anonymous server, and stopping
people from using such servers is not easy.

If an anonymous server was used to propagate information that was illegal according to the laws of the country in which the server resides, then police could probably be

able to use legal means to break anonymity. No one can totally rely on being anonymous, because there are known ways of breaking the security of anonymous servers.

From an ethical viewpoint, an important facility of anonymous servers is that you can send messages to the person who wrote particular anonymous messages. Thus, it is possible to use social pressure on people who misuse anonymity.

10.2 HUMAN RIGHTS ISSUES

The constitutions and laws in many countries contain sections which are applicable to electronic mail. For example, relevant sections say

- that the rights of free speech is important;
- that the right of every citizen to inform himself of what other people have publicly said is important;
- that the government (and sometimes private persons or organizations) are forbidden from eavesdropping on private mail and phone calls unless special rules are followed (for example, permission by a court for certain police investigations); and
- that the rights of citizens to privacy is safeguarded.

Thus, free speech, the right to communicate, and protection against eavesdropping may be also applicable to electronic mail. The extent to which such laws are valid for electronic mail may vary from country to country.

10.3 FREEDOM OF INFORMATION ACTS

Some countries have laws that require documents produced by government agencies to be available for inspection by any citizen, except when certain secrecy rules are in effect. These laws are normally not applied to phone calls unless they are recorded, but in most cases they are applied to electronic mail, since it is a written and recorded medium. This means that electronic mail communication in government agencies may be open to inspection by the public. This may also mean that the government agencies are not allowed to delete electronic mail messages except as permitted by archiving laws.

10.4 PRINTED MATTER

Some countries have special laws controlling printed publications. These laws are usually not applicable to electronic mail, but this can, of course, vary from country to country.

10.5 COMPUTERS AND PRIVACY LEGISLATION

Many countries have special legislation controlling computers and privacy. The goal of such legislation is to protect the privacy of individuals in relation to the processing of personal data in data files. Such national legislation is often based on some international agreements in this area:

- Guidelines on the protection of privacy and the cross-border flow of personal data, established by the organization for economic development (OECD) 23 September 1980.
- Convention of 28 January 1981 for the protection of individuals with regard to automatic processing of personal data, established by the Council of Europe.
- Proposal for a directive concerning the protection of individuals in relation to the processing of personal data, prepared by the European Community in 1990.
- Proposal for a directive concerning the protection of personal data and privacy in the context of public digital telecommunications networks, in particular the integrated services digital network (ISDN) and public digital mobile networks, prepared by the European Community in 1990.

The basic principle of these international agreements and national legislation is that people and organizations should not be allowed to store and process personal data about other people unless they do so according to special rules. Typical of such special rules are the following:

- A supervisory authority can control the use of computers for storing and processing of personal data.
- Those who wish to store or process personal data must either have permission from this supervisory authority or, in some cases, inform this supervisory authority. The authority may then regulate what personal information is to be stored and how it may be processed.
- People, if they have personal information stored in computers, must be notified of this, and/or may request a copy of what is stored about them and then can request that incorrect information be corrected.
- In some cases, for example, individuals may have the right to be excluded from address files used for market research and advertising.
- The legislation often regards the storage of certain information as especially sensitive and as subject to special control. Such information is data revealing ethnic or racial origin, political opinions, religious or philosophical beliefs, trade-union membership, and data concerning health or sexual life.
- Moving personal information from one data base to another may be restricted by special rules.

Such laws may effect electronic mail in several ways:

- Electronic mail systems include directories of users and what they have written. These are typical of the kind of personal information for which the computers and privacy legislation was intended, and there is usually no problem in applying the legislation to such information.
- Information about electronic mail users, like directory information, and information about messages they are sending and receiving is often moved between different electronic mail systems, and often from country to country. Because of the international nature of electronic mail, this may cause problems, if, for example, the computers and privacy laws forbid moving such information to countries who have not signed the OECD convention. One might compare this to postal organizations being forbidden to send mail to and from such countries or to phone companies being forbidden to connect phone calls to and from such countries.
- The text in electronic mail messages will, of course, often contain personal information, often exactly the kind of information which such rules say should be controlled especially strictly. For example, in electronic mail discussion groups, many messages may contain information about political, religious, and philosophical beliefs and may reveal a person's racial or ethic origin. A love letter may contain data concerning a person's sex life. Personal messages may also, of course, contain information about health: for example, someone sending a message that they cannot come to a meeting because of illness or giving health advice to friends with health problems, etc.

Note that computer and privacy legislation often conflicts with legislation about freedom of speech, which is intended to safeguard the rights of individuals to communicate, and especially to communicate freely, in areas like politics and religion. Many countries (Denmark, Finland, Germany, France, Austria) have exempted computer usage in newspaper offices from the computer and privacy laws in order to protect freedom of speech. For similar reasons, perhaps electronic mail should also be exempted.

This conflict between freedom of speech legislation and computer and privacy legislation is not easy to resolve. Usually, those who have encountered this problem resolve it by saying that storing personal information in word-processing documents, electronic mail messages, etc., should not to be controlled by the computer and privacy laws. These laws are should apply only to more structured ways of handling personal information.

However, there are still difficulties on where to draw the line between what is and is not permitted. Is it, for example, permitted to collect electronic mail messages so that you can easily check what a certain politician has said on a certain issues in those messages or what opinions on a certain issue have been voiced by different people?

Is it permitted to send via electronic mail a list of references to journal articles? Such a list can be seen as a structured data base of personal information and so is probably covered by the computer and privacy laws even if such laws only apply to structured information bases.

As an example, Sweden, which was one of the first countries to establish computer and privacy legislation, has had severe difficulties in trying to solve conflicts in interpreting these laws as they apply to electronic mail systems. This has included forbidding the use of certain electronic mail systems and forbidding the discussion of political issues in certain electronic mail systems! The Swedish supervisory authority has had problems in clarifying how to resolve the conflict between freedom of speech and computers and privacy laws.

10.6   COPYRIGHT LAWS

Copyright laws give authors the right to control the use of what they have written. In many countries, such laws can also apply to messages in electronic mail systems. The extent to which such laws are applicable to electronic mail may vary. Some providers of electronic mail services have notices in their contracts with customers that the customers are giving the providers a copyright license to use what the customers have written in the system, according to the normal principles used for distribution of messages in the system.

10.7   UNLAWFUL COMMUNICATION

One might believe that in a democratic society, freedom of speech would allow you to say anything you want in electronic mail. This, however, is not true.

Below are some examples of messages which may be illegal in many countries.

*   Slander,
*   Computer viruses,
*   Secret military information,
*   Privileged information supplied to lawyers, physicians, priests, etc.,
*   Personal information not allowed according to privacy legislation,
*   Copyrighted material, unless you have permission from the copyright holder,
*   Sedition (incitement to rebellion),
*   Racial agitation,
*   Pornography/obscenity,
*   Criminal conspiracy,
*   Disloyalty against your employers, and
*   Misconduct.

The exact definition of what kinds of speech are allowed and forbidden may vary much between countries, but some kinds, for example, child pornography, are forbidden in most countries.

Electronic mail, like almost any other tool, can be used for various kinds of illegal acts which may not be specific to the electronic mail medium, just as the telephone and the postal system can be used illegally. Of course, this will become more common with the wider use of electronic mail. A well-known example of this is the electronic mail system in the White House, in which Oliver North and his associates sent messages to each other concerning illegal funding of the Contras in Nicaragua. In that case, the actual messages had been erased, but not all backup copies were erased, and by court order, these backup copies were retrieved and used as evidence against North.

This example shows that a wise criminal would probably not choose to use electronic mail. A wise criminal uses the telephone carefully, since police may be listening. But, as the Oliver North example shows, police may be able to find what has been said in electronic mail, although the messages were not tapped when sent. This makes electronic mail even more dangerous than the telephone for the criminal.

In one case in Sweden in 1987, a person was sentenced to pay 15,000 kronor (about $2000) in damages for defamation of character. In a computer conferencing system he had distributed messages which implied that another person was a Russian spy. These messages had been read by about 100 people in the conference system. If this person had made the same statements by voice at a meeting, his risk of prosecution would probably have been lower because it would be more difficult to prove exactly what he said. A transcript of what he had written was given to the defamed person by a user of the conference system: this probably would not have been possible if his statement had been made by voice.

10.8   AGREEMENTS AND SIGNATURES

Contracts and agreements are very important legal concepts. Contracts and agreements can be formed in many ways, and there is usually no legal requirement that a contract must be written and signed. An exchange of electronic mail messages can thus be regarded as a legal contract. In such a case, when and where a contract is agreed to via electronic mail has been made must be clarified.

It is advantageous in disputes over contracts to be able to prove that a certain exchange of electronic mail messages, that result in a contract has occurred and to be able to prove who wrote the messages. There is thus a need for something corresponding to signatures on postal letters and contracts written on paper. There are also very secure methods for electronic signatures and seals (see Section 7.6.3). An electronic signature is actually more reliable than a signature on paper, since a signature on paper is very easy to forge. In one test, one-third of a group of people were not able to distinguish between their own signature and a forgery. Electronic mail might thus make contracts more secure. The main risk with electronic signatures is that the secret key for a person may be stolen. Advanced algorithms are employed to protect against this risk.

One way of getting even higher security would be to establish electronic archives, into which electronic messages and agreements could be sent and registered. If these archives were run by a third party, such as public notaries, they could provide very high security against falsification or false denials of computerized agreements.

10.9 LEGAL RECIPIENTS

It is sometimes important to distinguish between letters sent to an organization, letters sent to a private individual, and letters sent to an individual as employee of an organization. This can, for example, control who is allowed to look at the letter if the indicated recipient is not available and whether an official legal reply to the letter from the organization is expected. Some countries may have other special laws controlling official letters to private or government organizations.

How is this represented in electronic mail? One should first note that there is no rule that says that the recipient of an electronic mail must be a person. Even when a so-called interpersonal mail service is used, it is perfectly legal to address an electronic mail message to an organization, although all organizations may not be able to receive such messages. Many companies have a default mailbox with the name "Postmaster," to which mail to the company that is not addressed to a given individual can be sent. For example, you might send a message to

```
Postmaster@STANFORD.EDU or
Postmaster@SUMEX-AIM.STANFORD.EDU
```

when you want to reach the official organization "Stanford University."

Note that the personal name component is not mandatory in X.400 electronic mail addresses. The following addresses are thus allowed, even though all organizations may not be able to handle incoming mail with such addresses:

```
O=Stockholm University/ADMD=Sunet/C=SE or
OU1=Subscription department/O=Scientific American/A=CompuServe/C=US
```

In the 1988 version of X.400, there is an alternative to the personal name called "common name" which can be used to designate entities other than individual persons.

In ordinary postal mail, you sometimes indicate whether a message is to be delivered to an individual personally or to an individual as an employee of an organization, in the following way:

Format to indicate a personal letter	*Format to indicate a letter to the company*
John Smith	Company XYZ
Company XYZ	Att: John Smith
Box 1234, Small Town	Box 1234, Small Town

There is no directly corresponding facility in current electronic mail standards. However, X.400 has some facilities which might be used to indicate this.

On the P1 envelope, X.400 has a field called *alternate recipient allowed*. This indicates whether someone other than the named recipient is allowed to open the message. If this field is not included in a message, it should not be delivered to an alternate recipient. If, for example, you send a message to an individual who is no longer employed at the company, this field indicates that someone else should then open the message.

In the P2 heading, X.400 has a field called *sensitivity* with the allowed values *personal, private,* and *company-confidential.* The absence of this field means that the message is not sensitive in any of the three ways. The value *private* probably indicates that the message is not intended for the organization itself, but whether the absence of this field should be construed to mean that the message is legally intended for the whole company is not obvious.

10.10 WHICH LAW IS APPLICABLE

Since e-mail is such an international medium, it is sometimes difficult to know which country's laws are applicable. This is important since the laws regarding communication vary so much between countries. Suppose a person in a country which forbids pornography receives pornography through e-mail from a country where pornography is permitted, or the reverse. Who is guilty of illegal acts?

When an illegal act causes damage, should the laws in the country of the sender be used? Or the laws of the country where a person was hurt by the illegal act?

10.11 WHO IS LEGALLY RESPONSIBLE

In the case of phone and postal mail, we normally place the responsibility for the communication with the users of these services, not on the phone and postal companies. It seems natural to apply the same principle to e-mail. However, there is no sharp border between e-mail and data bases. The courts and lawmakers have not yet clarified this. A general tendency seems to be that police forces and prosecutors want the responsibility to be with the service providers, since it is easier to find and control them than their customers, but that they have not always succeeded in persuading the courts to share this view. The risk of placing the responsibility with the service providers is, of course, that this may force these providers to control and censor the communication in ways not compatible with freedoms of speech principles.

Who is responsible for illegal messages passed via anonymous servers (see Section 6.9)? Suppose a person in the United States sends a message via an anonymous server in Finland to recipients in the United States, and suppose that the message was illegal according to U.S. laws but not according to Finnish laws?

10.12 LAW ENFORCEMENT ACTIONS

Depending on the laws in different countries, law enforcement agencies may or may not be allowed to wiretap electronic mail, search your e-mail records, seize equipment used in the conduct of illegal communication, etc.

REFERENCES

[1] Templeton, Brad et al., *Emily Post for Usenet,* first version 1984, latest 1994, available from URL ftp://relay.cs.toronto.edu/pub/usenet/news.answers/emily-postnews.

[2] CSNET, *Draft guidelines on CSNET content,* developed by CSNET Executive Committee 1986.

[3] Code of conduct for EARN users, established by EARN Board of Directors, Geneva, 1986.

[4] DSV, *Konferenssystem för studerande vid SU/DSV, Information till studerande (Eng: Conference system for students at SU/DSV, information to students)* 1993.

[5] Eklund, Anne-Marie, *God ton och etikett i datorbaserade kommunikationssystem (Eng. Good form and etiquette in computer-mediated communication systems),* Department of Computer and Systems Sciences, Stockholm University, IDAK promemoria no. 47.

[6] Godin, Seth, *The Smiley Dictionary*, Berkeley, CA: Peachpit Press, 1993.

[7] Sanderson, David W. *Smileys*, Sebestopol, CA: O'Reilly and Associates, 1993

[8] Rospach, Chuq Von, *A Primer on how to work with the USENET community*, available from URL ftp://relay.cs.toronto.edu/pub/usenet/news.answers/usenet-primer, 1993.

[9] Palme, Jacob: *Legal and Ethical Aspects of Computer-Mediated Communication,* The Arachnet Electronic Journal on Virtual Culture, ISSN 1068-5723, June 30, 1993, Volume 1, Issue 4. Available on the Internet as ftp://byrd.mu.wnet.edu/pub/ejvc/PALME.V1N4.

Chapter 11

Research about Electronic Mail

The object of research about electronic mail is be to increase the functionality of electronic messaging systems, to develop standards, to make the systems more efficient, to understand better the processes involved in electronic mail, to evaluate cost/benefit aspects, to understand and regulate its legal aspects, and to adjust electronic mail usage to social norms.

Many different kinds of research on electronic mail have been done in different countries. One kind is behavioral science research, which looks at how people and organizations work and are influenced by electronic mail. Some results from such research is presented in Chapters 2 through 5.

Well-known researchers in this area are Roxanne Hiltz at the New Jersey Institute of Technology [1-6], Sara Kiesler at Carnegie-Mellon University [7, 8], Lillemor Adrianson [9], and Hans Köhler [10].

There is an interesting difference in the direction taken of this research in different countries. In the United States, the research seems to focus on criteria for success and how organizations are influenced by the introduction of electronic mail [5, 11]. In some European countries, the research is directed more towards finding out if the new technology has a good or bad effect on work environments [9]. The American research is thus directed more towards positive aspects (How to succeed?) and not towards negative aspects (Should we try to succeed?).

Some research on the communication process is related to linguistics. Such research studies the language used in electronic mail, the forms of interaction, how people plan and organize their communication, and which goals they have for their communication.

There is also some legal and behavioral science research into norms, control and accountability in electronic mail (see Chapter 10).

Another kind of research is more technical in nature. This is research about how to construct and build electronic mail systems. In such research, the definition and construction of electronic mail systems is often part of the research. This research is often similar to standards work in these areas. The research provides a basis for standards or is used to test standards and find out how to implement them. There is no sharp border between this kind of research and the behavioral science research, since behavioral science methods are often used to establish and evaluate user requirements and experiences.

Some different areas of research on the construction of electronic mail systems are:

- Clarifying the functionality needed as a basis for standards work.
- Testing standards to see if and how they can best be implemented.
- Developing techniques for distributed protocols and data bases needed in applications, for example, directory systems.
- Developing security techniques (see Section 6.13).
- Developing techniques for multimedia, that is, messages that contain a combination of text, picture, animation (moving pictures), and sound.
- Group communication and group processes. For example the European AMIGO-project [12, 13, 14]. An overview of the data model in several European projects in this area is given in [15].
- The use of electronic mail systems as a tool for long-distance education. For example, The Open University in the United Kingdom [16, 17] and the New Jersey Institute of Technology [6, 26].
- Using electronic mail systems as an aid to handicapped people as done by Magnus Magnusson and Margita Lundman at Handikappinstitutet in Stockholm.
- Hypertext, which is a research area closely related to electronic mail. Hypertexts are texts that you do not read linearly. Hypertext [18] may be written by one person, but it may also consist of electronic documents written by different people, which relate to each other, like comments, reviews, etc., and form hypertext structures. Such structures, created by the independent actions of many people, are expected to form a future electronic marketplace [19, 20]
- Computer-supported cooperative work. Researchers in this area try to develop computerized aids for different human cooperative work processes: discussions, joint text development, voting, task distribution and control, etc. Some of this research is directed towards support for simultaneous group processes, such as face-to-face meetings or audio and video conferencing. But many researchers also recognize the need for nonsimultaneous group processes and the need for a "group memory" [21]. Systems could be seen as split into three or four categories as shown in Figure 2.3.

The research in this area often uses very expensive equipment, like special meeting rooms with special built-in support tools. Large display screens visible to all participants are common in this area.

Special areas of human cooperation which this kind of research tries to investigate are electronic brainstorming, the generation of ideas, the formulation of alternative choices, the forming of policy decisions, etc.

Software for group support is today often called "groupware" [22]. Another often-used term is "computer mediated communications" [23, see especially Chapters 6 and 8]. Overviews of this area are given in [24, 25].

Part of the research in this area tries to develop languages for the description of group processes. The idea is that such languages might be used to program a computer to support human cooperative processes. There is an obvious risk that such methods might seriously restrict human activities, because, in real life, important human activities often involve handling of exceptions and special cases and computer systems which try to emulate human activities have difficulties in doing so. An examples of such a project is the AMIGO Advanced group [14]. This research is close to other research in the office automation area.

Researchers in electronic mail and related topics meet regularly at two recurring international conferences. One is the conference on Application Layer Protocols arranged by IFIP WG 6.5. The other is the conference on Computer-Supported Cooperative Work, sponsored by the Association for Computing Machinery, Special Interest Group on Computer-Human Interaction (SIGCHI) and Special Interest Group on Office Information Systems (SIGOIS).

REFERENCES

[1] Hiltz, Starr Roxanne and Turoff, Murray, *The Network Nation*, Reading, MA, Addison-Wesley, 1978, reprinted by MIT Press in 1993.

[2] Hiltz, S.R. et al.,. *Face-to-face vs. computerized conferencing: A controlled experiment*, New Jersey Institute of Technology, Newark, Research Report No. 12, 1980.

[3] Hiltz, S.R. and Kerr, E., *Studies on computer-mediated communication systems: A synthesis of the findings*, New Jersey Institute of Technology, Newark, Research Report No. 16, 1981.

[4] Hiltz, S.R. et al., *The effects of formal leadership and computer-generated decision aids on problem solving via computer: A controlled experiment*, New Jersey Institute of Technology, Newark, Research Report No. 18, 1982.

[5] Ritter (ed), "Computer-Mediated Communication Systems: dropouts versus users," In *Information Processing 89*, Amsterdam, Elsevier Science Publishers, 1989.

[6] Hiltz, S.R., *Collaborative Learning: The Virtual Classroom Approach*, T.H.E (Technological Horizons in Education) Journal, Volume 17, No. 10, June 1990, pp. 59-65.

[7] Kiesler, Sara et al., "Social psychological aspects of computer-mediated communication," *American Psychologist*, 39, 1984, 1123-1134.

[8] Sproull, Lee and Kiesler, Sara, *Connections—New Ways of Working in the Networked Organization*, Cambridge, MA: MIT Press, 1991.

[9] Adrianson, Lillemor, *Psychological studies of attitudes to and use of computer-mediated communication*, Göteborg Psychological Reports, University of Göteborg, Sweden, 1987.

[10] Köhler, Hans, *Inflytande och datorbaserade kommunikationssystem (eng.: Influence and computer-based communication systems)*, Teldok report 27, April 1987, Stockholm, Sweden: Televerket, 1987.

[11] Hiltz, Starr Roxanne and Turoff, Murray, "Computer networking among executives: A case study," (in *Proceedings of the Twenty-Fourth Annual Hawaii International Conference on System Sciences*, IEEE 1991.

[12] Speth, Rolf, *Research into Networks and Distributed Applications*, Amsterdam: North-Holland, 1988.

[13] Smith, Hugh (ed.), *Distributed Group Communication: The AMIGO Information Model*, *The AMIGO MHS+ Group*, West Sussex, UK: Ellis Horwood Limited, 1989.

[14] Pankoke-Babatz, Uta, *Computer-based Group Communication: The AMIGO Activity Model*, West Sussex, UK: Ellis Horwood Limited, 1989

[15] Hennessy, Pippa et al., *Modeling group communication structures, analyzing four European projects*, University of Nottingham, 1989.

[16] Mason, Robin and Kaye, Anthony, *Mindweave: Communication, Computers, and Distance Education*, New York: Pergamon Press 1990.

[17] Kaye, A., *Collaborative Learning through Computer Conferencing: The Najaden papers*. Heidelberg, Springer-Verlag, 1992.

[18] Rada, Roy, *Hypertext—From Text to Expertext*, London: McGraw-Hill Books, 1991.

[19] Turoff, Murray and Chinai, Sanjit, *An Electronic Information Marketplace*, Computer Systems and ISDN Systems 9 79-90, 1985.

[20] Malone, Thomas W. et al., "Electronic markets and electronic hierarchies," *Communications of the ACM*, June 1987.

[21] Turoff, M., "The anatomy of a computer application innovation: Computer mediated communications (CMC)," in *Technological Forecasting and Social Change* 36, 1989, pp 107-122.

[22] Johansen, Robert, *Groupware: Computer Support for Business Teams*, New York: The Free Press, 1988.

[23] Rapaport, Matthew, *Computer Mediated Communications*, New York: John Wiley & Sons, 1991.

[24] Wilson, Paul, *Key Research in computer supported cooperative work*, in [12].

[25] Ellis, C.A. et al., "Groupware: Some issues and experiences," *Communications of the ACM*, January 1991.

[26] Hiltz, Starr Roxanne, *The Virtual Classroom: Learning Without Limits Via Computer Networks*, Norwood, NJ: Ablex Publishing, 1995.

Chapter 12

User Interface Examples

This chapter contains some examples from the user interfaces of well-known e-mail software. There are thousands of different e-mail programs available, and my selection does not indicate in any way that these programs are better than other programs that were not included. The intention of this book to give an overview of all the different e-mail programs available and discuss their pros and cons. One aim of this chapter is to give you some ideas of how different user interfaces can be designed, so you have an idea of what to look for.

12.1 EXAMPLES FROM THE USER INTERFACE OF PINE

Pine is an e-mail system developed at the University of Washington, and used mainly for Internet mail. Its first version used a VT100-based user interface. This means that the interface uses only facilities available on VT100 terminals. A user can thus install a VT100 emulator on his personal computer (the public domain software Kermit includes a good VT100 emulator) and then connect to a Pine host and run Pine. A disadvantage of the VT100 interface is that full screen graphics and use of the mouse are not possible. Pine was specially designed to be easy for nonexperts to use. There is also a PC version of Pine, but what is shown here is the VT100 version.

When you enter Pine, you first go to a main window with a menu, from which you can get to various subwindows. For example, the subwindow for viewing incoming mail is shown in Figure 12.1.

```
 PINE 3.89   FOLDER INDEX              Folder: INBOX  Message 20 of 20 NEW

+ D 1    Jul  6 Inge Wallin         (4,040) Re: Reference group distance education
+ D 3    Jul  7 Mail Delivery Subs  (2,721) Returned mail: User unknown
  D 4    Jul  7 To: intfilter-proj  (4,914) Stanford news filtering system
+ A 5    Jul  7 roshandel@fokus.gm  (1,890) Re:SuperKOM access
+   6    Jul  7 Ulf Bilting         (1,048) Re: Internet-kurs (fwd)
+ N 7    Jul  6 Ingemar Joelsson    (1,514) Re: Reference group distance education
+ N 8    Jul  7 Julie Lancashire    (1,887) Contract
+ N 9    Jul  8 evaj@dsv.su.se        (850) Miscellaneous
+ N 10   Jul  7 Harald.T.Alvestran  (1,266) Re: Addressing X.400 from UNIX
+ A 2    Jul  8 Ulf Bilting         (1,173) Internet course
+ A 4    Jul  8 evaj@dsv.su.se      (1,124) Internet
+   5    Jul  8 Johan T Lindgren    (1,049) Re: Internet course
+ N 11   Jul  8 blum@igd.fhg.de     (1,164) Re: Question on OSI versus Internet i
+ N 12   Jul  8 Bertil Jansson Hog  (1,305) Internal courses
+ N 15   Jul  8 Lars Enderin Dialo  (1,125) Re: Duplicates to Nordpost
+ N 16   Jul  8 jussi@sics.se         (998) Re: Your Internet course
+ N 17   Jul  8 louise@dsv.su.se    (7,839) TC11 Swedish program
+ N 18   Jul  8 louise@dsv.su.se    (1,947) Re: The conference in may
  N 19   Jul  8 Tony Rutkowski      (2,144) Society Trustees - Election Results
+ N 21   Jul  8 tomaso@sics.se      (1,012) Re: Kommer Internets e-post-standarde

? Help         M Main Menu  P PrevMsg    - PrevPage    D Delete      R Reply
O OTHER CMDS  V [ViewMsg]  N NextMsg   Spc NextPage   U Undelete    F Forward
```

Figure 12.1   Pine window for viewing a list of incoming messages.

For each message in the inbox, there is one line with the date, sender, and first characters of the subject of the message. The two bottom lines on the screen always contain a summary of the most useful commands in the present window.

When a user first enters this window and there are only new messages, all the messages are marked with an "N" at the beginning of the line, as in the last four messages in Figure 12.1. As a user reads mail, he can choose to save the mail in folders, keep it in the inbox, or delete it. A "D" appearing first in the line indicates that a message has been marked for deletion, and that it will be deleted when the user exits Pine. An "A" appearing first in the line indicates that the user has written an answer to this message.

The messages you write yourself in Pine are automatically saved in a folder called "sent-mail" unless you explicitly choose to save them in some other folder.

Pine does not automatically purge old messages: all messages must be deleted explicitly by the user. This can be made simpler by deletion of a whole folder with one command. Pine also has a built-in aid to remind you to delete the old folder "sent-mail" once a month.

One useful feature of Pine is the address book. This is a personal list of the e-mail addresses of people to whom you frequently send mail. Figure 12.2 shows a window when looking at the address book in Pine.

```
PINE 3.89    ADDRESS BOOK              Folder: INBOX  Message 11 of 11

jaimed          Delgado, Jaime                     delgado@ac.upc.es
kerstine        Eklundh, Kerstin S.               kse@nada.kth.se
tommye          Ericson, Tommy                     M40@kom.komunity.se
pere            Eriksson, Per                      PERIXON@dsv.su.se
lfg             Forsberg, Lennart Umdac           lfg@biovax.umdc.umu.se
foutb           Forskarutbildningskommitten       foutb@dsv.su.se
awg             Gillner, Anders                    awg@sunet.se
gopher          gopher                             gopher@dsv.su.se
andrewg         Gordon, Andrew                     GORDON@NET-TEL.INTERSPAN
thomasg         Grundberg, Thomas                  THOMAS_GRUNDBERG@macexcha
roxanneh        Hiltz, Roxanne                     roxanne@eies2.njit.edu
jeroenh         Houttuin, Jeroen                   houttuin@rare.nl
erikh           Huizer, Eric                       Erik.Huizer@SURFnet.nl
mime            IETF-822 (MIME discussion list)   ietf-822@dimacs.rutgers.
itk             Informationsteknologikommissionen itk@utb.gov.se
intfilter       intfilter-projektet                intfilter@sics.se
isomess         ISO messaging                      iso-messaging-group@gec-
WG4             ISO/IEC JTC 1/SC 18/WG 4 secretaria nhirose@attmail.com
calle           Jansson, Carl Gustav               calle@dsv.su.se
rwj             Jesmajian, Richard                 rwj@ARCH2.ATT.com


? Help      M MainMenu   P PrevField   - PrevPage   D Delete     S CreateList
O OTHER CMDS E [Edit]    N NextField Spc NextPage   A Add        Z AddToList
```

Figure 12.2   Window showing the Pine address book.

There are three fields for each name in the address book. To the left is an abbreviation of the name which you can choose yourself so it will be easy to remember. You only have to indicate this name when you send a message to the person. The middle field shows the full name of the person. The right field shows the e-mail address.

When a Pine user gets a message, the user can transfer the e-mail address of the incoming message to the address book with one command. Entries in the address book are fully controlled by the user: nothing is added, changed, or removed except by user commands.

12.2 EXAMPLES FROM THE USER INTERFACE OF SUPERKOM

The user interface of SuperKOM is a VT100-interface, just like Pine. While most conventional message systems first give you a list of unread messages, most conference systems, like SuperKOM, gives you instead a list of conferences with unread contributions and tell you how many unread messages you have in these conferences, as shown in Figure 12.3. You can then proceed to read the conferences in your personally preferred order.

```
 Environment  Write  Read  Search  Organize  News  Conferences Help
Command ===> █Read next conference
   Unseen  Name (number)
       1   Macintosh announce (45010)
       8   ISO Protocols (43334)
       5   Use of the English language (43328)
      11   Macintosh user group (43330)
       5   Politics of Eastern Europe (43788)
       2   Poems (43398)

   You have 32 unseen entries
   You have 3 unseen letters




Text:                                          Line 1-10 of 10
Conference:                                    Connected
F1=Help F3=Quit F4=Print F5=Mark F6=Review F7/F8=Up/Down F9=Write F10=Join F11=News
```

Figure 12.3   List of news when entering SuperKOM.

It is also possible to get a list of personal mail, but this list will be shorter than in other mail systems, since it will not include group (conference) messages. In each conference, you can get a list of the messages in that particular conference.

Commands to SuperKOM can either be typed on the keyboard (in full or abbreviated form) or selected from a pull-down menu. Figure 12.4 shows an example of how to give a command to reply to a message.

```
 Environment  Write  Read  Search  Organize  News  Conferences  Help
Command ===>┌─────────────────────────┐
(107.537) Tu│write letter...          │  Palme QZ
Recipient: S│write own entry          │
Subject: Sup│message to letter-writers│
The Screen i│█comment on entry        │nix or MS-DOS/PC-DOES. This example
shows the in│personal reply           │ PC without graphics. SuperKOM will
then use the├─────────────────────────┤n the character sets of IBM PC and
VT100 termin│change entry             │s and windows. The advantage with this
is that the │change distribution...   │be used with most different kinds of
screens and │enter...                 │
            │cancel                   │
If we had 'ch│continue writing         │pabilities of some IBM PC-s, this would
have given a├─────────────────────────┤he program would then not be executable
on all PC-co│F3=Cancel                │ens.
            └─────────────────────────┘
We hope however, later to be able to develop a user interface using the
graphical capabilities of IBM and Macintosh.

Note that the same SuperKOM-code (with small changes) is used in Unix and on
PC-s. Also, the same code is used, whether the user process is executed in a
Text: (107537) SuperKOM screen interface        Line 1-19 of 34
Conference: SuperKOM experience                 Connected
F1=Help F3=Quit F4=Print F5=Mark F6=Review F7/F8=Up/Down F9=Write F10=Join F11=News
```

Figure 12.4   Giving commands to SuperKOM.

200

Figure 12.5 gives an example of how a SuperKOM entry looks like when you read:

```
(103.576) Tue, 12 Jan 1992 13:05 Paul Persson
Recipient: Nils Nielsen -- Received:  Fri, 24 Jul 1992 15:02
Copy Recipient: Marylin Stewart
Recipient: Management group
Recipient: Marketing group
Subject: The meetings tomorrow
I cannot come to our meetings tomorrow.
I have to be at home with a sick child.
(103.576)
```

Figure 12.5   Delivery information when looking at a message in SuperKOM.

Note that in this case the same entry had been sent as a personal message to two recipients, and as a conference entry into two conferences. If, after reading the entry above, you give the command "comment on entry," then you will start writing a comment which will be sent to everyone who read the commented entry, that is, all the recipients, both personal and members of the conferences, as listed in the message heading above. SuperKOM automatically produces receipt notifications for personal recipients, as is shown for Nils Nielsen in Figure 12.5.

The handling of addition and deletion of messages from the SuperKOM data base is very different from that of Pine. In Pine (like in and most other conventional e-mail systems) messages are kept until they are explicitly deleted by the user. In SuperKOM, messages are instead automatically purged after a certain time, unless the user has marked them as messages which should not be deleted. SuperKOM has both a personal data base for each user and a common data base for all users connected to the same server. Users of SuperKOM can use search keys on messages in the central data base. Such keys are one way of stopping messages from being purged. It is also possible to search for messages with certain keywords or combinations of keywords. This means that SuperKOM is both a mail system and an information-retrieval system at the same time. By giving keywords to a message, the user will logically enter this message into the information-retrieval system and at the same time protect the message from being purged. It is also possible to protect messages from being purged in the personal data base of an individual SuperKOM user.

Recipients can be added and subtracted from KOM entries when they are written and at a later date. When you are adding a recipient, you can type in the name of the recipient in an abbreviated form; KOM will look it up in the directory; if the abbreviation is ambiguous, KOM will list the alternatives and let you indicate which of the names to use.

The SuperKOM server data base is replicated between servers in much the same way as the Usenet News data base. Search keywords are also automatically replicated. The names of all senders of messages in SuperKOM are entered into the server directory, so that users can also search for external names in this directory.

201

A difference between the methods for replication in SuperKOM, First Class, and Lotus Notes is that, in SuperKOM, replication will be performed automatically to all servers where any user subscribes to a conference, while in Lotus Notes and First Class, replication only occurs when requested by the manager of the conference.

Figure 12.6 shows the subwindow for the "find" command used to search in the server directory of SuperKOM. Figure 12.7 gives an example of the search results. Note that the search found one conference which had neither "MSDOS" nor "MS-DOS" in their name. This is because this conference had one of these words added as a search keyword in the directory.

```
                               Find

Search key: MSDOS+MS-DOS

Find    (X) Conferences   ( ) People   ( ) Texts

Search in directory volumes for (X) Local names   ( ) External names

ENTER/RETURN=Search   F1=Help   F3=Cancel
```

Figure 12.6   Window for the *find* command in SuperKOM.

```
MSDOS Internals (435.345)
MS-DOS versus DR-DOS (343.212)
IBM PC and compatibles users group (561.349)
```

Figure 12.7   Search result example in SuperKOM.

12.3 EXAMPLES FROM THE LINE-ORIENTED USER INTERFACE OF EAN/ENVOY 400

EAN is an e-mail system developed in the early 1980s at the University of British Columbia in Vancouver. It is an example of a mail program which originally had a line-oriented user interface. That is the interface shown in this chapter. These kinds of interfaces are today considered old-fashioned, but they were common during the 1980s and there are still some people who prefer them. One group of people who prefer line-oriented user interfaces are the blind. A good mail system should have a line-oriented user interface in addition to fancy graphic interfaces.

EAN is a rather strict implementation of the X.400 standard. EAN has separate UA and MTA functions. The first thing that happens when you start EAN is that your UA software will start downloading messages from its MTA:

After that, as in most other systems, you get a printout of new messages in your mailbox (see Figure 12.8). Note the different format for giving the sender in different lines. The reason for this is that X.400 has two name fields, one containing the formal OR-address, and the other, called free-form-name, which gives the name in a more user-friendly form. When the free-form-name is available, EAN will show that. If it is not known, EAN will show the OR-address.

```
87  NU    Bernd Wagner              30 15:22 late AMIGO piloting
88  NU    "North American MHSNEWS   30 15:22 how does one get an x400 imp
89  NU    BCQ@SEARN.BITNET          30 15:22 ISO-work on group communicat
90  NU    BCQ@SEARN.BITNET          30 15:22 Thanks, Hugh, Julian and Ste
91  NU    Siri Jensen               30 15:22 Stoff om 'filing og retrieva
92  NU    BCQ@SEARN.BITNET          30 15:22 Conference = set with the sa
93  NU    Manel Medina              30 15:22 subject=conference?
94  NU    Steve Benford             30 15:22 Re:  subject=conference?
```

Figure 12.8   List of new messages from EAN.

If you ask EAN to show you a message, messages are shown according to the X.400 standard (see Figure 12.9). (The second column gives the status of the message, "NU" means "New Unread.") There is, for example, a delivery-date a send-date, and information on whether the message has been auto-forwarded. The message in the example has passed a P2-based distribution list, which is the reason why the *originator*[2]) and author (*from, authorizing users*[3]) are different.

```
> 94
Message inbox:94 -   Unread
Delivery-date: Fri, 30 Dec 1988 15:22:34 UTC+0100
Originator:    listmaster@xps.gmd.dbp.de
Send-date:     Fri,  2 Dec 1988 15:17:51 UTC+0100
From:          Steve Benford <sdb@computer-science.nottingham.ac.uk>
To:            <amigo_group@xps.gmd.dbp.de>
Message-ID:    573*sdb@computer-science.nottingham.ac.uk
Auto-forward:  true
Subject:       Re:  subject=conference?
...  ...  ...
```

Figure 12.9   Display of a message from EAN.

---

1   The computer types a period for each downloaded message to tell you that it is working.

2   This is the P1 originator. According to X.400, the P1 originator shall show the name of the UA which delivered the message to the MTS.

3   According to X.400 *Authorizing Users* can be used to give the name of a person who wrote or approved sending of a message; this field need not contain a full, correct OR-address.

Even though EAN is an X.400 implementation, the layout of messages, as shown in Figure 12.9, is much influenced by the Internet RFC 822 standard (compare this to the RFC 822 example in Section 8.6.4 above), even though EAN internally stores messages in the X.400 formats.

The figures "94" at the top of Figure 12.9, is a user command, asking to see message no. 94. This facility of letting just a number, as a command, ask for display of the message with that number, is common to many e-mail systems.

Figure 12.10 shows an example of how you write a reply in EAN The command "confirm" given by the user Figure 12.11, is a way to indicate that you want to get a delivery notification on this message. Other commands you can give at this stage are *high, normal,* and *low* to indicate priority and *personal, private,* and *confidential* to indicate secrecy level, all according to X.400.

```
> reply
To:          "Jacob Palme QZ" <JPALME@DSV.SU.SE>
In-Reply-To: <378737@QZCOM>
Subject:     Conference = set with the same subject?

... ... ...
.
Send options? confirm
```

Figure 12.10   Writing a reply with EAN.

Figure 12.11 shows an example of sending a message, which is not a reply, with EAN. No immediate checking is done to determine if the recipient really exists; if you have misspelled the recipient name you will be told this in a separate nondelivery notification at a later time. Note the single period which appears first in the next to last line in Figure 12.11. Such a single period is common in line-oriented user interfaces for e-mail systems and is the command to stop writing and send the message.

```
> compose
To: bilting@chalmers.se
Subject: Test message

... ... ...
.
Send options? personal low
```

Figure 12.11   Sending a message with EAN.

Figure 12.12 shows how this message looks like after entering. Note the fields *Importance* and *Sensitivity.*

204

```
> 96
Message inbox:96 -  Sent
Send-date: Fri, 30 Dec 1988 15:32:01 UTC+0100
From:       Sven Svensson <svens@qz.sunet>
To:         <bilting@chalmers.se>
Importance: low
Sensitivity: personal
Message-ID: 108*jacob@qz.sunet
Subject:    Test message

... ... ...
```

Figure 12.12   A message with importance and sensitivity according to the X.400 standard.

12.4 EXAMPLES FROM THE USER INTERFACE OF MEMO

MEMO was originally developed with a 3270 user interface. Such a user interfaces can be used from terminals which have a 3270 terminal emulator. This emulator is common, especially with IBM MVS mainframe computers.

Sections 12.4.1 and 12.4.2 will show excerpts from the MEMO user interface for a 3270 user, and, as a contrast, the MS Windows MEMO client.

12.4.1   MEMO 3270 Interface

As is common in MVS applications, Memo uses the word "menu" to mean what is usually called "window" outside the MVS area.

When you start Memo, you will first get into the mailbox menu. Figure 12.13 shows an example of that menu with the MEMO 3270 user interface.

```
Memo                        Mailbox - SMITH              93-10-08 14.08
Command =>
Select entry and specify    S - Select      D - Delete      R - Recall
action under A              C - Copy        E - Expand      P - Print

A   Memo title      File TY    Status       Memoid    Date    Time Note (   4 memos)
- --------------- ---- --  ------------- -------- -------- ----- ---------------
R New letter       ____      Received from TAYLOR  93-10-07 17.07 <-- top line
E New Statistics   ____      Received/read FRAWLEY  93-10-07 08.09
D Staff Meeting    ____      Received/read MARINO   93-10-07 10.29
_ United Grocers   ____  DL  Received/read MARINO   93-10-07 10.28 <-- bottom line

--------------------------------------------------------------------------------
F1=Help F2=Directory F3=Exit F5=New memo F7=Bkwd F8=Fwd F9=Commands F10=Actions
F11=Keys F12=Close F13=Top F14=Bottom F23=Standby
```

Figure 12.13   the Mailbox "menu" in the 3270 MEMO user interface

This window is the central hub of Memo. It shows a list of all the letters for the user, both sent and received letters. The letters are kept in this list until you explicitly delete them. Note that the identities of the recipients are given with eight character codes called "MEMOID." When you send a message, you have to know the MEMOID of the recipient. You can look up the MEMOIDs in the directory system.

As is seen in Figure 12.13, Memo produces automatic delivery notifications on all messages: you do not have to ask for them.

When you are looking at the screen in the figure, you can indicate with a character first in each line what you want to do with the message. In the example above, the letter "New letter" is marked with the character "R," which indicates that the user wants to fetch and read this letter. The letter "New statistics" is marked with the character "E" which is a request for full information about this letter, that is, which of the recipients have received it, etc. The message "Staff Meeting" is marked with the character "D" which means that it is to be deleted from the user mailbox.

When a user has an IBM 3270 type terminal, he can fill in these characters locally on the screen, without contact with the central computer. First, when all the lines have been entered, the user pushes the SEND key to get the computer to act on the requests. This reduces the time during which the user has to wait for a reply from the central computer. This user interface design is common on large computers of the IBM type.

12.4.2 Windows MEMO Version User Interface

Figure 12.14 shows an example of the user interface of MEMO with the MS Windows client. Note that user names are shown as Memo-IDs, compare this to the way user names are shown in the First Class user interface described in Section 12.5.

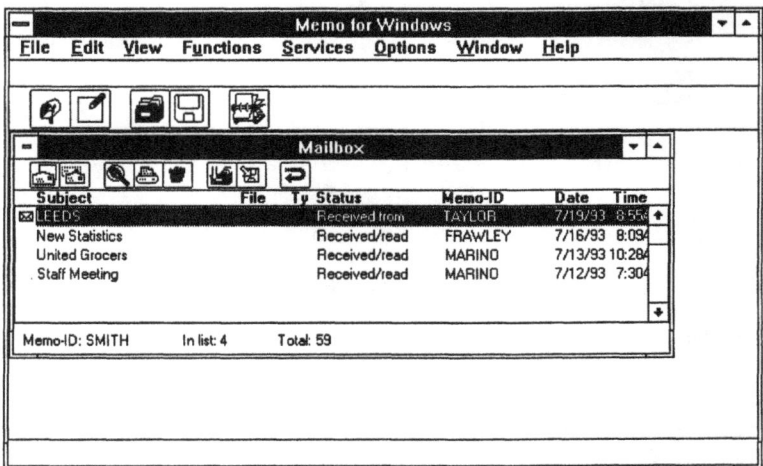

Figure 12.14   The mailbox menu with the MS Windows Memo user interface.

A problem in the design of user interfaces for electronic mail systems is the need for many windows: windows with lists of messages, windows showing messages, special windows for directory searches, etc. The Windows version of MEMO lets the user choose between cascaded (see Figure 12.15) and tiled windows (see Figure 12.16).

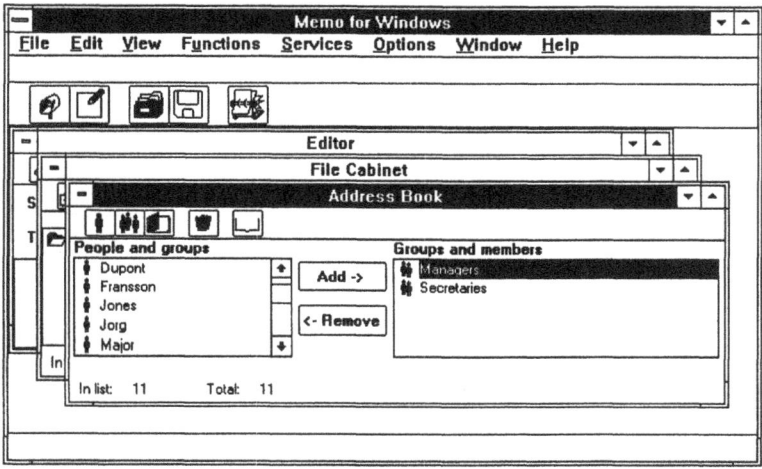

Figure 12.15   Using cascaded windows with Memo.

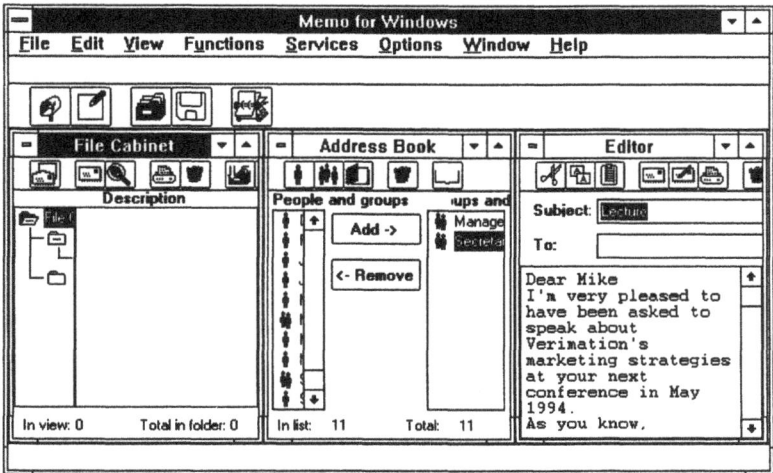

Figure 12.16   Using tiled windows with Memo.

12.5 EXAMPLES FROM THE USER INTERFACE OF FIRST CLASS

First Class is a popular e-mail and computer conferencing system which was initially developed for Macintosh computers but now can be used by Windows clients as well. The examples here are from the Macintosh First Class user interface.

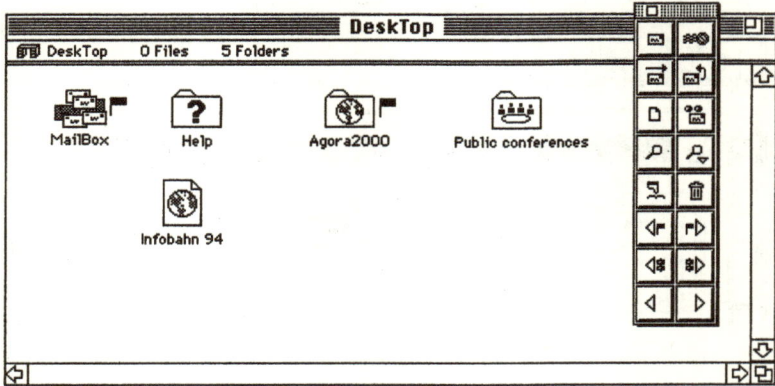

Figure 12.17   The DeskTop window with the Macintosh First Class client.

Figure 12.17 shows the screen when you first enter First Class. It is so similar to the ordinary Finder interface in the Macintosh file system that a user may not easily tell the difference. The MailBox icon opens the area for reading and writing personally addressed mail, the other icons opens groups of computer conferences. The flag beside some of the icons indicates that there are new items which the user has not yet read. Just like in the Macintosh Finder, a user can choose to see these windows as icons or as a list of items according to personal preference. The flag beside "MailBox" in Figure 12.17 thus says that the user has unread mail, and the flag beside Agora2000 says that the user has unread conference presentations of conferences in that subgroup.

The flag does not indicate that the user has unread new items in conferences within that conference subgroup. To see this, you have to open the Agora2000 subwindow. In my opinion, this is a mistake in the design of the First Class user interface. During the design of the SuperKOM system, the same problem was encountered, and was solved by allowing the listing of conferences with new items in them to be a linear list, not a structure of folders and subfolders. The advantage of a linear list is that the user can reorder the items according to personal preference, and that all conferences with new items are shown in the list without any need to open subwindows.

The floating palette in Figure 12.17 gives fast access to a number of common commands, like "show me the next message I have not yet read," and so forth.

If you double-click on one of the icons, a similar window is opened with a list of the conferences in that conference group, and if you click on a conference, you get a list of the messages in that conference in reverse order, so that you see the latest messages first (see Figure 12.18).

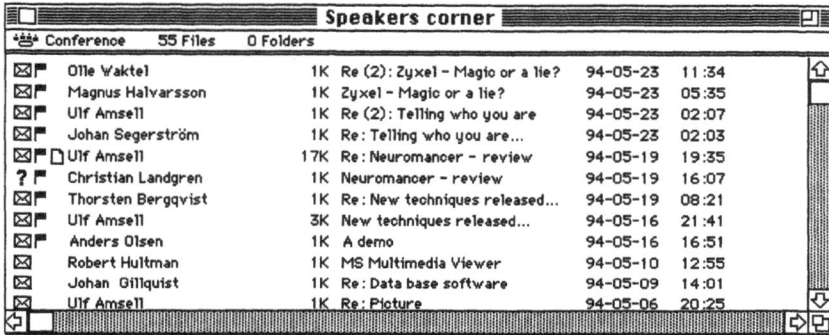

⊠⌐	Olle Waktel	1K	Re (2): Zyxel – Magic or a lie?	94-05-23 11:34
⊠⌐	Magnus Halvarsson	1K	Zyxel – Magic or a lie?	94-05-23 05:35
⊠⌐	Ulf Amsell	1K	Re (2): Telling who you are	94-05-23 02:07
⊠⌐	Johan Segerström	1K	Re : Telling who you are...	94-05-23 02:03
⊠⌐◻	Ulf Amsell	17K	Re : Neuromancer – review	94-05-19 19:35
?⌐	Christian Landgren	1K	Neuromancer – review	94-05-19 16:07
⊠⌐	Thorsten Bergqvist	1K	Re : New techniques released...	94-05-19 08:21
⊠⌐	Ulf Amsell	3K	New techniques released...	94-05-16 21:41
⊠⌐	Anders Olsen	1K	A demo	94-05-16 16:51
⊠	Robert Hultman	1K	MS Multimedia Viewer	94-05-10 12:55
⊠	Johan Gillquist	1K	Re : Data base software	94-05-09 14:01
⊠	Ulf Amsell	1K	Re : Picture	94-05-06 20:25

Figure 12.18   List of conference entries from First Class.

The flag beside some of the messages again marks those you have not yet read. Note that some messages can have a special type, the question mark indicates the special type "Request for information." The document symbol shows that this message contains an attachment. First Class also allows different fonts in the text of messages and embedded pictures. There is an interface to Internet mail and to Usenet News. A problem with such an interface is that special features, like message types, may get lost unless the standard you are interfacing with supports the same special features. This problem can be avoided if a system is designed from the beginning to be compatible with and provide features of a messaging standard like Internet mail (with MIME) or X.400. Neither Memo or First Class were designed this way.

209

Appendix A

Postal Addresses of E-Mail Organizations

Here are some postal addresses of organizations in the e-mail area. (Thanks to Markus Kuhn for most of this information.)

European Electronic Mail Association (EEMA)

> EEMA Executive Office
> Pastoral House
> Inkberrow
> Worcester WR7 4EL, United Kingdom
>
> Phone: +44 386 793 028
> Fax. +44 386 793 268
> Internet e-mail: eemaoffice@attmail.com
> X.400: C=gb; G=executive;S=office;O=eema; A=attmail;C=gb

U.S. Electronic Mail Association (EMA)

> Electronic Mail Association
> 1655 North Fort Myer Drive Suite 850
> Arlington, VA 22209, USA
>
> Phone: +1 703 524 5550
> Fax: +1 703 524 5558
> X.400: G=ema;S=ema;A=attmail;C=us

International Telecommunications Union (ITU, CCITT)

> International Telecommunications Union
> Place Des Nations
> CH-1211 Geneva 20, Switzerland

Japan Electronic Mail Association (JEMA)

> Japan Electronic Mail Association (JEMA)
> Nisso-bld, 5F
> 1-11-10 Azabudai Minato-ku
> Tokyo, 106 Japan
>
> Phone: +81 3-3583-5811
> Fax: +81 3-3583-5813
> X.400: C=jp; A=ati; O=jema; S=jema; G=office

Internet information

> InterNIC Information Services
> General Atomics (GA)
> P.O. Box #85608
> San Diego, CA 92186-9784, USA
>
> Hotline: +1 800 444 4345
> Internet e-mail: info@is.internic.net
> Phone: +1 619 455 4600
> Fax: +1 619 455 4640

BITNET

> BITNET Network Information Center;
> EDUCOM
> 1112 Sixteenth St., NW, Suite 600
> Washington, DC 20036, USA
>
> Phone: +1 202 872 4200

EUNET

EUnet European Office Address
c/o NIKHEF
Postbus 41882
1009 DB Amsterdam, Netherlands

Phone: +31 20 592-5109
Fax: +31 20 592-5155
Fax problems: 592-9444

HEPnet

CNAF, Istituto Nazionale Fisica Nucleare
(INFN)
viale Ercolani 8
I-40138 Bologna, Italy

Internet e-mail: Mailing@infn.it
X.400: C=it;ADMD=garr;
PRMD=infn;OU=infngw;S=Mailing
Phones: +39 51 498267 / +39 51 498211 / +39 51 498260 / +39 51 498286
Fax: +39 51 498135

IP networks

CIX
3110 Fairview Park Drive, Suite 590
Falls Church, VA 22042 USA

Phone: +1 303 482 2150
Fax: +1 303 482 2884
Internet e-mail: info@cix.org

Ebone

Ebone Secretariat
c/o RARE Secretariat
Singel 466-468
NL - 1017 AW Amsterdam, Netherlands

Phone: +31 20 639 1131
Fax: +31 20 639 3289
Internet e-mail: raresec@rare.nl
X.400: C=nl;ADMD=400net;
PRMD=surf;O=rare;S=raresec

ISO

International Standards Organization
Case Postale 56
CH-1211 Geneva 20, Switzerland

ISOC

Internet Society
1895 Preston White Drive, Suite 100
Reston, VA 22091 USA

Phone: +1 703 648 9888
Fax: +1 703 620 0913
Internet e-mail: isoc@isoc.org

CNRI (Corporation for National Research Initiatives)

Same postal address as ISOC

Phone: +1-703 620 8990
Internet e-mail: info@cnri.reston.va.us
IETF - CIX
Internet e-mail: cxii@es.net
X.400: S=cxii;P=esnet;A= ;C=us

European Academic Research Networks (RARE)

RARE Secretariat
Singel 466-468
NL - 1017 AW Amsterdam, Netherlands

Phone: +31 20 639 1131
Fax: +31 20 639 3289
Internet e-mail: raresec@rare.nl
X.400: C=nl;ADMD=400net;
PRMD=surf;O=rare;S=raresec

Appendix B

Standards Documents

B.1 ISO AND ITU STANDARDS

Standards under development in ISO are called DPs or CDs (draft proposal or committee drafts). When they are almost ready as a standard, they are called DISs (draft international standards).

ITU number	ISO number	Title
		MHS standards Common for ISO and ITU
X.400	10021-1	MHS: System and service overview
X.402	10021-2	MHS: Overall architecture
X.407	10021-3	MHS: Abstract Service Definition Conventions
X.411	10021-4	MHS: Message Transfer Service (MTS)
X.413	10021-5	MHS: Message Store: Abstract Service Definition
X.419	10021-6	MHS: Message Store: Protocol Specifications
X.420	10021-7	MHS: Interpersonal Messaging System
	12062	International Standardized Profiles AMH2n—Message Handling Systems
		MHS standards Only Issued by ITU
X.435		MHS: EDI Messaging System (will probably also be issued by ISO)
X.440		MHS. Voice Messaging System
F.401		MHS: Naming and Addressing for Public Message Handling Services
F.410		MHS: The Public Message Transfer Service
F.415		MHS: Interconnection with Public Physical Delivery Services
F.420		MHS: The Public IPM Service
F.421		MHS: Intercommunication Between IPM Service and Telex

ITU number	ISO number	Title
F.422		MHS: Intercommunication Between IPM Service and Teletex
X.480		MHS and Directory Conformance Testing
X.481-X.485		PICS Proforma for X.400

MHS Standards Only Issued by ISO/IEC

	ISO number	Title
	12062	International Standardized Profiles—AMH2n—MHS—Interpersonal Messaging

Directory System Standards

ITU number	ISO number	Title
X.500	9594-1	The Directory—Overview of Concepts, Models and Services
X.501	9594-2	The Directory—Models
X.509	9594-8	The Directory—Authentication Framework
X.511	9594-3	The Directory—Abstract Service Definition
X.518	9594-4	The Directory—Procedures for Distributed Operation
X.519	9594-5	The Directory—Protocol Specification
X.520	9594-6	The Directory—Selected Attribute Types
X.521	9594-7	The Directory—Selected Object Classes

General OSI Standards Including ROS and ASN.1

ITU number	ISO number	Title
X.200	7498	OSI: Basic Reference Model
X.208	8824	OSI: Specification of Abstract Syntax Notation (ASN.1)
X.209	8825	OSI: Specification of Basic Encoding Rules for Abstract Syntax Notation One (ASN.1)
X.217	8649	OSI: Association Control: Service Definition
X.218	9066-1	OSI: Reliable Transfer: Model and Service Definition
X.219	9072-1	OSI: Remote Operations Model, Notation and Service Definition
X.227	8650	OSI: Association Control: Protocol Specification
X.228	9066-2	OSI: Reliable Transfer: Protocol Specification
X.229	9072-2	OSI: Remote Operations: Protocol Specification
	10181	Information Technology—Security Frameworks for Open Systems

Character Set Standards

ITU number	ISO number	Title
IA5	646	7-bit coded character sets for information processing interchange
	2022	ISO 7-bit and 8-bit coded character sets—Code extension techniques
	8859-1	8-bit single-byte coded graphic character sets - part 1: Latin alphabet No.1

ITU number	ISO number	Title
T.61	6937/1	Character repertoire and coded character sets of the international teletex service. (ISO version contains a few additional characters not in the CCITT version. Note that X.400, even in its ISO version, refers to the CCITT version T.61, not to the ISO version 6937).
	10646	Universal Multiple-Octet Coded Character Set (UCS)

Other ISO Standards of Interest

	639	Code for the representation of names of languages
	3166	Codes for the representation of names of countries

B.1.1 How to Obtain Copies of ISO and ITU Standards

ISO standards can be bought from the national standards organization in your country, for example, ANSI in the United States, DIN in Germany, AFNOR in France, BSI in the United Kingdom, etc. or from ISO Sales, Case Postale 56, CH-1211 Geneva 20, Switzerland; e-mail sales@isocs.iso.ch. The price is fairly high. For those standards available both as ISO and ITU standards, the ITU version is usually much less expensive.

ITU recommendations can often be bought from the ITU member in your country, which may be the largest telecom company. They can also be bought from: ITU, Place des Nations, CH-1211 Geneva 20, Switzerland. Some of them can be downloaded using the Internet Gopher and connecting it to the Gopher server at info.itu.ch. These documents can also be downloaded from a mail server: send an e-mail message to itudoc@itu.ch (C=ch; admd=arcom; prmd=itu; s=itudoc) with the word HELP in the body to get more information. Finally, those documents available electronically can be downloaded through an X.25 connection (DTE address 228468111112) or a phone connection (+41-22-733 7575) using Kermit or Xmodem file transfer protocols).

A much more complete description of how to obtain ISO and ITU standards is given in [1].

B.2 INTERNET DOCUMENTS (A SELECTION)

Note that all these documents are not agreed-upon standards. Some of them are drafts or personal proposals. Some of them are de facto standards, but not officially accepted as Internet standards. The most important documents from the e-mail area are boldfaced in the list. Internet official standards are marked with an asterisk (*).

RFC 765	File Transfer Protocol (FTP)
RFC 791*	DARPA Internet Protocol (IP)
RFC 799	Internet Name Domains

RFC 807	Multimedia mail meeting notes.
RFC 819	Domain Naming Convention for Internet User Applications
RFC 821*	**Simple Mail Transfer Protocol (SMTP)**
RFC 822*	**Standard for the Format of the ARPA-Internet Text messages**
RFC 881	The Domain Names Plan and Schedule
RFC 886	Proposed Standard for Message Header Munging
RFC 917	Internet Subnets
RFC 920	Domain Requirements
RFC 921	Domain Name System Implementation Schedule—Revised
RFC 934	Proposed standard for message encapsulation.
RFC 952	Internet Host Table Specification
RFC 953	Hostnames Server
RFC 974*	**Mail routing and the domain system** *(How to use MX records)*
RFC 976	**UUCP Mail Interchange Format Standard**
RFC 985	Requirements for Internet Gateways -- Draft
RFC 987	See RFC 1327
RFC 1000	The Request For Comments reference guide
RFC 1006*	**ISO transport services on top of the TCP**
RFC 1012	Bibliography of Request For Comments 1 through 999
RFC 1026	See RFC 1327
RFC 1032	Domain Administrators Guide
RFC 1033	Domain Administrators Operations Guide
RFC 1034*	**Domain names—concepts and facilities**
RFC 1035*	**Domain names—implementation and specification**
RFC 1036	**Standard for interchange of USENET messages** *(describes the format for Usenet News)*
RFC 1047	Duplicate messages and SMTP
RFC 1049*	Content-type header field for Internet messages.
RFC 1056	PCMAIL: A distributed mail system for personal computers
RFC 1082	Post Office Protocol: Version 3: Extended service offerings
RFC 1090	SMTP on X.25
RFC 1113	Privacy enhancement for Internet electronic mail: Part I - message encipherment and authentication procedures [Draft]
RFC 1114	Privacy enhancement for Internet electronic mail: Part II - certificate-based key management [Draft]
RFC 1115	Privacy enhancement for Internet electronic mail: Part III - algorithms, modes, and identifiers [Draft]
RFC 1122	Requirements for Internet hosts - communication layers
RFC 1123*	**Requirements for Internet hosts - application and support**
RFC 1137	Mapping between full RFC 822 and RFC 822 with restricted encoding
RFC 1153	Digest message format

RFC 1154	Encoding header field for internet messages.
RFC 1168	Intermail and Commercial Mail Relay services
RFC 1197	Using ODA for translating multimedia information.
RFC 1203	**Interactive Mail Access Protocol: Version 3 (IMAP)**
RFC 1211	Problems with the maintenance of large mailing lists.
RFC 1225	**Post Office Protocol (POP)**
RFC 1279	X.500 and domains
RFC 1312	Message Send Protocol 2
RFC 1314	File format for the exchange of images in the Internet.
RFC 1319	MD2 Message-Digest algorithm
RFC 1320	MD4 Message-Digest algorithm
RFC 1321	MD5 Message-Digest algorithm
RFC 1324	A Discussion on Computer Network Conferencing
RFC 1327	**Mapping between X.400(1988)/ISO 10021 and RFC 822**
RFC 1328	**X.400 1988 to 1984 downgrading.**
RFC 1330	Recommendations for the phase I deployment of OSI Directory Services (X.500) community
RFC 1339	Remote mail checking protocol.
RFC 1343	**User agent configuration mechanism for multimedia mail format information**
RFC 1344	**Implications of MIME for Internet mail gateways**
RFC 1345	Character Mnemonics and Character Sets
RFC 1357	Format for emailing bibliographic records.
RFC 1421-1424	**Privacy Enhancement for Internet Electronic Mail: Part I-IV.** *(PEM, Security features for Internet mail).*
RFC 1425	SMTP Service Extensions.
RFC 1426	SMTP Service Extension for 8-bit-MIME transport.
RFC 1427	SMTP Service Extension for Message Size Declaration.
RFC 1428	Transition of Internet Mail from Just-Send-8 to 8bit-SMTP/MIME.
RFC 1456	Conventions for Encoding the Vietnamese Language.
RFC 1468	Japanese Character Encoding for Internet Messages.
RFC 1489	Registration of a Cyrillic Character Set.
RFC 1494	Equivalence between 1988 X.400 and RFC-822 Message Bodies
RFC 1495	Mapping between X.400 and RFC-822 Message Bodies
RFC 1496	Rules for Downgrading Messages from X.400/88 to X.400/84 When MIME Content-Types are Present in Messages
RFC 1502	**X.400 Use of Extended Character Sets**
RFC 1505	Encoding Header Field for Internet Messages
RFC 1506	A tutorial on gatewaying between X.400 and Internet mail
RFC 1521	**MIME (Multipurpose Internet Mail Extensions) Part One: Mechanisms for Specifying and Describing the Format of Internet Message Bodies**

RFC 1522	**MIME (Multipurpose Internet Mail Extensions) Part Two: Message Header Extensions for Non-ASCII Text**
RFC 1524	A User Agent Configuration Mechanism For Multimedia Mail Format
RFC 1556	Handling of Bi-directional Texts in MIME
RFC 1563	The text/enriched MIME Content-type
RFC 1591	Domain Name System Structure and Delegation
RFC 1616	X.400 (1988) for the Academic and Research Community in Europe
RFC 1664	Using the Internet DNS to Distribute RFC1327 Mail Address Mapping Tables
RFC 1685	Writing X.400 O/R Names

B.2.1 How to Obtain Copies of IETF (Internet) Standards

Send an e-mail message to rfc-info@ISI.EDU with the following text in the message body: "help: ways_to_get_rfcs." You will then get an e-mail reply which explains in detail how to get copies of IETF standards.

REFERENCE

[1] Kuhn, Markus, *Standards FAQ*, available from URL://rtfm.mit.edu/pub/usenet-by-group/comp.protocols.iso/Standards_FAQ

Further Reading

If you are interested in the contacts between people (which may have been modified by e-mail) then you might want to begin by a classic book [1]. It is not explicitly about e-mail, but still important. A classic work on the effects of CMC on social structures is [9]. That book, first published in 1977 and reprinted in 1993, prophesied much of what was going to happen. A good recent book with research results on changes to organizations as the result of CMC is [10].

A good introduction to OSI in general is given in [8]. Good introductory texts to X.400 are given in [2] and [3]. A good introduction to Internet mail standards is [4], and an introduction to MIME is given in [7]. Technical aspects of how to get e-mail to the intended recipients is covered in [11] and [12]. Useful reading are also the FAQs on OSI [5] and X.400 [6]. The standards themselves can also be read, of course. X.400 [13] and X.500 [14] have fairly good introductions in Part 1 of each standard. Market issues of e-mail are very comprehensively covered in [16].

For a long, annotated bibliography on electronic mail, see [15].

REFERENCES

[1] Allen, Thomas J., *Managing the Flow of Technology, Technology Transfer and the Dissemination of Technological Information within the R&D Organization*, Cambridge, MA: MIT Press, 1977.

[2] Radicati, Sara, *Electronic Mail: An introduction to the X.400 Message Handling Standards*, New York: McGraw-Hill, 1992.

[3] Betanov, Cemil, *Introduction to X.400*, Norwood, MA: Artech House, 1993.

[4] Rose, Marshall T., *The Internet Message: Closing the Book with Electronic Mail.* Englewood Cliffs, NJ: Prentice Hall, 1993.

l5] Kuhn, Markus, *Frequently asked questions about OSI with answers*, available from URL ftp://ftp.uni-padeborn.de/FAQ/comp.protocols-iso/comp.protocols-iso_FAQ, 1994.

[6] Alvestrand, Harald Tveit, *Frequently asked questions on comp.protocols.ISO.X.400*, available from URL ftp://aun.uninett.no/pub/mail/x400faq/FAQ-mhsnews.text, 1994.

[7] Grand, Mark, *MIME overview*, available from URL://ftp from ftp.netcom.com/pub/mdg/mime.ps and pub/mdg/mime.txt, 1992.

[8] Henshall, John and Shaw, Sandy, *OSI Explained; End-to-End Computer Communication Standards*, West Sussex, UK: Ellis Horwood Ltd., distributed by John Wiley & Sons Ltd.

[9] Hiltz, Starr Roxanne and Turoff, Murray, *The Network Nation*, Reading, MA: Addison-Wesley, Massachusetts, 1978. [Reprinted in an extended edition by MIT Press in 1993].

[10] Sproull, Lee and Kiesler, Sara, *Connections: New Ways of Working in the Networked Organization*, Cambridge, MA: MIT Press, 1991.

[11] Frey, Donnalyn and Adams, Ric, *A Directory of Electronic Mail: Addressing and Networks*, 3rd ed., Sebastopol, CA: O'Reilly & Associates, 1993.

[12] Frey, Donnalyn and Adams, Ric, *A Guide to Electronic Mail Networks and Addressing*, Sebastopol, CA: O'Reilly & Associates, 1989.

[13] CCITT Recommendation X.400 *Message handling: Service and system overview,* 1988 [almost identical to] ISO/IEC 10021-1, *Message handling systems, Part 1: Service and system overview*, 1991.

[14] CCITT Recommendation X.500 *The directory: Overview of concepts, models, and services*, [almost identical to ISO/IEC 9594-1], 1988.

[15] Thelen, Erik A., *Electronic mail: An annotated bibliography*, download by sending an e-mail message to Comserver@RPITSVM.BITNET with the text "Send Email2 Biblio."

[16] Blum, Daniel J. and Litwack, David M., *The E-mail Frontier Emerging Markets and Eveloving Technologies*, Reading, Ma., Addison-Wesley 1994.

Glossary

This glossary contains an annotated list of common terms in the electronic mail area. For a more complete glossary of X.400 terminology, see Annex A of X.400 Part 1 [1].

Absolute addressing
An electronic mail address, where the address is the same, independent of where the message is sent from. The antonym is relative addressing. See Section 7.2.

Abstract Syntax Language
See *ASN.1*.

Access Unit
Gateway between the MTS and other services such as postal delivery, fax delivery, etc. See Section 8.4.20.

Address
Information about a recipient which will enable a message system to deliver the message to its recipient. See also *Domain address, Absolute addressing, Relative addressing* and *O/R-address* and see also Sections 7.2 and 8.4.21.

ADMD
See *administration management domain*.

Administration Management Domain
A system of one or more X.400 MTAs run by a telecommunications service company. See Section 8.4.2.

Alert
Functionality, where the user is notified of, for example, incoming mail, even though the user is doing something else. Alerts can be produced by bells, flashing lights, etc. See Section 6.1.

Alias
The *directory system* (see Section 8.5) allows the storage of more than one name for an object or for a node in the DIT. One of the names are then the *Distinguished name*, and the other names are aliases.

All-in-one
Office automation software, including electronic mail, marketed by Digital Equipment Corporation.

Alternate recipient

Mail which cannot be delivered to the designated recipient is instead forwarded to the alternate recipient. This can be some kind of "postmaster," which handles incompletely addressed mail and tries to figure out who to deliver it to. See also *originator requested alternate recipient* and *redirection of incoming messages*.

Alternate recipient allowed

The MTA of the recipient is allowed, if it cannot deliver your message to the intended recipient, to let someone like a "postmaster" look at the message. See Section 8.4.16.

Alternate recipient assignment

Indication of a manual handler to which messages with incomplete addresses are to be forwarded.

ARPAnet

American computer network of research universities and companies. The technology for electronic mail was developed in this network. ARPAnet has grown into a network which today is called *Internet*. See Section 9.3.1.

ASCII

See *IA5*.

ASN.1

Abstract Syntax Notation One, language for computer-independent specification of data structures, used in many OSI standards including X.400 and X.500. See Section 8.3.2.

Asymmetrical encryption

See *Public key encryption*.

Asynchronous

Usually means messaging where the sender and recipient need not be active at the same time. Another term for this is nonsimultaneous.

ATLAS

The French telecom electronic mail service.

AU

See *Access unit*.

Audio

Content type for voice and sounds in *MIME*.

Authentication

Method of identifying with whom you are communicating. See Section 6.13.

Authorizing user

Person who authorizes the sending of a message in X.400. Sometimes used to indicate the writer of a message, if someone else than the writer actually enters the message into the electronic mail system.

Autoforwarding	Indicates that a message at or after delivery to the recipient UA is forwarded automatically to one or more additional recipients. Procedures for autoforwarding are defined in X.400 at both the P2 and the P1 sublayers. Different ways of forwarding at the P1 sublayer are called: *Recipient reassignment, Alternate recipient assignment, Originator requested alternate recipient, and Redirection of incoming messages.* See Section 8.4.16.
Base standard	See *Functional standard.*
Base64	Method of encoding 8-bit or binary data in *MIME* into 7-bit ASCII text. The text is split into groups of 24 bits, and each such group is split into 4 bytes of 6 bits each. Each such 6-bit byte is encoded with an ASCII character. See Section 8.6.6.
Basic encoding rules	See *BER.*
BER	*Basic encoding rules*, a standard for encoding *ASN.1* data into bit strings. See Section 8.3.2.
BITNET	International academic network consisting of thousands of computers. See Section 9.3.3.
BIX	*Byte Information eXchange*, computer conferencing services offered by *Byte* magazine in the United States.
Blind Copy	Recipient whose name is not divulged to certain other recipients of a message. See Section 8.4.13.
Body part type	Type of message body in X.400. A message can consist of several bodies of different body types. See Section 8.4.7. Be aware of the difference between *body part type* and *content type.*
BSMTP	*Batch SMTP*: A variant of the *simple mail transfer protocol* used in BITNET. See Section 8.7.
Bulletin board system	Another term for computer conference system. Sometimes bulletin board is used to refer to systems with more limited functionality than computer conference systems. Sometimes bulletin board is used to refer to systems which combine computer conferencing with data bases of files, which users can download. The files can contain documents, pictures, software, etc. See Section 7.5.
Business document	See *electronic data interchange* (EDI)
Caching	The operation of saving an entry received from another server, so that the next time someone asks for the entry, it need not be retrieved again. See Section 8.5.2.

Carbon Copy Recipient	A recipient who is sent a copy of a message whose primary recipient is different from the *carbon copy recipient*. The term CC is used in RFC 822; X.420 used the term *copy recipient*.
Case sensitive	A string which has a different meaning if the characters in it are changed from upper to lower case or the reverse.
CC	See *carbon copy recipient*.
CCITT	Previous name for the standards organization of the public telephone companies. Its name is now *ITU-T*.
CD	*Committee document*, draft version of an ISO standard.
Certificate	Information which can be used to ensure that an agent is not masquerading as someone else. The main component is usually the public key of the agent. The certificate itself is rendered unforgeable by encipherment with the secret key of the certification authority that issued it. See Section 7.6.4.
Certification authority	An authority which stores *certificates* in a trustworthy manner. See Section 7.6.4.
Chaining	Method for a server to find information by retrieving it from another server and returning the result to the client. See Section 8.5.2.
Circulation list	List of people who read certain messages in a designated order.
Closed conference	Computer conference with control over who may participate.
CMC	See:
	(1) *Computer-mediated communication*
	(2) *Common mail calls*
Common mail calls	Programmatic interface for between an application and a mail service, specially suited for X.400.
Common name	Name of an originator or recipient who is not a person, for example, a distribution list or an organizational entity. This was added to X.400 in 1988, since names consisting of surname and given name are suitable only when addressing people.
CompuServe	Electronic mail and other services offered in the United States and other countries by one of the largest companies of this kind. CompuServe also offers data bases of public domain software and other information.

Computer conference	Named group of users and a store of messages available to this group. Used in group support systems like conferencing systems and bulletin board systems. Communication between participants is asynchronous; that is, all need not be present at the same time.
Computer-mediated communication	Uses of computers for communication between humans. Electronic mail is one very important application within this area. See also *computer-supported cooperative work*.
Computer-supported cooperative work	Uses of computers to support cooperation between humans, usually in groups. Another similar term is *Groupware*. CSCW includes not only different-time applications but also same-time applications. See Figure 2.3 and chapter 11.
Conference	See *computer conference*.
Connection oriented network service	Transmission method where a connection is established between two systems and where several interactions can then be performed in sequence between the two computers. The connection is normally not shut down until one of the two computers requests.
Connectionless	Opposite of *connection oriented network service*.
CONS	See *connection oriented network service*.
Content	The terms "content" and "content type" are used in several different meanings for e-mail: (1) The part of a message which is contained in the envelope in *X.400*. The X.400 content consists of a heading and one or more body parts. See Section 8.4.6. (2) The part of a message which comes after the heading in *MIME*. See Section 8.6.6. (3) The binary file part of the file transfer body part in X.400. See Section 8.4.7. Note that the word "content" in MIME corresponds to the word "body" in X.400.
Content type	For each of the different meanings of the word *content* (see above) the term "content type" is used to designate the type of this content, out of the set of allowed types. For example, in X.400 the term *content type* is used to describe an indication on the envelope of the format of the contents in an X.400 message. Examples of such content types are *P2 (IPM-84), P22 (IPM-88), Pedi* and *Pvoice*. Note: be aware of the difference between *content type* and *body part type*.
Content-description	Attribute in *MIME* which gives a textual description of the content.

Content-ID	Attribute in *MIME* which uniquely identifies a content part in a message. (Compare with *message-ID*, which uniquely identifies a whole message, not part of it.)
Content-transfer-encoding	Way of coding data in *MIME*. The most common encodings are *quoted-printable, base64, 8bit, 7bit* and *binary*. Quoted-printable and base64 will encode 8-bit or binary data as 7-bit ASCII text.
Conversation	A series of messages that are directly or indirectly replies to each other. If each message is allowed to reply to not more than one other message, then a conversation will be a tree structure.
Conversion	The conversion of a body part from one character set to another character set. X.400 allows an *MTA* to convert messages before delivery. Conversion often causes some loss of information.
Conversion prohibited	Indication on the envelope that no character set conversion is allowed on this message.
Converted indication	Information from the *MTS* that some character set conversion has been done on the message.
Copy recipient	See *carbon copy recipient*.
Cross-referencing	Indication in an X.400 message header that a message refers to another message, using the related IPMS heading field. RFC 822 has a similar heading field called *references*. *Cross-referencing* was in the 1988 version of X.400 changed to *related*.
Cryptography	Principles, means, and methods for the transformation of data in order to hide its information content, prevent its undetected modification, and/or prevent its unauthorized use. See Section 7.6.1.
CSCW	See *Computer supported cooperative work*.
CSNET	American research network connected to and, to a large extent, part of Internet. See Section 9.3.1.
DASNET	American company providing message transfers between different mail system providers. See Section 9.3.6.
Deferred delivery	A message is stored in the MTS and delivered to the recipient at a time requested by the originator when submitting the message to the MTS.
Delivery	Transmission of a message from the MTS to the UA of the recipient.

Delivery notification	Notification to the originator and the MTA of the originator that a message has been delivered to the UA of one of its recipients. Delivery notifications can also be produced when a message is delivered to a distribution list expander or to an access unit. See Section 8.4.10.

For probes, the delivery notification indicates that the probe would have been delivered if it had been a message. |
Delivery time stamp	Attribute in an X.400 message indicating when the message was delivered to a recipient.
Dereferencing	Replacing an alias name with its *distinguished name*.
Deutsches Forschungsnetz (DFN)	The German academic computer network.
DFN	See *Deutsches Forschungsnetz.*
Dialcom	Electronic mail system and services in the United States. Dialcom is owned by British Telecom.
Direct connection	See *connection.*
Directory information tree	Tree structure of objects in the directory system. See Section 8.5.
Directory name	A name in the directory system can be either a *distinguished name* or an *alias*. See Section 8.5.1.
Directory service agent (DSA)	Server providing *directory system services* in the *X.500* directory system. See *Directory System.*
Directory system	Computer system storing directories of electronic mail (or other kinds of) addresses. See Section 8.5.
Directory user agent (DUA)	Client software serving one user of the directory system. See *directory system.*
DIS	*Draft International Standard*, draft version of ISO standard.
Disclosure of other recipients	Attribute on the envelope of an *X.400* message, indicating whether each recipient is to be told about other recipients of the same message. Note: this applies only to recipients on the envelope; recipients in the heading do not depend on this attribute.
Distinguished name	Globally unique name of an object used in the directory system. Each object can only have one distinguished name, all other names of the object are alias names. See Section 8.5.

Distribution list	List of recipients. The sender indicates the name of the list as recipient, and the message is delivered to all list members. See Sections 6.7, 6.7.2 and 7.4.
Distribution list expansion history	List of the distribution lists, which a message has passed on its way from the originator to the recipient. Delivered to the recipient UA at delivery according to X.400.
Distribution list expansion prohibited	Attribute on an X.400 message envelope, requesting that this message should not be resent via distribution list expansion.
DIT	See *directory information tree.*
DL	See *distribution list.*
DNS	See *domain naming system.*
Domain	Area of responsibility for handling electronic mail. See also *administration management domain* and *private management domain* .
Domain address	Address, organized into successively smaller areas (domains); compare to phone numbers with country code, city code, and local code. See Section 7.2.
Domain-defined attributes	Additional attributes in an *O/R-address* in addition to those attributes explicitly named in the *X.400* standard. For domain-defined attributes, both a type and a value is given in the name. The most important domain-defined attribute is DDA.RFC-822, which can be used to include an Internet e-mail address in an X.400 message address.
Domain naming system	Directory service on the Internet, which, given e-mail addresses, can return the domain address of the MTA serving this e-mail address, and which given domain addresses can return aliases, IP addresses, and other information.
DP	*Draft proposal*, draft version of ISO standard. Also known as *committee document (CD)*.
DSA	See *directory system agent.*
DUA	see *directory user agent.*
EAN	Messaging system based on the X.400 standard, which has been widely used. EAN was originally developed by the University of British Columbia in Canada. It has been marketed under the name *Envoy 400.*
EARN	*European Academic Research Network*. The European branch of *BITNET*. Merged in 1994 with *RARE* to form *TERENA*.

EDI	See electronic data interchange.
EDIFACT	A standard for exchanging EDI information via electronic mail or via other media.
EEMA	European Electronic Mail Association, the association of commercial e-mail service providers in Europe.
EFT	See *electronic funds transfer.*
EIES	*Electronic information exchange system,* Computer conferencing system developed by Murray Turoff at the New Jersey Institute of Technology. Was first operational in 1976. EIES 2, a completely rewritten distributed system, started operations in 1991.
Electronic data interchange (EDI)	Message for transferring data between computer applications. See Section 6.5, 8.2.5, and 8.4.23.
Electronic funds transfer (EFT)	Variant of *electronic data interchange* for the transfer of payments.
EMA	Electronic Mail Association, the North American organization of e-mail service providers.
EMISARI	The world's first computer conference system, developed by Murray Turoff in 1969.
Encoded information type	Information on the envelope of the character types used in the content.
Envelope	Part of a message indicating sender, recipient, trace information, etc., which is used by the MTS when transferring the message from the sender to the recipients.
Envoy 400	See EAN.
ESTMP	Extended *Simple Mail Transfer Protocol,* a facility for extending SMTP through agreements between SMTP servers to use extended facilities.
EUNET	The joint European UNIX net.
EuroKOM	Computer conferencing service for the European Community Esprit project. Run by the computer center at the University College in Dublin.
Expansion	The procedure in which the name of a distribution list on the message envelope is replaced by the names of the members of the list as recipients of the message.
Expiry date	Point in time, after which a message is no longer valid.

Explicit conversion	Conversion of the character set in a message requested by the originator.
Fax	See *Telefacsimile.*
FIDO	*Bulletin board system* for personal computers. By exchanging messages through the telephone, many FIDO computers can act as a coordinated network, Fidonet.
Filter	(1) Search query used in the *directory system* and in the *message store*. See Section 8.5. (2) Automatic process which sorts incoming messages for a user. The filter can put different messages into different folders, and can delete or mark-for-deletion certain messages.
FORUM	One of the world's first computer conferencing systems, developed in 1971 at the Institute of the Future. Also known under the name *PLANET*. The same name has also been used for a computer conferencing system under the MULTICS operating system.
Functional standard	Standard which defines subclasses (subsets of the functionalities) of another standard, called the *Base Standard*. Another word for Functional standard is *Profile*.
Funet	The academic network in Finland.
Gateway	Transfer unit between two nets with different protocols, which allows coworking between the nets. See Section 8.11.
GE QUICKCOM, GEnie	Electronic mail services offered in the United States by General Electric.
GO-MHS	Global MHS service.
Grade of delivery	*X.400* service allowing the sender to designate a message as *urgent*, *normal*, or *nonurgent*. This will influence the speed at which the message is handled by the *MTS*.
Grey book mail	Mail standard used in the *Janet* network. May be replaced by X.400 and/or Internet mail.
Heading	Part of a message giving the recipients information about and instructions on how to process a message. Note the difference between *heading* and *envelope*.
Hold for delivery	X.400 service where the sender of a message can instruct the MTS at what time to deliver a message.
IA5	7-bit character set much used in messaging. Also known under the names *ISO 646* and *ASCII*. See Section 8.2.1.

IANA	See *Internet Assigned Numbers Authority.*
Identification	Another word for *identifier.* See also *authentication.*
Identifier	Name of a message. See *IPMessageID* and *MessageID,* and Section 8.4.14.
IETF	See *Internet Engineering Task Force.*
IFIP	*International Federation for Information Processing.* Organizes regular international conferences on application layer protocols, including electronic mail.
Importance indication	X.400 service to indicate in the heading of a message that the importance is *low, normal,* or *high.* X.400 does not specify how this indication will influence the handling of the message. Note that importance indication is different from *grade of delivery.*
In-Reply-To	Heading field indicating a message to which the current message is a reply.
Incomplete copy	Indication in the X.400 message heading that some or all body parts are missing from this copy of the message.
Interpersonal message (IPM)	Letter sent to named personal recipients. In practice, IPMs are often sent to recipients other than persons, for example, to distribution lists, organizational entities, etc.
Internet	International net based on the TCP/IP networking standard. Internet consists of a large number of connected subnets run by different organizations and in different countries. There is thus no single owner or manager of Internet. Internet has its own e-mail standards, which in 1994 were more used than the X.400 e-mail standards. Internet has connections also to X.400 and other mail networks, so that Internet serves as the largest joint backbone for mail between users in almost every country of the world. See Sections 8.6 and 9.3.1.
Internet Assigned Numbers Authority	The central registration authority in IANA, which registers domain names, port numbers, MIME content types etc.
Internet Engineering Task Force (IETF)	The standards-making body of the Internet Society.
Internet Society	Organization of people and organizations interested in the Internet.
IP	Internet protocol, standard for the lower layers of the TCP/IP protocol suite.
IPM, IP-Message	See *Interpersonal message.*

IPMessage identification (IPMessageID, IPMIdentifier)	Globally unique message identification code in the P2 protocol. Called *IPMessageID* in 1984 and renamed to *IPM identifier* in 1988.
ISO	*International standards organization.*
ISOC	See *Internet society.*
ITU, ITU-T	International Telecommunications Union, the international organization for telecom companies. ITU-T is the branch in ITU responsible for standards development. ITU-T was known as CCITT before 1992.
Janet	The British academic network.
JEMA	Japan Electronic Mail Association, the Japanese organization of e-mail service providers.
KOM	A computer conferencing system whose first version was developed in 1978 in Sweden.
Language indication	Heading attribute of an X.400 message indicating the natural language of the message according to the ISO 639 standard. For example "en" for English. ISO 639 also allows "enUS" for the U.S.A. English dialect, but since the field was limited to two characters in X.400, such dialect information could be given with the 1988 version of X.400. In the 1994 version, the length was changed to five characters.
Latest delivery designation	Indication on the envelope that a message must be delivered before a certain time.
Listserv	Distribution list software used in *BITNET* and other nets. See Section 9.2.7.
Lotus Notes	Computer conferencing system marketed by Lotus. Has a distributed architecture with replications between servers.
Mailing list	See *distribution list.*
Management domain	See *administration management domain,* and *private management domain.*
Meeting	See *computer conference.*
Memo	Electronic mail system developed by Volvo and marketed by Verimation. See Sections 9.2.1 and 12.4.

Message handling system (MHS)	(1) System for electronic mail according to the *X.400* standard. *MHS* consists of an *MTS* plus a number of *UAs*. See Section 8.4.1. (2) *ISO* name of the X.400 standard. (3) An e-mail software product marketed by Novell.
Message origin authentication	Way of verifying that a message comes from the stated originator.
Message security labeling	Specification of the degree of sensitivity of a message. Can be used to ensure that the message is only delivered to recipients with a certain security clearance.
Message store	Mailbox in the server, accessed by the user via the P7 protocol. Each message store only stores the messages for one user, and is not a multiuser store facility. See Section 8.4.4.
Message transfer agent (MTA)	Server which receives messages from *UAs* and other *MTAs* and delivers them to *UAs* or other *MTAs*. See Section 8.4.1.
Message transfer system (MTS)	System of *MTAs*, which transfer messages from the originating *MTA* to the recipient *MTAs*. See Section 8.4.1.
Message-ID	Unique identification of a message in the Internet (RFC 822) standard. See also *IPMessage-ID*.
MHS	See *message handling system*.
MIME	See *multipurpose internet mail extensions*.
MMDF	Software for Internet mail *MTAs*. Often used together with *Phonenet*.
Mnemonic O/R-address	O/R-address with subfields in plain text, containing human-understandable names. See also *numeric O/R-address*.
MOTIS	Older name for *X.400* in *ISO* standards. Has been replaced by *MHS*.
MTA	See *message transfer agent*.
MTS	See *message transfer system*.
Multidestination delivery	Function that allows an originator to submit one message and ask the *MTS* to deliver it to more than one recipient.
Multimedia	Message containing a combination of text, pictures, and sound.
Multicasting	A service where a server can simultaneously ask several other servers for information. See Section 8.5.2.
Multipurpose Internet mail extensions	Extensions of the Internet mail standards to transfer messages in different character sets, to send binary files in mail, etc. Defined in RFC 1521 and 1522.

MX record	Record in the *domain naming system* storing information about e-mail addresses. Abbreviation of *mail eXchanger*.
Name server	Term for *directory systems* in the Internet. Name servers often translate only domains to Internet addresses, not translating the personal name part of the electronic mail address. See also *domain naming system*.
News control	Mechanism which protects a recipient from being shown the same message as "new" more than once.
Nondelivery notification	Notification in the P1 sublayer, indicating that a message could not be delivered to the *UA* or *DL* it was sent to. See Section 8.4.10.
Nonrecipient notification	Notification in the IPM sublayer, indicating that the recipient will probably never read this message. See Section 8.4.10.
Nonrepudiation of Origin	A way of ensuring the recipient of a message that it really comes from the originator, even if the originator later claims that he did not send the message.
Nonrepudiation of submission	A way of ensuring that the originator cannot at a later time state that he never submitted a certain message.
Notification	Message which can be understood by a computer program, often containing information about what has happened to ordinary messages. See *delivery notification, nondelivery notification, receipt notification, nonreceipt notification,* and Section 8.4.10.
NSFNET	High-speed network for academic usage in the United States financed by the National Science Foundation (NSF). Subnetwork within the *Internet*.
Numeric O/R-address	*O/R-address* consisting of numbers. Not often used. Instead, *X.400* systems usually use *mnemonic O/R-addresses*.
O/R-address, OR-address	Electronic mail address as used in X.400. See Section 8.4.21.
O/R-name, OR-name	A combination of an *O/R-address* and a *directory name*. Sometimes, only one of these two elements are included. (Note: In the 1984 version of X.400, O/R-name meant what is today called O/R-address.)
Object identifier	Globally unique identifying code, sold by standards organizations and used to name extended protocol units. See Section 8.3.3.
Obsoleting indication	Indication in an X.400 message heading that a message is a replacement for a previous message.

ODA	See *open document architecture*.
Open conference	See *public conference*.
Open document architecture (ODA)	A standard for exchanging word-processing documents via electronic mail or other media. See Section 8.2.4.
Open key encryption	See *public key encryption*.
Open systems interconnection (OSI)	Computer network standard, defined in seven layers, to facilitate development of standards for the interconnection of network equipment from different manufacturers. See Section 8.3.
Original encoded information types	Information on the envelope of which body types and character sets are used in the content of a message.
Originator	Name of the sender of a message in the X.400 standard.
Originator requested alternate recipient	Alternate recipient designated by the originator, to be used if delivery to the primary recipient is not possible.
OSI	See *open systems interconnection*.
P1	Protocol for communication between MTAs in X.400.
P2 and P22	Format for message content (heading and bodies) in X.400.
P3	Protocol for communication between a UA and an MTA in X.400, where messages can be downloaded and uploaded.
P7	Protocol for communication between a UA and an MTA in X.400, where the UA can manipulate a store of messages in the server. See also *Message Store*.
PDAU	See *postal delivery access unit*.
Pedi, P_{edi}	Format for *EDI* message content in X.400.
PEM	See *privacy enhanced mail*.
Personal letter	See *interpersonal letter*.
Personal name	Part of an X.400 *OR-address* containing the *given name, surname, initials,* and *generation qualifier* of the named person.
Phonenet	Protocol for communication between Internet mail servers through dial-up lines. Used by *MMDF*.
Physical delivery	Printing of electronic mail on paper for delivery through the postal system.

PICS Proforma	Short for *protocol implementation conformance statement form*, in which an implementation of a standard can report which facilities of the standard it supports. The X.400 *PICS Proforma* are published as *ITU recommendation*s X.481-X.485.
PLANET	See *FORUM*.
PortaCOM	Functional copy of the *KOM* computer conferencing system.
Postal delivery access unit	Unit for printing *X.400* messages on paper for delivery via the postal system. See also *access unit.*
PP	Originally public domain MTA software which also serves as a gateway between X.400 and Internet mail protocols. Also available in a commercial version. See Section 9.2.7.
Primary recipient	A recipient of a message who is not a *copy* or *blind copy recipient.*
Printable string	Restricted character set acceptable on all kinds of terminals. See Section 8.2.3.
Privacy enhanced mail (PEM)	*Internet* standards for secure messaging using cryptographic methods.
Private	(1) Anything not run by a telecom (PTT) company, according to ITU/CCITT terminology. (2) Anything not run by the government. (3) Standard not defined by an international standards organization like ISO, IEC, ITU or IETF. (4) Letter intended to be read only by a certain individual personally. (5) Computer conference or distribution list which is not available to anyone.
Private conference	See *closed conference.*
Private management domain (PRMD)	System of MTAs run by an organization other than a Telecom company.
PRMD	See *private management domain.*
Probe	Message which is sent to test if a certain UA can be reached. The probe is never delivered to its recipient, but it will cause a delivery or nondelivery notification to be returned to the originator. See Section 8.4.11.
Profile	Another word for *functional standard.*
Proof of delivery	Way of ensuring that a message has been delivered to the indicated recipient.
Proof of submission	Way of ensuring that a certain message has really been submitted.

PTT	"Public telephone and telegraph companies" or "post, telephone and telegraph companies."
Public conference	A conference to which some people, often anyone, can add themselves as members. Antonym of *closed conference*. See Section 6.7.
Public key encryption	Encryption method, where the encryption key need not be kept secret. The decryption key, however, must be kept secret. See Section 7.6.1.
Pvoice	Format for voice message content in X.400, defined in X.440.
Quoted-printable	Method of encoding 8-bit text into 7-bit text used in *MIME*. Most of those 8-bit characters whose first bit is 0 are transferred unencoded, all characters whose first bit is 1 and some of those whose first bit is 0 are encoded with "=" followed by the numerical value of the character as a hexadecimal number. See Section 8.6.6.
Quoting	Way of marking certain characters in *Internet* protocols to indicate that the characters are to be taken literally and not as syntactic separators. The most common methods of quoting are to put the character """" before and after the quoted text and to put the character "\" in front of a single quoted character. Warning: quoting is not very reliable and should be avoided.
RARE	*Reseaux Associes pour la Recherche Europeene*: European cooperative organization for academic and research network. Merged with *EARN* in 1994 under the new joint name *TERENA*.
Receipt notification	Message that a message has been read or at least handled in some way by its recipient. Belongs to the P2 sublayer. See Section 8.4.10.
Redirection disallowed by originator	Attribute on a message, indicating that this message should not be redirected.
Redirection of incoming messages	Service allowing a recipient to redirect his mail to some other mailbox. See also *alternate recipient*.
Referral	When a server cannot provide the information requested, the server can give the name of another server to the user agent which might have the requested information. See Section 8.5.2.
Related message	Reference from one message to another message which the message is related to. Also known by the names *cross-references* and *references*.

Relative addressing	Address which not only tells where the recipient is but also which route to use from the sender to the recipient. See Section 7.2. Antonym: *absolute addressing*.
Relative distinguished name	A name of a node in the directory tree, which is unique in relation to other nodes in the same branch of the tree. See Section 8.5.
Reliable transfer service (RTS)	Protocol in the OSI application layer for transferring information using underlying OSI layers.
Remote operations service (ROS)	Protocol in the OSI application layer, allowing two applications to send operations to each other. See Section 8.3.4.
Remote spooling control system (RSCS)	Protocol for file and message transfer used in BITNET. See Section 8.7.
Reply request	Indication by the originator that a reply from the recipient is wanted. In X.400, reply request is given per recipient, so that the originator can request replies from some but not all of the recipients of a message.
Reply-to	Indication in the message heading of where replies to a message should be sent. See Section 8.4.15.
Request for comment (RFC)	A series of documents containing *Internet* standards and other documents on the Internet. A list of RFCs can be found in Appendix B.2.
Return path	Address to use when sending a reply to a message along the reverse route through which the message was delivered.
RFC	See *request for comment*.
RFC 821	See *simple mail transfer protocol*.
RFC 822	Internet standard for the format of message headings. See Section 8.6.4.
ROS	See *remote operations service*.
Routing	The act in an *MTA*, when it chooses which MTA to forward a message to. See Sections 7.1 and 8.6.3.
RSA algorithm	Well-known method for *public key encryption*, based on the factorization of very large prime numbers.
RSCS	See *remote spooling control system*.
RTS	See *reliable transfer service*.
Screenmail	International electronic mail services provided by IBM.

Sendmail	Public domain software for MTAs using the Internet mail protocols. See Section 9.2.7.
Sensitivity indication	Indication in the X.400 message heading that a message is *personal, private* or *company-confidential*. This indication can cause a message system to request identification before delivery, to disallow printing on a shared printer, to disallow auto-forwarding, etc.
SGML	*Standardized general markup language*, A standard for coding of documents for printing. See also *ODA*.
Shadowing	Mode of cooperation between two distributed parts of a data base. The original of a piece of information is in one of the data bases. Every time the information is updated, the holder of the original will distribute the change to all holders of shadow copies. See Section 8.5.2.
Simple Mail Transfer Protocol (SMTP)	Protocol used in the *Internet* for forwarding messages between MTAs. Can also be used to enter mail from a mail client into the Internet mail transmission service. SMTP thus roughly corresponds to P1 and part of the P3 protocol in X.400. See Section 8.6.2.
Simultaneous	Communication where the sender and the recipient must be present at the same time, like an ordinary phone call.
Smart card	Plastic card in the shape of a credit card with a built-in microprocessor which might contain, for example, an encryption algorithm. See Section 7.6.1.
SMTP	See *simple mail transfer protocol*.
Spooling	Transfer of a message by a background process, where the sender need not wait while the transmission takes place.
STD	Internet Standard RFC.
Store and forward	Transfer of a message as a whole with intermediate storage at one or more intermediate stations, each of which takes over responsibility for forwarding the message to its recipient(s).
Subject	Most messaging standards have a field in the message heading indicating the subject of the message. This can be used, for example, by the receiving UA to sort messages by subject so that several messages with the same subject are read at the same time by the recipient. In Usenet News, a common feature is that a user can ask his UA to throw away all messages with a certain subject.
Sunet	The Swedish academic research network.

SuperKOM	Distributed computer conferencing system, a further development of the KOM system.
T.61	Character set used in teletex and X.400. See Section 8.2.2.
TCP	Method of transferring a document via Internet protocol networks, split up into several packets, so that the packets are joined together in the correct order into a copy of the original document at the receiving end.
TCP/IP	Standard for the packet-switched network used in Internet.
Telebox	Name used in many countries for the public mail services provided by the telecom companies.
Telecom Gold	Name of the public electronic mail services provided by British Telecom.
Telefacsimile	Sending of a document through the phone network in bit-mapped format, also known under the name *fax*. In this book, the word "fax" is mostly used. The X.400 standard has protocols for forwarding electronic mail via telefacsimile.
Telemail	Public messaging services in the United States provided by GTE Telenet.
Teletex	Network, similar to the telex network, but using the T.61 character set.
Telex	Older system for text communication through a direct connection between typing terminals. Very limited character set, only upper case characters, and a transmission speed of only 7.5 characters/second.
Telnet	Virtual terminal protocol used in TCP/IP nets.
TERENA	Trans-European Research and Education Networking Association. Formed in 1994 by a merger of *RARE* and *EARN*.
Trace	List, transmitted with a message, of nodes which the message has passed.
UA	See *user agent*.
Uninett	The Norwegian academic network.
Usenet news	Well-known distributed computer conferencing system. See Section 8.8.
User agent (UA)	Client unit handling the user interaction and connecting to a server.

UUCP	*UNIX-to-UNIX copy protocol.*
	(1) An international network of research computers using the UNIX operating system.
	(2) One of the protocols used to transfer information between nodes in this network.
Verify	Operation, where one *MTA* asks another *MTA* if it is capable of handling mail to a certain address. Used in the *simple mail transfer protocol* (SMTP).
Voice messaging	Messaging system for spoken messages.
White space	One character or a sequence of a characters which are shown as a white space with no ink when printed. White space can consist of the characters *space, horizontal tab, carriage return,* and *line feed.*
X.400	International standard for electronic mail. See Section 8.4.
X.500	International standard for directory systems. See Section 8.5.

REFERENCE

[1] CCITT Recommendation X.400 *Message handling: Service and system overview,* 1988
[almost identical to]
ISO/IEC 10021-1, *Message handling systems, Part 1: Service and system overview,* 1991.

Index

This is both a subject index and a person index. Italic reference numbers indicate person references. "Electronic mail" is abbreviated as EM.

246

250

251

260

Writing versus speaking, time for 25

X-OPEN, character set standards recommendation 85
X.214-216 91
X.25 91
   services 172
X.28 91
X.400 98 (see also P1, P2 P22, and P7 protocols)
   addressing 118
   ADMD name 119
   ADMD name mandatory or optional in OR-names 121
   authentication 123
   autoforwarding in 115
   body part type 105
   communication with other media 118
   comparison with Internet mail standards 142
   content of a message 103, 104, 105
   content type 105
   country name 119
   different versions of 125
   distribution lists 116
   distribution lists and notification handling 117
   domains and relaying 99
   EDI content type 122
   extensibility 122
   forwarding 106, 115
   functional model 98
   gatewaying to Internet 153
   IPM Identifier 112, 113
   IPMessageID 112, 113
   lists of standards documents 213
   loop control 118
   message body 103, 104, 105
   message headings 103, 104, 105
   message store 101
   message text bodies 105
   message transfer system (MTS) 98
   MHS and MTS 98
   naming 118
   notifications 108
   notifications and special delivery 110
   organization name 119
   originator 104
   P1, P2, P3 and P7 protocols 102
   P2 protocol, features of 103, 104, 105
   primary recipient 111
   protocol layers 91
   recipient indication on the envelope 110
   registration of e-mail addresses 173
   reply requests in 115
   responsibility flag on recipient names 111

   ROS 97
   security functions 123
   software 166
   time stamping 108
   use of ASN.1 for coding 91
   use of character set standards 86
   use of directory systems 102
   user interface example 202
   voice mail 123
X.411 (see also P1 protocol and message transfer system)
   layer for 91
X.413 (see P7 protocol and Message store)
   relation to other protocols 103
X.420 (see also P2 and P22 protocol)
   heading and bodies of 103
   layer for 91
X.500 126
   document list 214
   Schema 126

265

About the Author

Jacob Palme is a nontenured professor of computer science at Stockholm University and the Royal Institute of Technology, Department of Computer and Systems Sciences. Electronic mail and computer-mediated communication has been his primary interest since 1977. Before that, he worked with operations analysis, artificial intelligence research, and development of the Simula programming language. During the 1980s he was chairman of the joint European Community research projects GILT and AMIGO MHS+, and since 1987 he has been one of the Swedish representatives in the ISO/IEC group for developing standards for e-mail. Within that group, he is the main editor for group communication standards. He has been involved with the development of the KOM, PortaCOM, and SuperKOM electronic mail and computer conferencing systems: He has written eleven books. *Electronic Mail* is his first English-language book.

The Artech House Telecommunications Library

Vinton G. Cerf, Series Editor

Advanced Technology for Road Transport: IVHS and ATT, Ian Catling, editor

Advances in Computer Communications and Networking, Wesley W. Chu, editor

Advances in Computer Systems Security, Rein Turn, editor

Analysis and Synthesis of Logic Systems, Daniel Mange

Asynchronous Transfer Mode Networks: Performance Issues, Raif O. Onvural

A Bibliography of Telecommunications and Socio-Economic Development, Heather E. Hudson

Broadband: Business Services, Technologies, and Strategic Impact, David Wright

Broadband Network Analysis and Design, Daniel Minoli

Broadband Telecommunications Technology, Byeong Lee, Minho Kang, and Jonghee Lee

Cellular Radio: Analog and Digital Systems, Asha Mehrotra

Cellular Radio Systems, D. M. Balston and R. C. V. Macario, editors

Client/Server Computing: Architecture, Applications, and Distributed Systems Management, Bruce Elbert and Bobby Martyna

Codes for Error Control and Synchronization, Djimitri Wiggert

Communication Satellites in the Geostationary Orbit, Donald M. Jansky and Michel C. Jeruchim

Communications Directory, Manus Egan, editor

The Complete Guide to Buying a Telephone System, Paul Daubitz

Computer Telephone Integration, Rob Walters

The Corporate Cabling Guide, Mark W. McElroy

Writing Disaster Recovery Plans for Telecommunications Networks and LANs,
  Leo A. Wrobel

X Window System User's Guide, Uday O. Pabrai

For further information on these and other Artech House titles, contact:

Artech House
685 Canton Street
Norwood, MA 02062
617-769-9750
Fax: 617-769-6334
Telex: 951-659
email: artech@world.std.com

Artech House
Portland House, Stag Place
London SW1E 5XA England
+44 (0) 171-973-8077
Fax: +44 (0) 171-630-0166
Telex: 951-659
email: bookco@artech.demon.co.uk

www.ingramcontent.com/pod-product-compliance
Lightning Source LLC
Chambersburg PA
CBHW021429180326
41458CB00001B/194

* 9 7 8 0 8 9 0 0 6 8 0 2 1 *